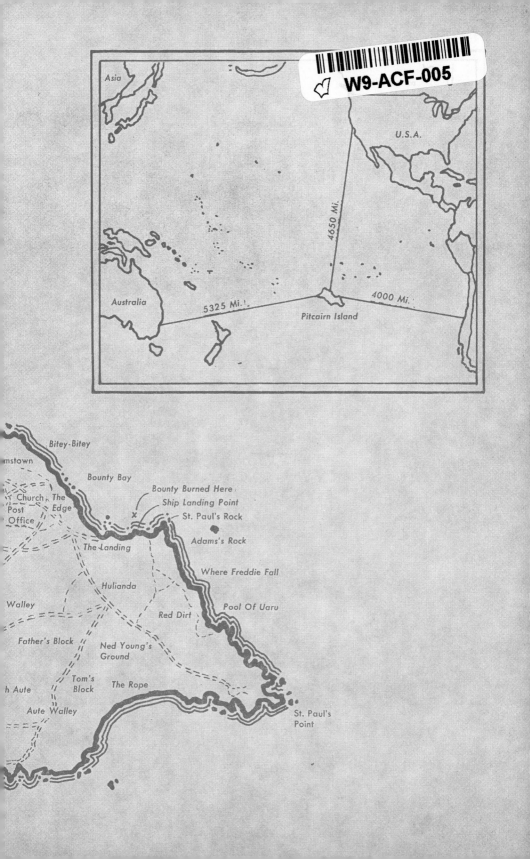

Asia

U.S.A.

4650 Mi.

Australia

5325 Mi.

Pitcairn Island

4000 Mi.

Bitey-Bitey

mstown

Bounty Bay

Bounty Burned Here
Ship Landing Point
St. Paul's Rock

Church The
Post Edge
Office

Adams's Rock

The Landing

Where Freddie Fall

Hulianda

Walley

Pool Of Uaru

Red Dirt

Father's Block

Ned Young's
Ground

h Aute Tom's
Block

The Rope

Aute Walley

St. Paul's
Point

PITCAIRN ISLAND

 Pitcairn Island

BY

DAVID SILVERMAN

THE WORLD PUBLISHING COMPANY

Cleveland and New York

GRATEFUL ACKNOWLEDGMENT TO

Mr. H. E. Maude, O.B.E., Senior Fellow, The Research School of Pacific Studies, The Australian National University (Canberra), who has rescued large areas of Pitcairn history from myth and elision, for permission to quote from his works listed in the Bibliography, and for invaluable assistance on many knotty problems of the Pitcairn story.

Dr. Harry L. Shapiro, Chairman of the Department of Anthropology and Curator of Physical Anthropology at the American Museum of Natural History, for permission to quote freely from his classic study of Pitcairn anthropology, *The Heritage of the Bounty*.

Captain and Mrs. Irving Johnson, for permission to use material from their books and magazine articles listed in the Bibliography.

The South Pacific Office and Commissioner T. R. Cowell, Suva, Fiji, for permission to use material in *A Guide to Pitcairn* and for information supplied.

Mr. Luis Marden for permission to quote from his article listed in the Bibliography.

Colonel Edouard R. L. Doty for sharing his childhood memories of Pitcairners who came to Tahiti in the early years of this century.

Others too numerous to mention for information and suggestions.

Published by The World Publishing Company
2231 West 110th Street, Cleveland, Ohio 44102

Published simultaneously in Canada by
Nelson, Foster & Scott Ltd.

Library of Congress Catalog Card Number: 66–24998

FIRST PRINTING 1967

To my wife,
Polly,
and the memory of my mother,
Hannah,
and my father,
Benjamin

❧ FOREWORD ❧

There is something about a remote and solitary island that touches a deep instinct in every man. Perhaps the sympathetic echo reaches back to a primal drive for sanctuary, for shelter from a hostile outside world. Doubtless it is this same basic urge that made us, as children, love to build tree-houses, and to seek out bowers, caves, and other secure and snug hideaways. In the desire to creep into an impregnable safe place man is one with the rabbit.

Such a place is Pitcairn Island, a fragment of volcanic rock thrust up from the deeps of the South Pacific Ocean just under the Tropic of Capricorn. Here dwell the descendants of a handful of men who had a more compelling reason to look for a hiding place than the universal pull toward secret islands. For to Pitcairn in 1790 fled the protagonists of history's most celebrated sea story—the mutiny on the "Bounty." This bizarre episode contains all the elements of melodrama: exotic setting, sex, piracy, murder, and exile, yet it has the advantage of being true, of having been written, as a friend of mine puts it, by the sure hand of God.

I first sighted Pitcairn Island against the polished metal glare of the sunlit Pacific on a November morning—late spring in the latitudes below the Line. The slate-colored wedge on the horizon was the only vertical element in the flat vastness of sea and sky. As the ship drew closer, the island slowly rose from the sea like a southern Gibraltar.

There are no anchorages or harbors at Pitcairn. The ship hove to a little less than two miles from the unbroken line of white surf breaking round the foot of the island. Low against the land we could see the white sails of the famed Pitcairn longboats standing toward us. As we watched, all three boats dropped their sails at the same instant, and the long oars flashed in unison as the boats pulled for our dangling Jacob's ladders.

We lay with engines stopped, rising and falling on the long slow swells of the Pacific, which roll down on the island after an unbroken fetch of more than 3,000 miles. The swells can be so high as to prevent disembarking of freight or passengers, but that day we were in luck, and the longboats made fast alongside with no trouble.

The barefoot Pitcairners swarmed up our ladders nimbly. My first impression of the islanders tallied with my last: I sensed frankness and an inner placidity in the strong clasp of their hand and in the disarming friendliness and sincerity of their smiling brown faces. The Pitcairners are big people—"strong made," as Captain Bligh wrote of Fletcher Christian, the mate who led the mutiny. Most of the men were well over six feet tall, and proportionally broad. The women were nearly as solidly built, and showed more markedly than the men the Polynesian cast of features inherited from the Tahitian women brought to the island by the mutineers.

The Pitcairners brought their island products and curios to sell or trade: bananas, pineapples, mangoes, and avocados, pandanus baskets, and carved wooden flying fish, sea birds, and turtles. Our ship had paused in her 20-day run from Panama to New Zealand to heave to off Pitcairn on the tenth day, and the passengers were eager to purchase fresh fruit. The ship's purser traded temperate zone staples such as flour, potatoes, and onions, for the luscious semitropical fruits.

After an hour's brisk trading, the islanders climbed down into their longboats and I went with them. Before casting off our lines, Parkin Christian, a handsome giant of over 70 who was Fletcher Christian's great-great-grandson, called out "A song for the Captain!" and softly at first, then with mounting volume, the Pitcairners began to sing the hymn "In the Sweet Bye and Bye." As the last strains died away, the beat of the ship's engines thumped against our boat's side, and our wet lines hissed like snakes as they were hauled aboard. In a swirl from the ship's propellers, we hoisted sail for the run to shore.

Foreword

Pitcairn is small, only two miles long by one mile wide. At one point a rocky cove, hardly more than a slight indentation in the ironbound shore, bears the impressive but misleading name of Bounty Bay. Just outside the line of breaking surf, we dropped the sails, unstepped the mast, and unshipped the rudder.

The oarsmen lay on their oars, keeping their eyes fixed on the boat captain. Standing in the sternsheets with a long steering sweep under one arm, the captain looked behind him to the advancing swells that passed under our boat, lifting it in place, then swept on to smash on the rocky shore. As an unusually high swell hunched its shoulders for the run ashore, the captain cried "Now!" With one movement, the men dipped their oars and the long blades flexed as they put their backs into a mighty pull. Borne on the crest of a wave that had come 3,000 miles to thrust us home, we shot forward, the men pulling the oars in short strokes to steer us to the left round a finger of rock. The sea broke astern in a welter of foam and we bumped against the Slide, a grid of logs and timbers slanting down to the water's edge from the boat-sheds on the shore.

A dozen men held each boat against the suck of the sea as we clambered ashore and unloaded the food, goods, and mails the ship had brought. The landing was barely wide enough for the wooden slide and the cluster of boat-sheds. Above it Ship Rock, a sharp-edged pinnacle of stone, soared 700 feet skyward. Behind the sheds a steep trail led to the living space, a more-or-less flat ledge 300 feet above.

When the mutineers and their Polynesian women landed on Pitcairn, the top of the island was heavily wooded, but the hardwood trees soon fell to the "Bounty's" axes, to make houses and fishing canoes. Today almost no timber trees remain; an undulating grassy savannah, broken by clumps of pandanus, coconut palms, and bush, covers the top of the island.

Except for the summit plateau, almost the only relatively flat place on Pitcairn is the ledge above Bounty Bay. Here the wooden houses of the inhabitants are scattered, nearly all out of sight of one another. The houses stand on stone piers; they are built of wood and once had thatched roofs, but now the unsightly but more practical corrugated iron takes the place of pandanus fronds. True to Polynesian custom, cooking is done in a small separate building, over a wood fire built on slabs of coral rock. Metal gutters run from the roofs to

ix

sunken concrete catchment basins, for there are no springs or streams on Pitcairn, and the people must depend on rain water.

When the mutineers first approached the uninhabited island, they descried a plumed waterfall cascading down the cliff face near Bounty Bay, and so it does to this day—for a few hours after a torrential rain. Fortunately, when it rains on Pitcairn the skies open and water falls in nearly solid sheets.

For two months I lived on Pitcairn, sharing the busy but tranquil life of the islanders, in an untroubled daily rhythm broken only by the fortnightly arrival of a ship. The day on Pitcairn, as on most tropical and subtropical islands, begins early. Shortly after dawn the islanders rise, and without food or drink, except, perhaps, for a cup of tea, trudge "up ah hill" to work their plantations. About eleven o'clock the people come down to their houses to have a hearty meal, and they do not eat again until eight or nine at night.

Goats, descendants without doubt of the original ones brought from Tahiti by the mutineers, roam wild over the northern half of the island. A fence keeps them from ravaging the plantations, but they effectively crop down most growing things on their side.

Since 1884 the Pitcairners have been Seventh-day Adventists, but unlike most Adventists, they eat meat when they can get it. Usually this is tinned corned beef from New Zealand, but on special occasions, such as Christmas, the islanders take up their "muskets," and then everyone eats boiled goat.

But the Pitcairners, true to their Polynesian heritage, love best to eat starchy roots such as taro, yams, and sweet potatoes, as well as the cause of all the trouble to begin with—breadfruit.

Afternoons, the people till their ground again, and all the while, during rest periods and spare moments, the men whittle and carve their flying fish and birds, and the women weave baskets and hats of strips of pandanus frond. Pitcairn has no shops or stores, so the islanders must send overseas for anything they cannot raise or make themselves. The sale of fruit and souvenirs brings in their only cash, which they send away for woodworking tools, fishhooks and line, printed yard goods, and other oddments.

High on the plateau, close under the highest point of land (1,100 feet above the sea) stands Pitcairn's wireless station. Here Fred Christian's son Tom twice a day talks to New Zealand and listens for calls from ships. The winds that blow almost constantly on the breezy plateau turn wind generators to charge the station's batteries.

Round a flat square of hard-packed earth stand the church, post office, and assembly building. Here hangs the island bell, which sounds to announce daily chores and unusual events. Three strokes call all able-bodied males between the ages of 16 and 60 to public work, such as repairing buildings or boats. Four strokes mark the distribution of mail.

Five strokes of the bell, repeated three times, is the most welcome sound on Pitcairn; it signals the sighting of a ship. Ship visits are vital because the passing vessels are the island's only material link with the outside world. Ships used to call approximately every two weeks, but a few years ago the larger of the two shipping lines that made regular stops at the island shifted its run to include Tahiti, and today only freighters with scant passenger accommodation touch at the island, about once a month.

There are no doctors on Pitcairn, and the Adventist pastor of the island, who has some medical training, takes care of most of the islanders' ills. For serious medical emergencies, Tom Christian must radio for help to any ship within hearing. Once a vessel that had called at the island only two days before turned around and raced back because Tom's sister was stricken with acute appendicitis. They took her aboard and the ship's doctor treated her as the ship continued her voyage to the United Kingdom, but it was too late. They buried her at sea.

One can grasp the true isolation of Pitcairn only from the top of the island. There, leaning into the prevailing easterlies of summer that rattle the pandanus fronds and send ripples through the tall grass like the billows of the sea below, one can turn in a complete circle and see nothing but the white-flecked cobalt disk of the Pacific, enclosed by a ring of horizon as hard and unbroken as if drawn with a compass. One can almost sense the enormous distances of the Great South Seas— 3,500 miles northeast to Panama, 3,500 miles southeast to New Zealand.

And so, with the men fishing, planting, and carving, and the women cooking, sewing, and weaving baskets, the placid Pitcairn days glide one into another in a dreamlike suspension of time as it is marked by clocks and calendars. Yet paradoxically in this oasis of peace where, except for the brief flurry of a passing ship, one day seems much like any other, the days and weeks, because uncounted,

Foreword

slip by with a stealthy swiftness. One day merges almost imperceptibly into another, the stars of the seasons wheel slowly across the sky, and the heavy rains of summer give way to the bright blue days of what passes for winter on this mild island at the edge of the tropics.

At last the day came when I had to sail away from Pitcairn on an American brigantine. When I sighted her topmasts rising over the horizon, I remembered the words of Fred Christian. He had said: "I always say Fletcher Christian find a good place to hide."

I agree.

Luis Marden

⚜ PREFACE ⚜

The story of the Pitcairn Island settlement by nine of the "Bounty" mutineers and their entourage of Polynesian men and women, together with a half dozen corollary tales, has been told and retold for more than 150 years. The "Bounty" saga, of which Pitcairn is a constituent part, has been the inspiration for two expensive and widely circulated motion pictures, as well as several less costly. The Pitcairn story has sired an indeterminate number of poems (including a poor one by Bryant and an uneven one by Byron), and a veritable spate of novels, tracts, purportedly factual accounts, short stories (including one by Mark Twain), and even an "Operatick Ballet Spectackle." Interest in Pitcairn is not confined to the Anglo-Saxon world; it has been the subject of books in French, German, Swedish, and Serbo-Croatian.

The attraction has been principally that of a superlative yarn or of a dramatic instance of human regeneration through religious devotion. Sometimes it has been forgotten, for the purpose of arriving at the neat conclusion of "a strong harmonious chord of simple piety," that the story did not end in the first quarter of the nineteenth century, but has continued to this day with the Pitcairn community still in being and still in danger. After the movie fades out and the house lights go on, life continues on the remote Pacific Island, where the progeny of the "Bounty" mutineers arise, perchance, to dig yams, repair boats, or carve or weave a curio.

Preface

The Pitcairn community, occupying an isolated and inaccessible two-square mile island in the vast Pacific, and seldom exceeding two hundred souls in its 175 year history, has attracted the persons and interest of many distinguished (and undistinguished) men representing diverse interests or maritime accidents. Its visitors have included admirals, archaeologists, anthropologists, divers, historians, journalists, noblemen, and novelists. To say nothing of adventurers, church dignitaries, government officials, missionaries, officers of the British Navy, whalers, sealers, yachtsmen, and shipwrecked sailors.

The Pitcairn story, if only in dim outline, is known to many. Its various aspects recall many of the classic cliches, legends, stories, and parables of the Western world. Pitcairn is the very prototype of the man-and-woman-cast-up-on-an-island which has become a cartoon genre. It is the Bali Hai of the song, "that special island." It is the dream nurtured by Melville and others of a South Seas paradise, complete with Fayaways. It is the Swiss Family Robinson. It is Robinson Crusoe with sex. It is Adam and Eve and the apple. It is the Fall—and the Redemption. It is the story of the Exodus, the Revelation, and the Promised Land. It is Utopia. Unplanned and imperfect Eden, Pitcairn has survived many precalculated versions of the perfect community.

Pitcairn embraces in compact and focused style most of the central problems of the human condition. Malthus could have found no more dramatic example than Pitcairn to support his thesis had he delayed its publication for a few years; Pitcairn anticipated the current population explosion. To the so-called color problem may be ascribed the devastating warfare the little community managed to promote without benefit of flags, kings, boundary disputes, or rivalries for commercial markets, or economic ideologies.

As an unplanned experiment in crossbreeding of two disparate races, in cross-culturation, and in human inbreeding (possibly the most intensive of which there are good records), the Pitcairn society is of unique interest to anthropologists, ethnologists, and eugenists.

For the moralist, the philosopher, the student of Utopias, and the religious, the Pitcairn story offers a treasure-filled mine of texts from which each can draw according to his predilection. Pitcairn has aspects of interest to students of medicine and dentistry, sex, education, government, language, economics, and colonialism. The lawyer will note with interest the way in which legislation was tailored to the terrain, its sheer bulk, and the treatment of the problem of land inheritance. The Pitcairn story makes available to the social scientists a controlled (by isolation) experiment difficult to duplicate in the random outer world, with interesting lights on such subjects as class, caste, and color, community property, morals, and alcoholism.

Omitting THE BOMB (the Pitcairners managed to reach the edge of extinction without it) and such pressures of urban living as the insufficiency of parking space, there are few questions we face today that did not confront those voluntarily shipwrecked settlers and their descendants. How they coped with these problems is the Island story which this book proposes to tell, updating it and calling attention to facts and aspects which seem to have been slighted, despite the wealth of attention Pitcairn has received.

It has been suggested that, because of the minuscule character of the community, it will not do to rest too much weight on the Pitcairn experience. Contrariwise, it may be argued that, because of this very reduction in scale and the accompanying intensity of focus (complicating factors being at a comparative minimum), many aspects of the human situation are exposed on Pitcairn with greater clarity than would be possible in the case of a more diffuse and complex society. As in any history, the morals deducible will depend more on what the reader brings to the story than on the tale itself.

Probably more has been written of the Pitcairn community than of any group of comparable size. Nonetheless, the history of Pitcairn Island presents several unique problems. As its most acute scholar, Mr. Maude (1) puts it: ". . . the main chroniclers were either primarily concerned with the Bligh versus Christian controversy or in painting an edifying picture of moral regeneration; for these purposes they were content to use, as their source material, virtually nothing except the reports or published narratives of a few naval officers, in one or two instances adding traditional information obtained from the islanders of the second generation."

Moreover, the period from the founding of the Pitcairn Colony in 1790 to its discovery by Captain Folger in 1808 is shrouded in a cloud of hearsay. There is hardly a statement that can be made about this eventful time that does not rest ultimately upon hearsay testimony, or even hearsay on hearsay. If this does not offer a sufficiency of difficulty, compounded by the strongly conflicting nature of this hearsay testimony, there is the necessity for relying on the reports of visitors to Pitcairn (some of whom stayed for only a few hours or did not even land) for a considerable part of the story. These reports, when rendering the visitors' own observations, rather than hearsay, are frequently invaluable, but subject to the well-deserved skepticism traditionally applicable to travelers' tales.* Not only are the stories these visitors relayed suspect because of their hearsay nature, but because there is frequently good reason to doubt that the visitors transmitted accurately what was told them.

To ignore the many conflicts and lacunae in evidence in the interest of a smoothly running account, however tempting an expedient, is a course which has been rejected. Because of the way in which Pitcairn history has transpired and the not inconsiderable mysteries and problems it encompasses, any arbitrary reading must gloss over difficult and insoluble points. The Pitcairn story is not neat. That is why so many of its chroniclers have frankly resorted to the novel. Any attempt to "prettify" the tale by excision or trick lighting can only add another superfluous distortion to a story already excessively bizarre.

Time is of the utmost materiality in the Pitcairn story; it is not all of a piece as we scan 175 years. There were fat years and lean years, periods when nature smiled and crops exceeded needs, and periods of drought that imposed cruel deprivations on the Islanders. There were times when three ships were hove to off Pitcairn and times when the inhabitants searched the horizon for weeks or months in the vain hope of sighting a vessel. There were dramatic changes in morals, customs, law, dress, and every facet of community life. There were also seeming changes in mood within short intervals. One visitor might find the Islanders smothering differences to present a picture of superhuman harmony; the next might find festering frictions broken out in a rash of recrimination that exaggerated a normal amount of discord into a picture of unbridled animosity.

---

* If it were not enough that "travelers' tales" has become a synonym for dubiety, we are constantly warned, especially in the case of the South Seas, by the travelers themselves against heeding the reports of their predecessors. Typical are the fulminations of Herman Melville in his introduction to *Typee*. It is difficult to decide whether his warnings are bolstered or weakened by the fact that Melville was able to kite a few months' experience in the South Pacific islands and access to prior accounts into a reputation as an authority on South Seas life. No man had more influence in creating the Western image of Polynesia. *See* Anderson, Charles Roberts, *Melville in the South Seas* (New York, 1939).

Preface

One amusing and dramatic instance of confusion of time occurred when Sir Cyprian Bridge, commenting on a murder committed
on Pitcairn, suggested that it could not have happened "in the days of
John Adams." To which Montgomerie retorted that this indicated
ignorance of the slaughter which occurred in John Adams' time. Sir
Cyprian was, of course, referring to the period *after* Adams' personal
regeneration, Montgomerie to the *preceding* period.

To avoid such difficulties, *Pitcairn Island* has been organized
around separate subjects, each dealt with from beginning to end,
rather than juggled together in one chronology. This method serves
the further purpose of making more readily available those aspects of
the story which appeal to special interests, whether in the field of
philology or philately. It is hoped that this will prove a useful and
clarifying device, even at the expense of occasional repetition.

SOURCES OF THE STORY

The Pitcairn saga is not simply a story, it is a literature. Whereas
the voyage of the "Bounty" to Tahiti, the mutiny, the punitive
expedition of the "Pandora," and the court-martial can be recon-
structed from public records, logbooks, official correspondence, and
other evidence admissible in a court of law, our knowledge of what
happened in the first twenty years of the existence of the Pitcairn
Colony rests almost entirely on hearsay, and contradictory hearsay at
that. Short of giving this hearsay an arbitrary reading, it is necessary
to examine the literature in which it was developed, as well as other
publications pertinent to our understanding. It seems logical to examine this literature beforehand.

Pitcairn Island was settled by nine of the "Bounty" mutineers
and a menage of Polynesians that included twelve women, six men,
and an infant girl. The character and background of these settlers are
of material interest for the story. For that reason and to refresh the
reader's memory, the next chapter briefly recounts the oft-told tale of
the voyage of the "Bounty" and the mutiny and the sketchily-told
story of the acquisition of the Polynesian menage with a view particularly to whatever light it may throw on the twenty-eight persons who
initiated the Pitcairn Colony.

Of necessity we must be drawn into some involvement with the

Bligh versus anti-Bligh controversy, raging without abatement after 175 years. Bligh is a historical part of the Pitcairn picture; though he never set foot on that remote island, he has at least a shadow claim to the title of "Father of Pitcairn."

Bligh is the first entrant in the literary sweepstakes. Expelled into the "Bounty" launch with eighteen "loyalists," and arriving at Timor after a historic voyage of six weeks, he immediately issued a stream of letters and reports. Bligh arrived back in England on March 14, 1790, in the temporary role of hero. Before the year was out, George Nicol, Bookseller to His Majesty, published at London Bligh's account under the catch-all title of *A Narrative of the Mutiny on Board His Majesty's Ship Bounty; and the Subsequent Voyage of Part of the Crew in the Ship's Boat from Tofoa, one of the Friendly Islands, to Timor, a Dutch Settlement in the East Indies.* This was followed in 1792 by Bligh's *A Voyage to the South Sea for the Conveying of the Bread-fruit Tree to the West Indies, including the Narrative of the Mutiny.*

Shortly after Bligh's return, a punitive expedition to capture the mutineers was sent out in the "Pandora" under Captain Edward Edwards, described by McKee as a "savagely ruthless officer beside whom Bligh appears more as a fussy old woman than a grim tyrant." For histrionics, its troubled journey rivaled that of the "Bounty." Arrived at Tahiti on March 23, 1791, Edwards rounded up the fourteen surviving of the sixteen men who had elected to remain when Christian and his contingent sailed the "Bounty" to an unknown destination. When the "Pandora" was wrecked on the Great Barrier Reef, Captain Edwards lost four of his caged prisoners by drowning. He returned to England with the remainder, all of whom were put on trial for mutiny.

The first account of the voyage of the "Pandora" was that of its surgeon, George Hamilton, issued at Berwick in 1793 under the title *A Voyage Round the World in His Majesty's Frigate, Pandora.*

The alleged mutineers were tried in September of 1792 in the absence of Bligh—"the part of Hamlet was omitted." (Bligh was on his second breadfruit expedition, successful save for the ironic anti-climax that the West Indian slaves, for whom this succulent delight was intended, proved as indifferent to its taste as to the arduous labors and multiple tragedies which its procurement entailed.)

Two of the alleged mutineers, one on trial, Midshipman Peter

Heywood, and one absent by his own preference, Fletcher Christian, had powerful relatives and friends. Heywood's friends exercised strenuous efforts in behalf of his life and reputation, which gave rise to a considerable literature of its own.

Heywood was convicted and pardoned, along with Boatswain James Morrison, of whom more later. Four alleged mutineers were acquitted and four convicted, one of the latter, A. B. Muspratt, winning pardon by reason of a legal technicality. The other three swung from the yardarm of H.M.S. "Brunswick" on October 29, 1792, in expiation of the guilt of all their fellows.

The Heywood case permeates a great deal of the early Bounty-Pitcairn literature; his exculpation was one of the chief reasons for the book written by his stepdaughter, Lady Belcher, under the title *Mutineers of the Bounty and Their Descendants in Pitcairn and Norfolk Islands* (London, 1870).

While Heywood's case was literally a matter of life or death, Fletcher Christian, then a leading citizen of Pitcairn, could be tried only at the bar of public opinion. This did not dilute the energy with which his barrister brother, Edward Christian, teacher of law and editor of legal works, pursued the matter. Edward could not exculpate Fletcher of the charge of mutiny, but he could attempt to mitigate his crime and the damage to his reputation by establishing what was not at issue in the court-martial: namely, that the mutiny was provoked by the unbearable misconduct of Bligh.

In his assault on Bligh, Edward Christian gathered testimony from members of the "Bounty" crew and in 1794 issued a pamphlet consisting of the abridged minutes of the court-martial kept by Stephen Barney, Muspratt's attorney, and an Appendix in which Edward adduced the testimony (not separately identified) of various "Bounty" men in support of his argument that his brother was a fine chap diverted from the proper conduct natural to him by the intolerable Bligh. Bligh's "Answer" was published in the *British Critic* for December 1794, followed by a "Short Reply" from Edward Christian.*

The excitement over the "Bounty" story eventually subsided; the looming shadow of Napoleon helped cast it in the shade. The last glimpse of the "Bounty" vouchsafed the eighteenth century world

---

* Bligh's Narrative and the rare Minutes and Appendix, Bligh's "Answer," and the "Short Reply" are most readily accessible in a facsimile edition published by Georgian House at Melbourne for The Australiana Society.

Preface

was its departure from Tahiti for an unknown destination on September 23, 1789. It was easy to assume that Christian and his cohorts had met with some maritime disaster in a time when shipwreck was commonplace and the limitless Pacific scantily charted.

In 1808, eighteen years after the settlement of Pitcairn, an American Captain, Mayhew Folger, in the sealing vessel "Topaz," discovered the Colony. Of the fifteen young males who had landed on Pitcairn, John Adams, alias Alexander Smith, was the lone survivor. Adams' account, as reported by Folger, indicated that all the other men had met violent ends. The Colony, numbering thirty-five, included some nine or ten of the Tahitian women who had settled it and twenty-four or twenty-five children of varying ages, some verging on adulthood.

Captain Folger's was the first account of the fate of the "Bounty" and its final complement. It reached the British Admiralty on May 14, 1809, in the form of a dispatch from Rio de Janeiro by Sir Sidney Smith, commander in chief on the Brazil station, which was conveyed from Valparaiso by Lt. Fitzmaurice and included a copy of the "Topaz" logbook entry. The Admiralty chose to ignore the report for conjectural reasons.

Captain Folger's brief visit to Pitcairn is also memorialized in his letter of March 1, 1813 to the British Admiralty and in his letter to his friend, Captain Amasa Delano. The fullest account of Folger's visit comes from Delano's salty *The Voyages and Travels of Amasa Delano* (Boston, 1817) which reprints the letter. It is allegedly based on what Folger told Delano; its accuracy is highly suspect.

The next visitors to Pitcairn, again accidental, arrived in 1814 in command of the British ships of war "Briton" and "Tagus." This encounter is reported in a letter by Captain Staines to the Admiralty under the date of October 18, 1814, in a private account by Captain Pipon, now in the Mitchell Library in manuscript form* (partially quoted in a variety of publications), and in the book published in London in 1818, written by one of the officers, Lt. J. Shillibeer, *A Narrative of the Briton's Voyage to Pitcairn Island*. Shillibeer, like some subsequent reporters, never went ashore on Pitcairn.

In 1825, Captain F. W. Beechey arrived at Pitcairn on express orders from the Admiralty in H.M.S. "Blossom." His visit resulted in

* Banks Papers, Brabourne Collection, Vol. 1, pp. 17–51, M.L. Ref. A 77.

the most complete report, embodied in Beechey's *Narrative of a Voyage to the Pacific and Bering Strait,* two volumes (London, 1831). Beechey's account is further distinguished by being based in part on purported quotations from a diary of Midshipman Edward Young, not mentioned by anyone else and not to be found. Because of its comprehensiveness and detail, Beechey's has received wider acceptance than other accounts and is the basis for most of the many versions of early Pitcairn history.

Visits by Frenchman Moerenhout in 1829 are described in his *Voyage aux îles du Grand Océan* (Paris, 1837). Probably because of its inaccessibility and its not having been translated into English, this valuable account has been ignored by many of those who related the Pitcairn story.

The reports of others who touched on Pitcairn in intervening and subsequent years all form part of the Pitcairn source material. What distinguishes the accounts named is that they all report versions of the 1790 to 1808 history of Pitcairn related to the visitors by John Adams, who died in 1829.

Unfortunately for the peace of mind of Island historians and the curious, each of the four versions, although based largely on what the writers were told by Adams, was materially different from the others in outlining the fate of the deceased settlers. If this inconsistency and the hearsay nature of the evidence were not a sufficient objection, Adams himself was the beau ideal of the impeachable witness. His self-interest in clearing himself of the guilt of mutiny* and many circumstances reflecting on his veracity would have provided a cross-examiner with an invitation to destroy his credibility. The visiting captains, however, readily accepted what Adams told them, and pictured him as a kindly patriarch, completely regenerated and full of good will, piety, and deep religious feeling.

There are reasons to suspect that this view was more ingenuous than Adams himself. Adams told Captain Pipon that he was not "in the smallest degree concerned in the mutiny, he being at the time it happened, sick in bed." Adams told Captain Beechey that he was "sleeping in a hammock" and, on learning of the mutiny, returned and remained in the hammock until he saw Christian issuing arms,

---

* To Moerenhout, however, Adams admitted that he immediately accepted the proposal of mutiny when awakened from a deep sleep. This admission was made, of course, long after the danger of punishment had evaporated.

when "he turned out again and went for a cutlass." The record clearly fixes Adams as one of the most active in the mutiny, the third man who came on deck armed, and as having stood over Captain Bligh with loaded musket and fixed bayonet.

If one overlooks Adams' fabrications as natural in one who retained a healthy fear of the yardarm which had claimed three of his shipmates, there remains the circumstance that Adams alone, of all the males who landed on Pitcairn from the "Bounty," survived to greet Folger and subsequent visitors. Adams, who "went for a cutlass" when it seemed propitious, was a man born to take care of himself and obviously not above tailoring the truth to that end.

Accounts based on the four named visits are the main sources of early Pitcairn history as reported in the Bounty-Pitcairn literature. They are supplemented only slightly by the *Pitcairn Island Register Book*, much quoted from even before its publication in entirety at London in 1929, under the aegis of the Society for Promoting Christian Knowledge, with an introduction by Sir Charles Lucas. This record of the annals of the Colony was started by John Buffett in 1823 and its entries for 1790 to that date must have been based on what was told Buffett by the inescapable Adams.

One further resource, long neglected, was brought to light by Mackaness (1931) and Maude(1) (1958). Jenny (her mouth-filling, vowel-happy Tahitian name was Teehuteatuaonoa) was Pitcairn's first emigrant in 1817 and the only one of the settlers not to die on Pitcairn.

After her return to Tahiti, she was interviewed on three separate occasions. The first interview, Jenny(1), was reported in the Sydney *Gazette* for July 17, 1819 and reproduced in other newspapers. The second, Jenny(2), in 1824, is reported by Otto von Kotzebue in his *A New Voyage Round the World*, two volumes (London, 1830). The last, Jenny(3), "an account dictated to the Rev. Henry Nott in the presence of Captain Peter Dillon and communicated by the latter verbatim," was published by the Bengal *Hurkaru* for October 2, 1826, and is more readily available in the *United Service Journal*, pt. 2, pp. 589–593, 1829.

These accounts, even the allegedly "verbatim" account, unfortunately do not reach us in Jenny's own words. Besides the indirect nature of the quotations, there are obvious errors made by the reporters, such as mistakes in nomenclature, and a suspicion of a strong editorial instinct at work arises from a close reading. Nonetheless, these accounts are invaluable. Jenny had no axe to grind. There are no major inconsistencies in the stories she related at considerable intervals; they check out with known facts in all but a few instances, and Jenny was an eyewitness to most of the events described. These accounts and similarly neglected accounts by Captain King, an 1819 visitor, and John Buffett, Pitcairn's first immigrant in 1823,* provide a means of checking Adams' variant stories and developing a clearer picture of the first decade of the Colony, albeit many questions remain.

One might assume that the doubts created by incomplete and conflicting stories would be dissipated in this particular milieu by the seemingly inevitable development of an oral tradition. Dramatic, bloody, and mortal events occurred which intimately concerned every member of a tiny community almost completely illiterate. The adult survivors of this holocaust, with the exception of Adams, were all women who derived from a tradition where it was commonplace to recite from memory one's ancestors for generations back. In their country, stories existed *only* in oral form. It would seem that the least we are entitled to expect is an epic.

As Dr. Shapiro discovered in 1934, this expectation was not matched by fact; all that the Pitcairners knew was what they had read in the same books commonly available to outlanders. The answer may lie in the anxiety of the Islanders to conform to the image of piety and goodness broadcast by the early reports.

The spate of books describing Pitcairn, beginning with the anonymously published work of Sir John Barrow (*The Eventful History of the Mutiny and Piratical Seizure of H.M.S. Bounty*, London 1831) emphasized this image and passed over the era of savagery and slaughter as too horrendous to do more than outline for the purpose of contrast with the present happy condition of the Colony. Under these circumstances, it is conceivable that any oral tradition which may have existed was stifled in deference to the prevailing picture of an island Eden.†

Barrow's book is remarkable on a number of counts. It became

---

* Extract from the "Journal of Captain Henry King" of the "Elizabeth," *Edinburgh Philosophical Journal*, Vol. III (1820), pp. 381–388; and "A Narrative of twenty years' residence on Pitcairn's Island," *The Friend*, Honolulu, 1846, Vol. 4, pp. 2–3, 20–21, 27–28, 34–35, 50–51, 66–68.
† The scraps of oral tradition exhumed by later writers, Brodie, Young, and O'Brien, add only little of a solid nature to the story, although not without interest.

known that it was the work of the Secretary to the Admiralty, so that it reflected a quasi-official Navy view of the "Bounty" affair. And what a view!

Mutiny was of course inexcusable under any circumstances, but Bligh was clearly not a gentleman and had been guilty of conduct unbecoming an officer of the Royal Navy. (As a natural consequence, no doubt.) Barrow's volume was the first to put between two covers the six principal strands of the story: the "Bounty" expedition, the mutiny, Bligh's voyage in the "Bounty" launch to Timor, the punitive voyage of the "Pandora," the court-martial, and the Pitcairn Island settlement. It is the oldest version still in print; brought out in 1914 in *The World's Classics Library*, with an introduction by Admiral Sir Cyprian Bridge, it was reprinted in 1928, 1935, 1936 (twice), 1944, 1947, 1951, and 1960.

Barrow's book was also the reopening gun of the Bligh-against-everybody warfare, marked by few and brief armistices since. The mutiny of the tiny "Bounty" has inspired more discussion and controversy than all other maritime mutinies combined. The major part of the argument has swirled around Captain Bligh—Bligh against Christian or Heywood, Bligh against the "loyalists" (one can easily imagine him complaining that, with such "friends" as Fryer and Purcell, he needed no enemies), Bligh against the friends and relatives of the real and alleged mutineers, Bligh against Royal Navy standards of marine command and what constitutes a proper "gentleman and officer," Bligh against a fluctuating public opinion as to his character and conduct. Only one, Montgomerie, has suggested that the fault might lie in the stars; for most the question is merely who was to blame and how much. The Niagara of controversy indicates the existence of a copious stream of factual disputes to feed it. Curiously, the essential physical facts, if not always the motivations of the actors, are written large and clear in the extensive record, and the postulated stream is a small and unimportant trickle.

The Barrow view of Bligh dominated for a century; frequently echoed in the interval, it did not meet strong opposition until the 1930s. Then occurred a resurgence of interest and the record was scrutinized anew and combed with much thoroughness.

Geoffrey Rawson's sympathetic biography, *Bligh of the "Bounty,"* was published in London in 1930, followed shortly by the monumental work of Professor George Mackaness, *The Life of Vice-*

Preface

Admiral William Bligh, first published at Sydney in 1931, and issued in a revised edition in 1951.

The Mackaness work is by all odds the most scholarly and thorough of any in the field, and, while only incidentally concerned with the Pitcairn story, throws invaluable light on the Pitcairn mutineers and includes liberal quotations from unpublished documents pertinent to the early history of the Colony. Mackaness is determinedly and scrupulously "fair," if sympathetic, to his controversial subject. If Bligh emerges smelling considerably better than his nineteenth century characterizations would suggest, it is as a result of the facts which his biographer has culled from the record and analyzed with studied reasonableness.

This painstaking biography is almost beyond praise, but apparently not beyond exception, both by those adherents of Bligh, such as Montgomerie (*William Bligh of the Bounty, in Fact and in Fable,* London, 1937), who find Dr. Mackaness' portrait insufficiently rehabilitory, and those still unwilling to discard the tag of villainy. The latter, submerged by "rehabilitory" forces for decades, have found a new leader in Alexander McKee (*H.M.S. Bounty,* New York, 1962), who has not only resurrected and embellished all the old charges against Bligh, but has unearthed new and even more damaging ones.

Apparently something about the "Bounty" story inevitably involves the emotions of those who study it; there are no neutrals. What must be the unconsciously funniest line in the whole vast literature contains an appeal to the "impartial observer" (save the mark!) by one of the most partisan commentators. Scrutiny of the many differing interpretations indicates that it is the particular "slant" or scale of values of the analyst, rather than what is thrown on the scales, that determines the reading.

Thus, for one example, it may be plausibly argued that the lash was a cruel and inhuman punishment (it was) and that, hence, its employment could not be justified. With equal plausibility it may be urged that the lash was an essential form of discipline in the context of the times, so recognized and widely administered by most Navy captains with less restraint than that employed by Bligh.

One other book, the manuscript of which was completed in the 1790s, though first published by the Golden Cockerel Press in 1935, deserves special mention. This is the so-called *Journal of James*

Morrison, boatswain of the "Bounty." His *Journal,* handwritten by himself, purports to be based on a notebook or diary (like Young's, missing) contemporaneous with the events described therein, which include the "Bounty's" southward voyage, the mutiny, the wanderings of the "Bounty" until the split-up at Tahiti, the life of the men remaining there and later taken into custody by Captain Edwards, and the return voyage of the "Pandora." For an important part of the story it is the only or chief source. The manuscript of the *Journal,* after a sojourn with Peter Heywood and his heirs, and apparent disappearance for a time, wound up in the Mitchell Library.

If there were a need for controversy, the Morrison *Journal* could by itself supply it. Cogent attacks have been mounted against the possibility that Morrison's notebook could have survived the vicissitudes of the "Pandora" and Morrison's imprisonment, but even the harshest critic of Morrison's *Journal,* Montgomerie, admits that "it contains a good deal of the truth." And Maude(1) finds it possible "to verify so many of his statements from other sources that one is left in no doubt as to its reliability, at least where his own personal interests are not concerned."

Morrison's account is invaluable for the Pitcairn story because of the light it throws on characters involved therein and the circumstances preceding the final voyage of the "Bounty." The character of the founders of the Pitcairn Colony is of the essence in evaluating the bloody events of the first decade, as indicated by the statement of Montgomerie, a man with a pretty gift for plain speaking: "So far were the mutineers from being a nest of love birds, turned to evil ways by the cruel conduct of Bligh, it seems obvious that the moment the hand of authority was removed from them they showed themselves as quite unfit to manage their own lives."

The authorities and sources cited in this chapter are far from exhaustive, as further citations and separate chapter bibliographies will indicate. The reader interested in exploring the source material and the secondary use made thereof is referred to the awesome bibliography in Mackaness and to the authorities which Mr. Maude* has made available in *In Search of a Home: From the Mutiny to Pitcairn Island* (1789–1790), Journal of the Polynesian Society, vol. 67, pp. 106–116, Maude(1); *Tahitian Interlude,* Journal of the Poly-

---

* Harry E. Maude, O.B.E., Institute of Pacific Studies, Canberra, Australia.

nesian Society, vol. 68, pp. 115–138, Maude (2) ; *A Social and Administrative History of Pitcairn Island* (typescript 1941), Maude (3) ; chapter entitled, ''The History of Pitcairn Island,'' Maude (4), in *The Pitcairnese Language,* New York, 1964. A selective bibliography of the most frequently cited sources will be found on page 246, and should be consulted to identify authorities designated by name.

For whatever interest it may hold, there are here listed some of the poems, novels, and short stories inspired by the Pitcairn saga, plus an ''Operatick Ballet Spectackle.'' It seems that it was not enough for this bizarre yarn to stagger the imagination; it must also stimulate it.

POEMS

Bryant, William Cullen, *A Song of Pitcairn Island.*
Byron, Lord George, *The Island, or Christian and His Comrades.*
Coleridge, Samuel Taylor, *The Rime of the Ancient Mariner.* The connection of this famous poem with our story is conjectural, but see *Wake of the Bounty,* by C. S. Wilkinson (London, 1953).
McGilchrist, John, M.D., *The Mutineers* (1859).
Mitford, Mary Russell, *Christina, or the Maid of the South Seas* (1811).

NOVELS

Becke, L. and J. W., *The Mutineer* (1898).
Christian, Fletcher, *Letters from Mr. Fletcher Christian* (London, 1796).
Christian, Fletcher, *Voyages and Travels of Fletcher Christian* (London, 1798). This and the preceding volume, although purporting to be factual accounts, have been declared forgeries, and are given the designation ''novel'' for that reason.
Chaumier, Captain Frederick, E.N., *Jack Adams, the Mutineer,* 3 vol. (London, 1838).
Goss, Sylvester T., *The Life of Alexander Smith* (Boston, 1819). Purporting to be derived from a manuscript in the hand of John Adams, alias Alexander Smith, but obviously a fiction.
Merle, Robert, *The Island* (New York, 1964), translated from the French. While admittedly inspired by the Pitcairn story, it departs therefrom deliberately.

Preface

Nordhoff, C. B. and Hall, J. N., *Pitcairn's Island*. It is interesting to
note that, while in the first two novels of the "Bounty" trilogy,
Mutiny on the Bounty and *Men Against the Sea,* the authors
stuck close to the facts, in their version of the Pitcairn story they
drew freely on their imagination.

Rutter, Owen, *Cain's Birthday* (London, 1930).

Whiteing, Richard, *The Island* (New York, 1899).

Wilson, Erle, *Adams of the Bounty* (1958).

SHORT STORIES

London, Jack, "Seed of McCoy" (in *South Sea Tales,* New York,
1911).

Twain, Mark, "The Great Revolution in Pitcairn" (in *The Stolen
White Elephant,* 1882).

OPERATICK BALLET SPECTACKLE

Pitcairn Island: A Romantick Operatick Spectackle, founded on the
recent discovery of a numerous Colony, formed by, and descended
from the Mutineers of *The Bounty Frigate.* First performed at
the *Theatre Royal, Drury Lane,* on Wednesday, April 17, 1816.
With new and select Musick, new Scenery, Dresses and Embellish-
ments. Printed by C. Lowndes, Marquis Court, Drury Lane. Sold
at the Theatre only.

✾ CONTENTS ✾

"The history of your island will long, I may say always, be a wonder." From a letter of Robert Folger, son of the discoverer of the Pitcairn colony, Capt. Mayhew Folger, to Rosalind Amelia Young of Pitcairn Island.

". . . the best of all South Seas stories is a very famous, lurid, and sentimental melodrama. It starts with institutionalized brutality, dips into psychopathology, goes heavily into sex, fights a war, proceeds with exploration in a Crusoeish vein, declines into lethal violence, and finishes on a strong harmonious chord of simple piety." J. C. Furnas, *Anatomy of Paradise.*

"I distinctly recall that you paused, after the narrative, and commented that you would rather go to Pitcairn than anywhere else in the world." Dr. Harry L. Shapiro, anthropologist, describing a lecture by Professor E. A. Hooton, in his "Epistle Dedicatory" of *The Heritage of the Bounty.*

". . . I now thought it the most eligible place in the world, a place free from temptation, and with no hindrance to prevent a man becoming a christian. . . . I found something more was necessary, beside reading and prayer to become a christian, and although secluded as it were, from the world, I found that the heart of man was the same . . ." John Buffett, Pitcairn's first immigrant in 1823. *A narrative of 20 years' residence on Pitcairn's Island.*

"Mais il faudrait les bien comprendre, avoir leurs gouts, leurs vertus." J. A. Moerenhout.

"The ship is moor'd and we are now our own masters." Answer given to mutiny leader Christian by mutineers Sumner and Quintal when asked to explain an unauthorized shore leave at Tubuai.

xxx

Part One

THE BOUNTY EXPEDITION,
THE MUTINY,
FINDING PITCAIRN

☙ THE BOUNTY EXPEDITION ☙

It all began with the breadfruit tree.

First discovered on the voyage of Mendana de Neyra in 1598, it remained for William Dampier, whose collection of *Voyages* was published in 1729, to extol its virtues as a nourishing food, and for the accounts of Cook's voyage to Tahiti in 1769 to spread its fame. Not the least appealing feature of the breadfruit plant was the effortlessness with which its bounty could be achieved. As Lord Byron put it in *The Island, or Christian and his Comrades:*

> The Breadtree, which, without the ploughshare, yields
> The unreap'd harvest of unfurrow'd fields,
> And bakes its unadulterated loaves
> Without a furnace, in unpurchased groves,
> And flings off famine from its fertile breast,
> A priceless market for the gathering guest.

It was only inevitable that such irresistible attractions should command the fancy of the West Indies planters who found themselves under the painful necessity of feeding their slaves. They began to agitate for the transplantation of this estimable plant to their clime. The Royal Society for Promoting Arts and Commerce offered a gold medal to the first to accomplish this. Sir Joseph Banks, president of the Royal Society, proposed an expedition to Tahiti to King George III early in 1787. That monarch, in his day as devoted to geographical

3

explorations as some of our present rulers to interplanetary ones, gave his approval. A 33-year-old lieutenant, to be known to history as "Breadfruit Bligh," was appointed on August 16, 1787, to command the expedition.[1]

THE CAPTAIN

Bligh's selection was merited by his sound record as sailing master with Captain Cook on his third and fatal voyage to the South Seas in the "Resolution," by his extensive services in the Navy and the merchant fleet, and by his superlative knowledge of naval surveying and cartography. Since merit was not always paramount in Navy appointments, it may have been of equal importance that he was given support by his wife's uncle, Duncan Campbell, who today would be described as a "shipping tycoon." Campbell sold to the British Navy the trading ship, originally named "Bethia," which, symbolically renamed and refurbished for its mission, became the immortal "Bounty." Campbell not only "put forward Bligh's qualifications" to that influential patron of the geographical arts, Sir Joseph Banks, but won his telling support for the appointment. Banks did not yet know Bligh personally, but knew of him and had obtained for Bligh a share in the profits of the official account of Cook's third voyage. He was to become Bligh's lifelong friend, patron, and advocate.

THE SHIP

Adherents of Bligh have urged, not without justification, that the "Bounty" was too small for its mission. Its proud master described it in his *Narrative* in the following fashion:

> Her burthen was nearly 215 tons; her extreme length on deck, 90 feet ten inches; extreme breadth, 24 feet 3 inches; and height in the hold under the beams, at the main hatchway, 10 feet 3 inches. In the cock pit were the cabins of the surgeon, gunner, botanist, and clerk, with a steward room and store-rooms. The between decks was divided in the following manner:—the great cabin was appropriated for the preservation of the plants and extended as far forward as the after hatchway. It had two large sky-lights, and on each side three scuttles for air, and was fitted with a false floor cut full of holes to contain the garden-pots, in which the plants were to be brought home. The deck was covered with lead,

and at the foremost corners of the cabin were fixed pipes to carry off the water that drained from the plants, into tubs placed below to save it for future use. I had a small cabin on one side to sleep in, adjoining to the great cabin, and a place near the middle of the ship to eat in. The bulkhead of this apartment was at the after-part of the main hatchway, and on each side of it were the berths of the mates and midshipmen; between these berths the arms-chest was placed. The cabin of the master, in which was always kept the key of the arms, was opposite to mine. . . . The ship was masted according to the proportion of the navy: but, on my application, the masts were shortened, as I thought them too much for her, considering the nature of the voyage.

THE "BOUNTY" ROSTER

The "Bounty" roster has been the subject of so much derogation and praise that one might conclude that it was actually two rosters because of the improbability of a single roster giving rise to such opposing views. It was remarkable on at least two counts; as far as can be ascertained, it listed no men with criminal records and no pressed men. The indefatigable Dr. George Mackaness reported that, "Careful search has been made to ascertain whether any of the crew of the 'Bounty' had criminal records. No evidence has been discovered. If they had, they were probably careful to keep the fact dark. On the other hand for such special service as that on which the 'Bounty' was engaged the men were usually specially recommended."

And Alexander McKee, after noting that thirty-two men had deserted and been placed on the vessel's "Run" list while she was waiting to sail, comments that it "was nothing very unusual" and that, in consequence, "the most discontented men had, therefore, already discharged themselves."

The reader familiar with the press gang method of recruitment commonly employed by the Royal Navy and the conditions of Navy service will not wonder that desertion in port was common and was the chief reason why crews were rarely allowed shore leave. The press gang frequently filled a Navy ship's roster with the social dregs of port city streets and jails, inevitably garnishing it with criminals and "hard cases."

If only for negative reasons, the "Bounty" roster was at least several cuts above what was characteristic of a Royal Navy ship of the late eighteenth century. The unusual voluntary character of the

"Bounty" roster may have resulted from the fact that the ship, though armed with 4 short four-pounder carriage guns and 10 half-pounder swivel guns, was not on a war mission and was bound for a destination of well-advertised attractions. (The tales brought back from the South Seas by the early voyagers of luscious food, benign climate, and complaisant nymphs were mouthwatering.) It may have been in part because Bligh was given a rather free hand in the selection of his officers and crew. Fletcher Christian, master's mate, and midshipmen Heywood, Stewart, and Hallet were all personal selections of Bligh, and all the other officers, in accordance with Navy custom, were required to meet his approval. He also picked at least several members of the crew.

This may be the place to note that Bligh himself, at various times, especially after the vain attempt to round the Horn, commended his crew in strong terms. More frequently he rated them so harshly as to render inevitable the conclusion that never a captain sailed with so sorry a gang of landlubbers. (It is interesting to note, in this connection, that the peerless Captain Cook, on his first voyage to the Pacific, complained sharply in his log of the quality and conduct of his first and second lieutenants, one of the midshipmen, and other members of his company. Was this par for the course? or was incompetence rife in the Navy?)

Bligh's supporting cast on the "Bounty" was not beyond reproach, especially when viewed from his perfectionist stance. The surgeon, Thomas Huggan, in addition to dubious competence, suffered from unappeasability of alcoholic appetite and spent practically all his time in his cabin in a valiant effort to surmount this distressing condition, relinquishing the unequal contest only when he succeeded in drinking himself to death after arrival at Tahiti.

Master John Fryer proved to be a prickly character, almost as intransigent as Bligh himself.

Midshipman Peter Heywood, whose guilt or innocence of mutiny became a *cause célèbre*, was all of fourteen years of age when he boarded the "Bounty" and was sixteen at the time of the mutiny.

Purcell, the carpenter, as a warrant officer was highly conscious of his special status and consequent exemption from flogging. An early unionist, he was quick to call his captain's attention to his claimed immunity to ordinary duty and to his proprietary rights in his tools.

Midshipmen Hayward and Hallet, beachcombers without portfolio, developed a disconcerting talent for falling asleep on watch at crucial moments.

The recreation department was represented by Michael Byrne, the "blind fiddler," whose presence Bligh explains on the ground that "some time for relaxation and mirth is absolutely necessary" and that, because of the difficulty in getting a man to play the violin, he "preferred at last to take one two-thirds blind than come without one."

Despite the absence of pressed men, the roster included a generous sprinkling of the "hard cases" common in Navy service—tough bully boys like Quintal, McCoy, Master-at-Arms Churchill, and Thompson. These were of the type whose propensity for violence lay just beneath the skin. To control them was the function of the lash. It did not always prove a sovereign remedy.

The list of potential troublemakers would not be complete without mention of Fletcher Christian, master's mate, young, ardent, and thin-skinned. Though Bligh, when not berating him, gave Christian many tokens of favor, such as appointing him acting lieutenant in the course of the voyage, it was Christian who was to prove Bligh's undoing. Christian had boasted that he knew how to handle his Captain, but repeated tongue lashings pierced his fragile armor—Christian was much too human to give Navy duty priority over his own passions.

Considerable controversy has centered on the question whether the officers of the "Bounty" were inferior or superior. Sir John Barrow takes the former view, and Sir Cyprian Bridge, in his introduction to the 1914 edition of Sir John Barrow's book, holds the latter view. Bridge supports his position by reference to the superior social position of Christian, Young, Heywood, Stewart, Hallet, and Hayward. (This matter of class is part of the warp and woof of the whole story, although direct discussion thereof is strangely neglected by most commentators. (See pages 139 ff.)

From H. S. Montgomerie comes the statement that the "presence in a ship's company of ambitious men, educated above the general level of their respective stations but lacking in ballast, was liable to lead to difficulties." Mackaness takes the side of Barrow. He places weight on the derelictions of the officers reported in Bligh's private and unpublished log. These entries certainly support the argument that the officers were guilty of grievous neglects of duty and did not meet Bligh's standards of naval conscientiousness and duty. Curiously, though, Dr. Mackaness fails to answer his own question as to whether "Bligh's men were above or below the average."

That Christian and Lebogue, the sailmaker, had sailed with Bligh on two previous voyages, and several other members of the crew on at least one, has been much made of—by both sides. Like many facts in the Bounty-Pitcairn story, it is of ambivalent purport. The Bligh adherents argue that Bligh could not have been the cruel bully pictured to a gullible public, or else Christian would certainly not have sailed with him for a third time. The counterargument is obvious. Montgomerie's solution is that Bligh, "for all his many merits, was not a good judge of character." McKee suggests that Bligh, a Cornishman and Celt, was predisposed by a "temperamental affinity to people less stolid than the Anglo-Saxons" to favor Manxmen in selecting his officers.

One other point frequently raised by Bligh supporters—the lack of Marines—should be discussed before setting sail for Tahiti. Marines formed a police force on most Navy vessels because, as Geoffrey Rawson puts it in his *Last Voyage of the Pandora*, "Mutiny was in the air. . . . the isolated case of the 'Bounty,' with its special circumstances, was soon to be followed by serious and prolonged outbreaks in the British fleets. . . . Admiral Byng was executed for his failure to raise the siege of Minorca. The great crime was mutiny. . . . Bligh . . . lived in times when the triangle and the gallows were there for all to see."

The constant threat of mutiny was the result of manning Navy ships so largely with the bitterly unwilling, and otherwise dubious, products of the press gangs and of permitting conditions so cruel as to test the endurance of amiable men, let alone that of "hard cases." Navy service was characterized by pitiful pay, maggoty food, scurvy, infrequent shore leave, and no certainty of discharge, to say nothing of the frequently brutal discipline necessary to enforce acceptance of such harsh conditions.

Plain flogging was not at the top of the punishment list. Even the simpatico Captain Cook employed the lash ungrudgingly, much more so than Bligh. Cook, incidentally, carried Marines with him to the Pacific. Marines were employed to make mutiny impossible. Captain Bligh complained, in an oblique way, of the lack of Marines *after* the mutiny. Their absence may be attributed to reliance on the picked nature of the crew and its special mission, or to the lack of space on the ship, or simply to Navy parsimony.

THE VOYAGE

The "Bounty" sailed from Spithead, England, on November 28, 1787, got stalled by unfriendly winds at St. Helen's, and finally got under weigh on December 23. A few days later occurred the first of the incidents used to support the attack on Bligh, who served as purser as well as commander, an expedient not uncommon on small vessels. On airing some casks, Bligh found two cheeses missing and accused the crew of stealing them. Hillbrant, the cooper, bravely protested that the cheeses had been taken to Bligh's house while the ship was in port, whereupon he was threatened with a "damn'd good flogging" if he said any more, and the cheese allowance was stopped. On the next banyan (meatless) day, no cheese was issued. The seamen refused the butter issue on the theory that acceptance would be tacit admission of theft of the cheeses. John Williams reinforced the resentment of the crew with his declaration that he himself had carried the cheeses to Mr. Bligh's house "with a cask of vinegar and some other things. . . . "

The "Bounty" now battled fierce gales all the way to Tenerife in the Canary Islands, where it arrived on January 6. Reprovisioning included twenty-three pumpkins which were to figure in the next rift, again involving the perennial question of food. Favored by better weather, the voyage continued southward, amidst grumblings of the crew against insufficiency of the ship's fare. Many of those sympathetic to Bligh are inclined to dismiss these complaints as routine griping. The judicious Mackaness characterizes many of them as "somewhat frivolous." It may be questioned whether this viewpoint takes sufficient cognizance of the importance of food to men subjected to strenuous physical labor and to the monotony of protracted sea voyages; the crew had steeled itself to overlook the lack of quality (to put it politely) in their rations, but could not ignore insufficiency.

Bligh, intending to make for Tahiti without stopping, put his company on two-thirds allowance of bread. This was accepted without complaint; but when Bligh, desirous of disposing of the pumpkins before the now warmer latitudes completely spoiled them, issued them in lieu of bread at the rate of one pound of pumpkin for two of bread, the men "refused and on Mr Bligh's being informed of it, he came up in a violent passion, and calld all hands, telling Mr Samuel (Bligh's loyal clerk) to call the first man of every mess and let him see who would dare to refuse it or anything else that he should order to be served, saying 'You dam'd infernal scoundrels, I'll make you eat grass or anything you can catch before I have done with you.' "

This edict was accepted, more grudgingly by the officers than by the men, but discontent was reinflamed when the "beef and pork [began] to appear very light, and as there had never yet been any weigh'd when open'd, it was supposed that the casks ran short of their weight, for which reason the people apply'd to the master and begg'd that he would examine the business and procure them redress." Bligh's answer was to threaten with a flogging any future complainants. James Morrison, from whose *Journal* we have been quoting, goes on to accuse Bligh of snatching for himself "all the prime pieces" when a cask was broached and to complain of the sparing issue of "pease & oatmeal." In his unpublished answer to Morrison, Bligh designates Morrison a villain and vehemently, though unconvincingly, denies his charges.

Early in March, Bligh "gave to Mr. Fletcher Christian, whom I [Bligh] had before directed to take charge of the third watch, a written order to act as lieutenant." To this promotion over the head of Master Fryer, Alexander McKee attributes Fryer's animosity to Bligh. The plausibility of this bit of "mind-reading" is somewhat impaired by the fact that it is unsupported by any concrete fact in the record, and that there are indications to the contrary.

The first flogging took place on March 11. The victim, subjected to twenty-four lashes, was Matthew Quintal, later to take active part in the mutiny and to become one of the founding fathers of Pitcairn. The offense was "insolence and contempt to the Master," as Bligh put it in his log book, apparently adding the words "to the Master" at a date much later than the original entry. In his published *Voyage*, he attributes Quintal's punishment to a complaint by the Master of "insolence and mutinous behavior."

The next alimentary difference of opinion occurred two weeks later, when Bligh issued, in lieu of the day's allowance of "pork and pease," a sheep which Bligh's log described as "killed" and Morrison's *Journal* as "dying." According to Morrison, "it was divided and most part of it thrown overboard, and some dried shark supply'd its place for a Sunday dinner, for it was no other than skin and bone."

Frivolity of a sort characterized one disciplinary incident at this time. George Mackaness tells it well:

> From an entry made in Bligh's log-book, but afterwards crossed out in pencil, though still legible, we find that Bligh stopped the grog from John Mills and William Brown, the gardener, for refusing to dance in the evening as usual. This certainly savours of harshness on the part of Bligh, for Brown was at the time ill with rheumatism and on the sick-list. In his excess of zeal for the health of his crew, Bligh certainly exceeded the bounds of discretion when he tried to make a sick sailor dance the hornpipe, though, after all, the stopping of a man's grog for a few days can hardly be considered very severe punishment. On the other hand, it is significant that both Mills and Brown accompanied Christian to Pitcairn.

The "Bounty" now reached the justly dreaded region of Cape Horn—at the wrong season, as Bligh had feared. His orders called for him to make passage around this cape as first choice, and his seaman's pride and, possibly, fear of future criticism caused him to battle storms for a cruel and debilitating month before exercising the option of sailing around the Cape of Good Hope, an option which he had foresightedly extracted from the Admiralty before leaving England. It was now April 21 and in another month the "Bounty" reached Simon's Bay, Capetown. On the day of arrival, just before going ashore, Bligh "punished John Williams with six lashes for neglect of duty in heaving the lead." Williams was to become a mutineer and member of the Pitcairn contingent.

After refitting and reprovisioning, and with his men refreshed, Bligh took off again on the first of July. Adventure Bay in Tasmania was reached on August 21, and anchor was dropped with a view to obtaining wood and water, and perhaps some fish and game. Here occurred two incidents involving carpenter Purcell. In the first, he apparently refused to take lying down his Captain's criticism with respect to his conduct of a wooding party, and, in the second, he refused to assist in hoisting water into the hold.

In the first case, Bligh ordered Purcell back to general ship duty, because "I could not bear the loss of an able working and healthy man." In the second case, when Purcell stated that "he would do

anything in his line, but as to that duty he could not comply with,''
Bligh threatened to cut off his provisions, ''which immediately brought
him to his senses.''

In October, after resumption of the voyage, the first death on
board ship occurred, that of able seaman James Valentine, of ''asthmatic complaint'' and, quite likely, of mistreatment and neglect by
Surgeon Huggan, whose prowess with the bottle apparently exceeded
that with the knife. Captain Bligh was more than a little annoyed.

Bligh was further exasperated by Master Fryer's refusal to
countersign various ship's account books, as was necessary to their
validation, unless Bligh would certify that Fryer ''had been doing
nothing amiss during his time on board.'' Bligh refused to accept this
condition, and Fryer refused to sign.

Bligh called all hands aft, had the Articles of War read, whereupon Fryer yielded, saying, ''I sign in obedience to your orders, but
this may be cancelled hereafter.''

The result of these contretemps, according to Morrison, was that
''Mr. Bligh and his mess mates, the Master and Surgeon, fell out, and
separated, each taking his part of the stock & retiring to live in their
own cabins, after which they had several disputes & seldom spoke but
on duty; and even then with much apparent reserve.''

The significance of the account book episode is obscure. Mackaness puts it down to ''cantankerousness'' on the part of Fryer. McKee
suggests that it was an attempt by Fryer to protect himself against
blame for any ''fiddle'' in the accounts, such as that indicated in the
cheese and, possibly, other incidents. It does make clear that the
mutual detestation of Fryer and Bligh was antecedent to their cheek
by jowl proximity for forty-one days in the ''Bounty'' long boat.

TAHITI AHOY

Relief was now just over the horizon. On October 25 the crew
sighted the promised land—Tahiti of the golden haze and the bril-
liantly-hued tavern tales, paradisical isle of sailors' dream shore
leaves. Strangely enough, it turned out to be at least as good as
advertised.

The hospitable Tahitians, although subjected to bloodshed and
venereal invasion on previous visits by discoverer Wallis in 1767 and

by Cook and Bougaineville, treated the visitors as though they were manna or the fulfillment of some ancient prophecy of the coming of white gods. Lord Byron wrote:

"Kind was the welcome of the sun-born sires,
And kinder still their daughters' gentler fires."

Tars whose lack of social position would have made it difficult to achieve a kind word in their class-conscious homeland were treated with a courtesy more genuine and heart-warming, if less ornate, than royalty might receive in the courts of Europe. Instead of hard bargaining for sexual favors with case-hardened and unappetizing Portsmouth hacks, fresh and amiable girls were readily available. In the worst event, a nail was the required fee. Besides love and friendship, fresh pork, fruits, vegetables, and sunshine poured in on the seamen.

THE POLYNESIAN WAY

The Englishmen immediately fell in with the Polynesian institution of "taio." A "taio" was, roughly speaking, an adopted friend; but the full implications of "taioship" are possibly beyond the understanding of outsiders to this day. In theory, it involved a sort of blood brotherhood in which the participants exchanged names and loyalties. In practice, it meant that the "Bounty" sailor became a house guest of his "taio" whenever he had shore leave, and reciprocated by bringing gifts of whatever was his own or could be pilfered from the ship. That "taioship," whatever it might mean to the British, was more than a trading arrangement to the Tahitians is indicated by instances in which they risked their lives for their new found "taios."

The difficulty of defining "taioship" exemplifies the inadequacy of Western comprehension of the Polynesian way and view of life. Such understanding is important to our story, because the mothers of the Pitcairn Colony were all Polynesians, and because it might illuminate the murky question of how the Polynesian entourage which the "Bounty" took to Pitcairn was acquired.

Boswell early recognized the difficulties and the dubious authenticity of South Seas reportage:

13

I said I was certain that a great part of what we are told by travellers to the South Sea must be conjecture, because they had not enough of the language of those countries to understand so much as they have related. Objects falling under the observation of the senses might be clearly known; but everything intellectual, everything abstract—politicks, morals, and religion, must be darkly guessed. Dr. Johnson was of the same opinion.

Despite the accretion of linguistic and anthropological information in the interval, Boswell's suspicion is well-founded. For one example, what were Westerners to make of a society, famous for its love of children, in which the aristocracy (*Ariois*) were strolling comedians who practiced infanticide while permitting commoners to multiply at will? Probably not much more than the Polynesians could make of a society in which the upper classes treated the underdogs as though they were medieval serfs and hung them for theft of a rabbit, while the lower classes exalted God for assigning them to their destined station.

Difficulties are compounded when we reach the favorite topic of sex in Polynesia. Many of the early accounts indicate that this ancient pastime suffered practically no restrictions in the land of the golden haze. True, sex was not affected by Western conventions, but it was surrounded by a different set of taboos. These taboos were incomprehensible to the visitors and, hence, they violated them in the same ignorance in which they denied their existence.

Thus, to cite one instance from Newton A. Rowe's *Voyage to the Amorous Islands* (London, 1955), describing the discovery of Tahiti by Captain Wallis:

> They [the Tahitians] said that the Englishmen were ashamed of nothing, and had led them to public acts of indecency never before practised among themselves. From their experience with the men of the "Dolphin" they undoubtedly derived the belief that open, public and unabashed fornication was the white man's custom; was, in fact, his mode of greeting the opposite sex at sight. The experiences of subsequent navigators . . . show that they . . . believed . . . such was the custom of the Tahitians.

And Cook, one of the "subsequent navigators," though stating that "Chastity is but little valued," added that "none but the more common would yield to the embraces of our people." (Class again!)

If problems were lacking in this "Paradise of the World," as Captain Bligh described it, he found it necessary, despite absorption

14

with gathering his precious breadfruit plants and "buttering-up" and playing gracious host to local royalty, to introduce a little trouble in the form of British naval discipline.

The first lashing marked the second week at Tahiti. The offender was Alexander Smith, alias John Adams, who was to become a notable of Pitcairn history. The offense was failure to prevent the theft of the cutter's gudgeon by a native. The punishment was twelve lashes, administered in sight of the Tahitians. Their pleas for mercy, although bringing no remission of punishment, elicited from Bligh a tribute to the Tahitian women as being "the most humane and affectionate creatures in the World."

Thievery was apparently as natural to the metal and nail-hungry Tahitians, who possibly understood the "Bounty" to have an inexhaustible supply, as "stinginess" was to their British visitors. In the Tahitian deontology, there could be no doubt which was the graver sin.

Purcell was placed under close arrest for a day because he refused to cut a grindstone for Bligh's host on the ground that: "It will spoil my chisel. Though there is a law to take away my clothes, there is none to take away my tools." (This sea lawyer and precursor of unionism was to be the only one of the "loyalists" against whom Bligh preferred charges on his return to England.)

Twelve lashes fell on Lamb, the butcher, because he allowed his cleaver to be stolen, and on Thompson for "insolence and disobedience."

Once more, even in this port of plenty, trouble arose over food rations. Before landing, in emulation of Cook, Bligh posted a notice requiring the sailors to channel all personal trading with the natives through a "provider" appointed for that purpose. Despite this injunction, individuals made bargains for pigs, brought them on board only to have them confiscated by Bligh, who served them out as "ship's allowance at one pound pr man pr day." This brought on a running battle of stratagems in which the Tahitians outwitted Bligh by cutting up the pigs for their "taios" and covering them up with leaves, breadfruit and coconuts.

Shortly after the new year 1789 began, Bligh was afflicted with that bane of all ships' captains, and most particularly those who anchored off Tahiti—desertion. Able seamen Muspratt and Millward, and no less than the ship's corporal, Churchill, were the culprits. They took with them eight muskets and ammunition.

Midshipman Hayward, whose bent for falling asleep on watch was held responsible for this dereliction, was disrated and put in irons for eleven weeks.

The deserters were eventually rounded up and awarded so many lashes (forty-eight each for Muspratt and Millward, twenty-four for Churchill) that application was divided into two installments—a dubious mercy.

If this were not trouble enough, Bligh had another occasion to berate his sailing master, Fryer, and boatswain, Cole, when inspection proved new replacement sails to have become mildewed and rotten.

The next victim of the lash was Isaac Martin; the offense was striking a native in a quarrel, the nature of which was obscure, but may have resulted from an attempt to recapture some stolen object. On the plea of local chieftain Tinah (Otoo) to lessen the punishment, Bligh reduced it from twenty-four to nineteen lashes.

The next offense, potentially the most serious of all, went unpunished, because the culprit could not be identified. It involved the cutting of the ship's cable, which could have brought the expedition to an inglorious end on the Tahitian shore. Bligh was not to learn for many years that a "taio" of the enchained Hayward, incensed at the treatment of his British friend, had cut the cable with the hope of beaching the "Bounty" and thereby releasing Hayward from Bligh's clutches.

"Bounty" discipline was extended to the natives when Tinah turned over to Bligh for punishment a Tahitian who had purloined part of a compass, a water cask, and bedding. One hundred lashes, which the victim miraculously survived—and then irons. Five days later this local Houdini managed to escape by breaking "the lock of the bilboa bolt" and jumping overboard. Bligh blamed this on the mate of the watch, Mr. Stewart, and again scolded his officers in his log.

More than five months after reaching Matavai Bay, the "Bounty," richer by 1015 breadfruit plants, was towed out to sea on April 4 to start the long voyage home through the awesome perils of Torres Straits, which later proved a death trap for the "Pandora."

The prolonged stay at Tahiti has been the subject of much criticism. Everyone seems agreed that the lengthy exposure to the manifold delights of Tahiti, including the "Circean blandishments of

16

the Otaheitean women,'' made Bligh's job more difficult. Disputed is whether so long a stay was necessary and, if so, why.

One reason given is that the breadfruit was in flower and could not be transplanted for some time; another, that the time was required to cut and transplant the shoots. A third theory suggests that the real reason was that Bligh had to wait for favorable winds to negotiate the Torres Straits, which the Admiralty had ordered him to do on the return voyage. (On his second and successful breadfruit expedition Bligh reached Tahiti in April and left with more than 2660 plants in July.) Even granting the necessity for the extended stay at Tahiti, some Bligh critics have suggested that he should have taken the ''Bounty'' out at intervals for ''dry runs'' to keep his crew up to the mark.

PRELUDE TO THE MUTINY

Departure from Tahiti was not a complete leave-taking of the Society Islands. First there was a courtesy call to be made at Huaheine to gather details about the death of Omai, a native who had accompanied Cook in the ''Resolution'' to England, where he was lionized by London society.

On April 12, John Sumner was subjected to twelve lashes ''for neglect of duty.''

On the 23rd the ''Bounty'' anchored at the Island of Annamooka, and on the 25th, wooding and watering parties were sent on shore, one of them under the command of Christian. Arms were issued, to be ''kept in the boat, and there only to be used.''

Within an hour of landing, an axe and adz had been filched by the natives, bringing down Bligh's wrath on his next-in-command. Christian complained of the difficulty of controlling the islanders.

''Are you afraid of a naked set of savages while you have arms?'' was Bligh's scornful question. Christian replied, ''The arms are no use while your orders prevent them from being used.'' Apparently this wrangle was part of a running battle. The journal* of Master Fryer for the 21st records a quarrel in which Christian told his captain:

---

* *Narrative of the Mutiny*, by John Fryer, Master. An undated Ms. presented in 1887 by the late Hugh Rump of Wells to the United Service Institute.

"Sir, your abuse is so bad . . . I have been in hell for weeks past with you."

After another theft from a shore party, this time of a spade and a grapnel, Bligh threatened two local chiefs who had come on board that he would keep them there until return of the grapnel. (The spade had been recovered.) According to Morrison, Bligh set the chiefs to peeling coconuts for his dinner, but finally released them when they "cried bitterly." Bligh again took occasion to berate his officers in his log.

Matters were approaching climax. It was now April 27, the day before the mutiny, when the famous coconut imbroglio occurred. This is not referred to in either Bligh's log or *Narrative*, but is testified to by various members of the crew and vividly described by that born reporter, James Morrison.

To assess the cause and effect of this hassle in its proper light, recall that the crew had but shortly left the *dolce vita* of Tahiti; that there had already been a sharp reversion to shipboard discipline and the fearsome scoldings of Bligh; and that there lay before the sailors a year's journey, including passage through the largely uncharted and potentially murderous Torres Straits, under a captain whose tongue lash could draw as much blood as his cat-of-nine-tails.

In this context, a straw may have sufficed, but the affair of the coconuts was of a weight commensurate with the subject matter. Save for the wound it inflicted, the men might still have swallowed their grievances and the mutiny might never have been born. But let Morrison tell the story:

> In the afternoon of the 27th Mr Bligh came up, and taking a turn about the quarter deck when he missed some of the cocoa nuts which were piled up between the guns, upon which he said they were stolen and could not go without the knowledge of the officers, who were all call'd and declared they had not seen a man toutch them, to which Mr Bligh replied "then you must have taken them yourselves," and ordered Mr Elphinstone to go and fetch evry Cocoa nut in the ship aft, which he did. He then questioned evry Officer in turn concerning the number they had bought and coming to Mr Christian ask'd him. Mr Christian answer'd "I do not know, sir, but I hope you don't think me so mean as to be Guilty of stealing yours?" Mr Bligh replied "Yes, you dam'd Hound, I do. You must have stolen them from me or you could give a better account of them. God damn you, you Scoundrels, you are all thieves alike, and combine with the men to rob me.—I suppose you'll steal my yams next, but I'll sweat you for it, you rascals. I'll make half of you jump overboard before you go through Endeavour Streights." He then

call'd Mr Samuel and said, "Stop these villians' grog and give them but half a pound of yams to-morrow, and if they steal them I'll reduce them to a quarter." The cocoa nuts were carried aft and he went below. The officers then got together and were heard to murmur much at such treatment. . . .

Notwithstanding the bitter charges he had hardly finished uttering, Bligh invited Christian to dinner an hour later. The invitation was declined on the ground that Christian was "unwell." Bligh, by his own account, accepted this excuse at face value and "was concerned rather than suspecting his integrity and honor." If it were anyone but Bligh who made this statement, we should be required to regard it as the ultimate in outrageous disingenuousness.

We are touching here close to the heart of Bligh's character and its connection with the mutiny, and this is perhaps the best place to assess it, though the uprising remains to be described. It is characteristic of the difficult side of Bligh's nature that he could overlook the likelihood that his categorical charge of thievery had angered his Acting Lieutenant to the point where he found it impossible to break bread with his maligner.

Witness after witness, friendly and hostile, united in describing Bligh as a man of "passion" or "passionate man." No reference was intended to his amorous propensities, about which the record is silent. The connotation was that which we would attach to "quick-tempered" or "hot-tempered" or "trigger-tempered." The most remarkable thing about this temper or passion was, not the ease with which it was aroused, nor the violent hand motions which accompanied it, but the suddenness and completeness with which it exhausted itself. Apparently a cathartic process was involved; Bligh had only to give vent to his anger in most cases to be relieved of his bile. It was frequently a case of out of mouth, out of mind.

Some of the objects of his wrath grasped this aspect of Bligh without effort and shrugged off his outbursts as mere fume; others were not so discerning or were incapable of accepting apparent insults at less than face value.

An example of the former type was Boatswain Jewell, whom Bligh had upbraided, according to one witness at the court-martial of Bligh, for "unofficerlike" misbehavior toward his subordinate officers of the "Warrior," as "an infamous Scoundrel, an audacious Rascal, a Vagrant and a Dastardly Villain." Despite these encomiums and the

19

fact that Bligh had told Jewell that "if he had him in a Dark Corner he would do his Business for him" and that Bligh had once shaken Jewell and torn his shirt—when placed upon the stand, Jewell testified that Captain Bligh was "very hot and hasty, but I believe the words are no sooner escaped him, then his passion ends. I put no particular interpretation to what he said."

An example of the type who could not shrug off Bligh's verbal abuse was Fletcher Christian. Despite his previous boast that he knew how to handle Bligh, he allowed himself to be wounded by Bligh's forked tongue to the point where he was ready to do something so desperate as "jump overboard" in fulfillment of Bligh's prediction.

As for Bligh himself, and this was the "blind spot" which was to lead him into a succession of pitfalls throughout his career, he found it impossible to comprehend that the relief of his feelings which resulted from his tongue lashings did not similarly attend the object. If he were willing to forget that he had made a charge of thievery, why should not the accused?

It was this default of imagination which, in the case of the "Bounty" mutiny and subsequent troubles in Bligh's career, triumphed over his competence, conscientiousness, and courage. It was this failure to sense the effect of his words which was responsible for Bligh's unfeeling reply to a letter from the mother of alleged mutineer Peter Heywood.* Otherwise we should have to attribute its callousness to a monstrousness too great to impute to crueler men than Bligh. It was this consummate obtuseness that was responsible for the fact that Bligh did not gradually ease his men from the delights of their shore leave into the rigors of shipboard, but instead heightened the contrast by impatiently plunging them into the grim world of harsh seafaring discipline and frequent scoldings. It was this matchless insensitivity that made it possible for Bligh to author an entry in the log immediately after the mutiny indicating that he had been commanding a happy ship "in the most perfect order" up to the day of disaster—and mean it!

---

* Wrote Bligh: "His baseness is beyond all description, but I hope you will endeavour to prevent the loss of him, heavy as the misfortune is, from afflicting you too severely."

⚜ THE MUTINY ⚜

But to return to Christian, left quivering and "beside himself" with indignation and lacerated pride; he complained bitterly to Purcell of his treatment and of the future outlook for the voyage, stating that he "would rather die ten thousand deaths than bear this treatment" and that "to be counted a thief is more than I can bear."

As if to prove that he was not merely letting off steam, Christian proceeded to tear up his letters and records, to give away his Tahitian mementoes, and to build a crude raft of staves and planks and nails scrounged from Purcell, which he planned to use to depart the "Bounty" for a nearby island.

According to Morrison's account, finding that he could not effect his escape

> . . . in the first and middle watches, as the people were all a stirring, he went to sleep about half-past three in the morning. When Mr Stuart [Midshipman Stewart] call'd him to relieve the watch he had not slept long, and was much out of order, and Stuart beg'd him not to attempt swimming away, saying "the people are ripe for anything," this made a forcible impression on his mind and finding that Mr Hayward the mate of his watch (with whom he refused to discourse) soon went to sleep on the arm chest which stood between the guns and Mr Hallet not making his appearance, he at once resolved to seize the ship.

The first man Christian approached was bully boy Quintal, who refused the scheme on the ground that it was too dangerous, but suggested that Christian try another.

Martin, the next prospect, was all for it, without a moment's thought, and immediately enlisted Corporal Churchill, who brought over Thompson and other seamen. Execution of the mutiny now turned on gaining control of the ship's arms, stowed in a chest on top of the main hatch at the after end of the forecastle.

Keys to the chest were in the possession of Coleman, the armourer, from whom Christian obtained them, after waking Coleman, on the pretext that he wanted to shoot a shark.

21

Midshipman Hallet, asleep on the forecastle arms chest, was ordered back to his watch by Christian, and the mutineers were quickly armed, Quintal now joining in and accepting a weapon.

Taking along Churchill and Burkett, Christian descended to Bligh's open cabin door and announced to his captain, "Mr. Bligh, you are my prisoner." Bligh, instantly awake, commenced shouting for help despite the blade of a cutlass at his throat. As if to accent the wildly impromptu nature of the mutiny, Churchill was now forced to roar up for something with which to tie up Bligh, which something turned out to be a sounding line, to the horror of naval purists. Hands tied behind his back, Bligh was taken up and stood against the mizzen mast.

Here Bligh tried to win over his crew with admonitions and threats, until silenced by Christian's, "Mamu, sir! Not a word or death is your portion." After a vain effort by Fryer to effect a reconciliation or compromise, and after confused efforts to determine what had not been forethought, namely, who was to be expelled from the ship and in what, the haphazard upshot was that eighteen men and Bligh were placed in the open launch. Twenty-five men remained on the "Bounty," including three midshipmen and Christian.[2]

The whole course of the mutiny, from conception to Bligh's departure in the launch, was run in the space of three or four hours and was marked by such confusion that Morrison reported that the seamen "hardly knew what part they had acted in the business." Many members of the crew did not even know what had taken place until after Bligh was brought up on deck. There was no formal choosing of sides; even on the crucial question of who were to stay on the "Bounty" and who were to go in the launch, the line of demarcation was not clear, so that some anxious to go were required to stay, and some who pleaded to stay were forced to go.

In the light of these and other corroborating circumstances (for once all the writers are agreed!), Bligh was clearly in error in postulating a deep and long-planned conspiracy as a prelude to the mutiny. Sharp difference of opinion, however, develops over Bligh's theory that the mutiny was attributable solely to the desire of the men to return to the "Circean blandishments" and easy living of Tahiti. His argument is bolstered by his statement that, when the launch was cast adrift, the cry "Huzza for Otaheite" resounded on board the "Bounty."

As usual, there is support in the record for both sides. Doubtless their taste of Polynesian delights aggravated the men's grievances against Bligh and the hard life on board ship, and the possibility of recapturing those joys was a strong factor in the mutiny. On the other hand, a number of circumstances in the subsequent wanderings of the "Bounty," as will appear, suggest that Tahiti was the last place in all the vast Pacific that Christian had in mind as a future home, because, obviously, it was the first place to which the long arm of the Admiralty would reach. But it is unprofitable to analyze the mutiny as though it were a reasoned venture; reasoning, such as it was, came after the mutiny, not before.

But we have left Bligh and his eighteen men in the 23-foot launch, at the beginning of their epic battle against unfriendly seas, savages, broiling sun, and hunger. We shall not follow them, as has been done in a number of colorful accounts previously cited, except to transport them across 3,168 miles of trackless waters to Timor (a voyage of forty-one agonizing days) in a sentence, pausing to remark that this was Bligh's "finest hour," in which his intransigent virtues found their fullest value and expression. Bligh's consummate seamanship, his stubborn courage, and his qualities of leadership, limited though they might be, effected this classic of navigation in the face of obstacles of wind, weather, supply, and morale which would have staggered a lesser man.

TROUBLE AT TUBUAI

The "Bounty," with Christian in command, headed for Tubuai, one of the Austral group, about 300 miles southward of Tahiti. Most of Bligh's painfully collected breadfruit plants were tossed overboard, and Christian took possession of the cabin. Apparently Christian had Tubuai in mind as a place of permanent settlement. Sighting of the island by Cook in 1777 was reported in the narrative of his voyages available in the ship's library. Unfortunately, the initial reception by the islanders was anything but friendly, and fighting broke out in which twelve Tubuaians were killed and many injured. Christian and the men decided to return after first picking up some livestock (absent from Tubuai) and, possibly, female companions at

Tahiti to provision their future home. Christian may have been motivated by hunger for his Tahitian Isabella.

At Tahiti, the trusting natives swallowed wholesale Christian's story that Bligh had met Cook (long dead—unbeknown to them) and that the "Bounty" had been sent back for more supplies. This the Tahitians provided with a lavish hand—460 hogs, 50 goats, fowl, dogs, cats, and other provisions, including the bull and cow which Cook had left at Matavai. According to Morrison, Christian was beloved, "but on the contrary none liked Mr Bligh tho they flatter'd him for his riches."

The "Bounty" left Tahiti for Tubuai loaded with these provisions and "9 men, 8 boys, 10 weomen and one female child, some of which hid themselves below till we were at sea." These human additions to the ship's complement may have contributed to a more friendly reception by the Tubuaians on the second visit, since they were closely related ethnically and spoke a similar dialect. When it was explained that the seamen and their Tahitian friends wanted to settle on Tubuai, one of the chiefs granted them a plot of land near the shore. Here preparations were made for the building of an ambitiously grandiose fort, 125 feet by 120 feet, to be protected by the ship's guns. But developments soon made it clear that Tubuai was not to be the untroubled paradise envisioned by Christian.

Christian had already been confronted with the problems of command when Sumner and Quintal took an unauthorized shore leave. Christian met their argument that "The ship is moor'd and we are now our own masters" by clapping them in irons at the point of Bligh's pistol. The building of the fort proved irksome despite the example Christian set by pitching in himself. The livestock created problems with the Tubuaians on the unfenced island. Rivalries between Tubuaian chieftians imperiled the status of the settlers. Quarrels with the natives became frequent—they apparently did not have the generous attitude toward sharing their women which the mutineers had learned to expect in Tahiti.

When, against this unpromising background, Christian proposed taking the masts out of the "Bounty" and dismantling her, building houses and settling down, the crew began to grumble and ask for an armed expedition to get them each a woman to live with. They "refused to do any more work till evry man had a Wife." Christian suggested persuasion instead and refused a demand for more grog. The crew responded by breaking the lock of the spirit room and taking it by force.

At this crisis, Christian abandoned command for democracy. On September 10th, he called all hands to a conference in the ship's great cabin. A proposal to return to Tahiti "and there Seperate, where they might get Weomen without force" was carried by a vote of sixteen to nine after Christian made a dramatic plea:

> Gentlemen, I will carry you, and land you, wherever you please. I desire none to stay with me, but I have one favour to request, that you will grant me the ship, tie the foresail, and give me a few gallons of water, and leave me to run before the wind, and I shall land upon the first island the ship drives to. I have done such an act that I cannot stay at Otaheite. I will never live where I may be carried home to be a disgrace to my family.

To which Mr. Young, seconded by seven others, replied, "We shall never leave you, Mr. Christian, go where you will."

Departure from Tubuai, involving the rounding up of the livestock, was not accomplished until after a sanguinary battle with the Tubuaians in which the natives suffered heavy, and the crewmen light, casualties. When the "Bounty" sailed, she carried aboard a friendly Tubuaian chief named Taroamiva, who fled possible death at the hands of his offended countrymen, as well as other Tubuaians.

THE PITCAIRN PARTY

The "Bounty" reached Matavai Bay on September 22. They had divided the ship's stores as had been agreed, and each member of the crew made the fateful decision whether to stay at Tahiti or leave with Christian. The split-up, with characteristic disregard for logic, did not follow closely the line which might be anticipated, namely, that those clearly guilty of mutiny would leave and those clearly innocent remain.

The eight men who decided to throw in with Christian and who were to wind up at Pitcairn were Edward Young, midshipman, John Mills, William Brown, Isaac Martin, William McCoy, John Williams, John Adams (alias Alexander Smith), and Matthew Quintal. Five were clearly involved in the mutiny. Brown, the gardener's assistant, was clearly innocent, and we have no clue as to why he joined. The majority is of the opinion that Young, likewise, had no part in the mutiny, and the few dissenting voices offer no evidence for their contrary position.

The case of Martin was somewhat equivocal. Bligh seemed of the opinion that Martin was on his side. As a counterweight to the two or three "innocents" who followed Christian into the unknown, there remained on shore men clearly guilty, such as ringleader Churchill, Thompson, Millward, Ellison, and Burkett. The latter three swung for mutiny after being picked up on the punitive expedition of the "Pandora," and the first two would have swung with them had they not been providentially killed. Some of the others who remained could face court-martial with dubious assurance in the light of the Navy canon which equated inaction with hostile action in the case of mutiny.

At any rate, one can but wonder how the future of Pitcairn would have been affected if this momentous split had taken a slightly different line; if, for one example, the sensible and ingenious Morrison had joined Christian instead of one of the "hard cases" like Quintal or McCoy.

Before sailing from Tahiti, Christian held a last beachside conference with Stewart and Heywood. He assumed complete and sole responsibility for the mutiny. He advised his shipmates on the politic procedure which they, as innocents, should follow when a punitive man-of-war reached Tahiti. He then shook hands and returned to the "Bounty," which sailed suddenly and without notice the following morning, September 23, 1789.

On board, besides his eight shipmates, livestock and plants, Christian carried a human cargo of Polynesians which included six males, two Tubuaians, three Tahitians, and one Raiatean, nineteen females, and a babe in arms. The significant question of how these passengers without ticket were acquired has been strangely neglected in most accounts. Generally it has been assumed that they were voluntary "joint adventurers," motivated in the case of the women by amorous attachments and, in the case of the men, by friendship or a lust for travel and adventure.

With the aid of Jenny(3) and several other neglected clues, Maude(1) has been able to reach the conclusion that, "with the exception of Taroamiva and his companions, 'who were now become very fond of Mr. Christian and would not leave him,' and probably of Christian's wife and Jenny herself, the natives on board the 'Bounty' were in fact kidnaped against their will; blackbirding was now added to mutiny.''*

This charge is supported with the statements that Christian had announced that he would be staying at least overnight, that the women were invited on board ''with the feigned purpose of taking leave'' (Adams to Beechey), that the anchor cable was quietly cut, and that ''by the time the natives discovered they had been tricked she was a mile outside the reefs.'' Further that, ''Even so, one of the women jumped overboard and set out for shore: Jenny says that most of the remainder would have liked to have followed suit, but lacked the courage.'' After the selection of ''permanent female partners . . . one each for the mutineers and three in all for the natives . . . the ship headed for Moorea, only nine miles from Tahiti, where a canoe came out from the shore on which the six surplus women who, as Jenny puts it, were 'rather ancient,' were permitted to depart.''

It seems clear that Christian, in his anxiety to insure against further trouble from lack of sufficient women, was willing to countenance the blackbirding which he had scorned to employ at Tubuai. Quite possibly enough women could have been recruited, had time allowed, but Christian was in a sweat to leave. There are suggestions in the record that he had reason to fear an attempt to capture the ''Bounty'' by his ex-shipmates or the Tahitians, and that he feared the possibility of defection by those committed to him. He may have also apprehended the sudden arrival of a British man-of-war, however unlikely this event so soon after the mutiny. His motivation is conjectural, his impatience manifest.

As for the six Polynesian men, despite Adams' statement that they were brought along as ''servants,'' we can only guess as to what, if anything, they intended in boarding the ''Bounty.'' The key to their treatment by the mutineers was sounded when the six ''rather ancient'' women were released, leaving the six men with only three female partners. Here was seed for trouble with the venture barely under weigh.

---

* This theory draws support from Im Thurn, Sir Everard, and Wharton, Leonard C., *The Journal of William Lockerby*, Hakluyt Soc. ser. 2, vol. 52. Also, the account of First Officer Newell of the ''Sultan,'' which visited Pitcairn in 1817 (*New England Galaxy*, vol. 4, January 12, 1821) describes the mutineers as ''securing them [the Polynesians] under hatches,'' cutting the cable and putting to sea. Buffett states that ''some of the females were taken against their will.''

This unfortunate result derived from the improvised nature of the departure from Tahiti. Improvisation was the hallmark from the beginning; the mutiny itself had been improvised, the failed Tubuaian settlements had been improvised, the split-up had been improvised, and now the composition of the future Pitcairn Colony was improvised. Sufficient unto the day.

❦ FINDING PITCAIRN ❦

The time for the haphazard was now clearly past; death and capture could be averted only by finding a viable refuge.

When Christian left Tahiti on September 23, he was a man who knew what he wanted, but not where to find it in the multi-islanded Pacific. He was "in search of a home" for his entourage—a home which was remote, inaccessible, uninhabited, defensible, and capable of sustaining a human community. The Tubuaian experience had dramatized the importance of finding an uninhabited island, causing Christian to rule out several appealing landfalls when investigation proved them to be peopled.

He was to travel for some four months and seven thousand miles before he reached his destination some twelve hundred miles from his starting point. He was to crisscross the South Pacific three times, visiting the Cook, Tonga, and Fiji Islands. Maude(1) traces in detail the wanderings of the "Bounty," which he "ranks with the epics of Pacific exploration." This long-neglected epic, pieced together by Maude(1) in a fascinating exercise of historical detective work, included a vain search for the "lost islands" of Mendana and Quiros, the discovery of Raratonga, and a trading visit with the Tongans at Tongatapu.

One of the vessel's stops was the occasion of an incident which reveals the tenuous nature Christian's command was assuming. When a native ventured on board and admired the pearl shell buttons on his jacket, Captain Christian gave him the jacket. Then, according to Jenny(3), "He stood on the ship's gunwale showing the present to his countrymen when one of the mutineers shot him dead. He fell in to the Sea. Christian was highly indignant at this. He could do nothing

more, having lost all authority, than reprimand the murderer severely. . . ."

That morale on the "Bounty" was deteriorating is indicated by
Jenny's statement, probably referring to a later date, that "all on
board were much discouraged; they therefore thought of returning to
Tahiti." The fruitless search for a refuge and the seemingly endless
voyage, any party atmosphere having long since been dissipated, were
dispiriting.

Christian found the answer to his quest in the ship's library, for
its size certainly one of the most influential in history. (It was later to
provide the basis for the promulgation of Christianity on Pitcairn.)
In a volume of Hawkesworth's *Voyages* was a description of an island
discovered by Carteret in 1767:

> . . . it appeared like a great rock rising out of the sea: it was not
> more than five miles in circumference, and seemed to be uninhabited; it
> was, however, covered with trees, and we saw a small stream of fresh water
> running down one side of it. I would have landed upon it, but the surf,
> which at this season broke upon it with great violence, rendered it impos-
> sible. I got soundings on the west side of it, at somewhat less than a
> mile from the shore, in twenty-five fathoms, with a bottom of coral and
> sand; and it is probable that in fine summer weather landing here may
> not only be practicable but easy. . . . It lies in lat. 20° 2′ south: long.
> 133° 21′ west.* It is so high that we saw it at a distance of more than
> fifteen leagues, and it having been discovered by a young gentleman, son
> to Major Pitcairn of the marines, we called it PITCAIRN'S ISLAND.

Here was exactly what the doctor had ordered. Christian must
have read and reread this description with avidity. Now all that
remained to do was to find this pimple on the Pacific and the travelers
would have a home. The clue Carteret had given was imprecise. With
the imperfect tools at hand in his time, Carteret had placed Pitcairn
too far west. "A weary period of tacking in the teeth of the southeast
trades," possibly along the latitude given, which was substantially
correct, brought success.

On the 15th of January, 1790, the Bounty sighted the "promised
land," Pitcairn Island, "in the evening, when the setting sun would
have lighted up the heights of Goat-house Peak and the Ridge." As it

---

* Maude (1) says: "The latitude given in this account is an obvious slip, for in
his chart of Pitcairn Carteret states it to be 25° 02′ S. and 133° 30′ W. Its actual
position is 25° 04′ S. and 130° 16′ W., or nearly 200 miles to the east of Carteret's
reckoning."

was to do to many others, surf-bound Pitcairn offered the weary voyagers the back of her hand for welcome. Rough seas made landing impossible for several days. On the third day a boat was put over and Christian and some of the men rowed to shore on the western coast of the Island for a tour of inspection.

Christian returned to the "Bounty" two days later in an obviously happy frame of mind. He pronounced good what he had seen— the wayfarers had found a home at last. The "Bounty" was run into an indentation in the northern shore, later distinguished as "Bounty Bay," and preparations were made to unload passengers and stores.

Thus began the eventful history of the Pitcairn Island community.

⚜ NOTES: PART ONE ⚜

1. For the story of Bligh, the voyage of the "Bounty," the stay at Tahiti, and the mutiny, George Mackaness is the most complete and outstanding authority. He relies greatly on Bligh's published and unpublished writings and on James Morrison's *Journal*. Among many interesting readings of the story, selected from a plethora of literature, are Barrow, McKee, and Montgomerie.
2. For the history of the Pitcairn contingent from the mutiny to the establishment of the Pitcairn Colony, Maude(1) is most valuable.

THE PITCAIRN MYSTERY

1790 TO 1808

❧ THE MYSTERY ❧

The Pitcairn community, initiated in 1790, was not discovered until eighteen years later. Of fifteen young men, nine English and six Polynesian, who landed from the "Bounty," only John Adams was still alive. Several of the original twelve Polynesian women were missing, and there was an increment of some twenty-four or twenty-five children ranging in age from infancy to seventeen or eighteen.

What happened to the rest? What was the life of the Colony like in its eighteen uninspected years?

No published attempt to answer these questions, which constitute the Pitcairn "mystery," has included a close reading of discrepant accounts, largely derived from Adams, recorded by Folger, Pipon and Staines, Beechey, and Moerenhout, whose visits to Pitcairn were made in 1808, 1814, 1825, and 1829. Few have made use of the invaluable reports of interviews with Jenny, one of the settlers, after her return to Tahiti in 1817, or of accounts by Captain King and John Buffett, Pitcairn's first immigrant in 1823. Most writers of Pitcairn history have ignored contradictions and have accepted Beechey's version because it is most complete in outline and detail.

One who attempts to analyze and reconcile the variant reports, plus the scraps of tradition retailed in Brodie, Buffett, Young, O'Brien, and others, may well conclude that the course adopted was the better part of valor. Neat and completely satisfying conclusions are unattainable. Nevertheless, use of the neglected accounts and a search for agreements, rather than differences, in the various versions offer the possibility of considerable clarification of the bloody history of the first decade of the Pitcairn settlement.

❦ THE SCENE ❦

The most imaginative scene designer could hardly invent a more appropriate set than Pitcairn Island for the variegated cast of self-shipwrecked characters and the turbulent story they were to enact. The dramatic topography created by its volcanic origin, with steep ascents from rock-girdled shores, peaks reaching to one thousand feet contrasting with valleys, was accented by lush green foliage, by the small size of the island, and by the heavy surf which beat on this "great rock rising out of the sea" and emphasized its isolation.

That isolation is apparent only to the initiated from its location at 25° 04′ S. and 130° 16′ W. "The Southern Seas are empty to the ice-caps of Antarctica." Pitcairn's nearest neighbors are the uninhabited atolls of Oeno, 75 miles northwest, Henderson (Elizabeth), 105 miles east-north-east, and Ducie, 293 miles east. All four are now called the Pitcairn Islands Group. Valparaiso and Panama are roughly 4000 miles distant, Sydney 5000 miles, and even Tahiti is 1200 miles away.

The area of Pitcairn is roughly comparable to that of Central Park, but this allusion does not suggest the mountainous terrain of Pitcairn, only a small part of which consists of land approaching the level quality of the Park. Nor does it indicate the inaccessibility of harborless Pitcairn, which can be reached only by small boats, weather not forbidding, which land on a slight indentation glorified by the name "Bounty Bay." Beach is very scanty and shingly, and one is hardly ashore before being confronted by a steep climb of several hundred feet up the aptly named "Hill of Difficulty" to the village, plateaus, and valleys found on higher ground.

Small, inaccessible, and isolated as Pitcairn was, the settlers discovered that it had been previously inhabited by Polynesians. They found human skeletons, idols, and many stone tools. In what was apparently a version of the *marae*, or holy grounds, of their predecessors, stood rough-hewn stone gods. Excavated skulls were discovered resting on pearl shells. Stone hatchets, spearheads, and a bowl were among the remnants. A cave contained pictographs of the sun, moon, stars, a bird, and men.

This earlier settlement has been attributed to the Polynesian custom of sending conquered tribes off in their canoes to scrabble for themselves, a procedure not unlike that whereby the mutineers cast the vanquished Bligh and the "loyalists" into the "Bounty" launch with the implied invitation to avail themselves of whatever the Pacific might offer. The previous habitation indicated Pitcairn's ability to support human life; the unexplained disappearance of the community suggested that life on Pitcairn was not without hazard—a suggestion soon to be verified.

❦ THE CAST OF CHARACTERS ❦

THE MUTINEERS

John Adams (alias Alexander Smith), Able Seaman. John Adams, poor-house alumnus and for three decades lone survivor of the fifteen males who landed from the "Bounty," became theocratic king of Pitcairn Island in all but name. He is a pivotal, if oversimplified, figure in Pitcairn history. This near-illiterate Island Moses set the course for the future of the community. To his reluctance to part with the truth, or his faulty memory, or his notion of what might best serve his purposes at a given moment, we owe much of the confusion surrounding the early history of the Colony.

Captain Bligh, in his no-nonsense style, pictured Adams in his "Description of the Pirates" as "aged 25 years, five feet five inches high, brown complexion, brown hair, strong made, very much pitted with the small pox, and very much tatowed on his body, legs, arms and feet; he has a scar on his right foot, where it has been cut with a wood axe." In later years, he developed a notable corpulence.

Adams' "Bounty" career included twelve lashes at Tahiti, in sight of the natives, for failure to prevent the theft of the cutter's gudgeon, a punishment not abated by pleas for mercy from Tahitian chiefs and their wives. The record establishes his active participation in the mutiny, despite Adams' attempts to disavow or mitigate his guilt. Scarcely a distinction, his name appears on the ship's venereal disease treatment list; he was debited with thirty shillings for treatment by Surgeon Huggan and assistant Ledward. The list included seventeen members of the crew debited with from fifteen to forty-five shillings.

Adams shipped under the name of Alexander Smith, probably because he had deserted from another ship. Amasa Delano's suggestion that he adopted the name John Adams from the American president must be rejected, in the light of evidence identifying Adams. Adams himself wrote:

"I was born at Stanford Hill in the parrish of St. John Hackney Middellsex of poor But honast parrents My farther was drouned in the Theames thearfore he lef Me and 3 More poore Orfing Bot one was Married and ot of All harmes."

This brief sketch is corroborated by a published interview[1] with Adams' brother, a waterman at Union Stairs, who wore the fire coat of the London Assurance and was "of course, a steady character." Said the brother, "We are natives of Hackney and were left orphans, being brought up in the poor-house."

Another attempt at autobiography by Adams, "unequal to the task" in four tries, ended abortively after the following statement: "The Life Of Jon Adams Born November the 4 or 5 in the Year Sixty Six att Stanford Hill in the parrish of St. John Hackney My father was Sarvent to Danel Bell Cole Marchant My father drowed in the River Theames."[2]

It was in the poorhouse that Adams acquired whatever rudiments of literacy he brought to Pitcairn and some acquaintance with the tenets and liturgy of the Church of England. These fragments were to prove of singular potency in the history of Pitcairn Island.

John Adams belonged, in the ordinary course of events, to that class of anonymities likely to come to attention only when they have transgressed some law. Nonetheless, he was able to impress deeply the early visitors to Pitcairn, who tended to throw caution to the winds in extolling his merits as a kindly, wise, thoroughly regenerated, and deeply religious and moral patriarch.

It would be possible to fill a bulky volume with the encomiums paid him. J. A. Moerenhout, after noting that Adams had long been justly celebrated in Europe, commended him to the plaudits of *"la dernière postérité."*

An even more telling weight might be accorded the testimonial resulting from Otto von Kotzebue's interview with Jenny, if the reporter's accuracy were not somewhat suspect. As he tells it, Jenny "had a very high opinion of her Adams, and maintained that no man in the world was worthy of comparison with him."

The standard picture of Adams in Pitcairn literature as a completely regenerated rascal, benevolence and piety incarnate, while not without basis, is much too simplistic and pat to encompass the record, as it will appear. It should not be forgotten that, not only was he the leader of the community when the first ships visited Pitcairn, he was the only man on the Island who had experience of life off that tiny rock, that he monopolized the visitors, that he was unlikely to be contradicted in any statement he made, and that he had a shrewd sense of what the visitors might like to hear in response to their questions and the ability to project a sympathetic picture of the artless man of profound sincerity and good will.

Adams' education, whatever its academic limitations, was sufficient for a diploma in that school which teaches the resourcefulness necessary to survival in a world where underdogs are expendable. The man "who went for a cutlass" when it seemed propitious was not the toughest of the mutineers who landed on Pitcairn. He was not the meekest, the one with the most blue blood, nor the best educated. John Adams was the one who survived, notwithstanding his "Bounty" nickname of "reckless Jack," and left the most indelible mark on the community.

Adams arrived at Pitcairn as the consort of Oburaei, although he had paired off with Jenny during the Tubuian adventure. Oburaei bore him no children. By Vahineatua he had three daughters, Dinah, Eliza, and Hannah, and by the consort of his latter years, Teio, one son, George.

William Brown, Botanist Assistant. William Brown, born in Leicester, was appointed assistant to David Nelson, the "Bounty" botanist, "to help with the plants," on the recommendation of Sir Joseph Banks, suggesting a horticultural background. Little is known of his pre-"Bounty" history, although there is a suggestion that he had worked at Kew Gardens.

Bligh described him as, "aged 27, five feet eight inches high, fair complexion, dark-brown hair, slender made; a remarkable scar on one of his cheeks, which contracts the eye-lid, and runs down to his throat, occasioned by the King's evil [scrofula], is tatowed." Brown was down on the V.D. list for forty-five shillings.

He was the man whose grog Bligh "stop't" (along with Mills's) for refusal to dance to the fiddle of Blind Byrne, in defiance of Bligh's dictum that it was "conducive to their health." Brown had been complaining for some three weeks of rheumatic pains, which Surgeon Huggan diagnosed as mild scurvy, a condition which Bligh refused to admit could exist on his ship, in view of the fact that he employed all the latest measures against the dread affliction.

There is not the smallest bit of evidence in the record to tie Brown to the mutiny, and we have no clue as to why he joined the Pitcairn party rather than remain at Tahiti. He arrived at the Island as consort of Teatuahitea (Sarah). The indications are that he was the mildest man in the party of nine. Brown left no progeny on Pitcairn Island.

Fletcher Christian, Master's Mate and Acting Lieutenant. Fletcher Christian, twenty-six, leader of the mutiny and of the Pitcairn party, is the member of the community about whom we know the most, not only because of his leading role in the story of the voyage and the uprising, but because he came from an old and influential family and, hence, was in no danger of the anonymity which ordinarily engulfed such men as Adams, Mills or Williams.

Although frequently designated a Manxman because of his family's long association with the Isle of Man, Christian was born in Cumberland in 1764. He was distantly related to William Wordsworth, and there is some indication that he attended the Cockermouth Grammar School at the same time as his illustrious neighbor, as well as a local poet, Isaac Wilkinson, who characterized Fletcher as "mild, generous, open, humane, sincere" and "quick of spirit."[3] Other friends and acquaintances testified to these qualities, including some of the crew members; there can be no doubt from the record that he had a likable personality. The Bligh detractors are fond of pointing out that even those who suffered by Christian's actions had no harsh word to say against him, whereas even those who owed their lives to Bligh's skills disparaged their captain.

The most hostile witness to his character was a former shipmate, Edward Lamb, whose letter to Captain Bligh on October 28, 1794, was apparently "drawn to order" to serve as makeweight in the controversy between Bligh and Edward Christian, Fletcher's barrister brother, who was attempting to rehabilitate the mutineer's reputation by destroying that of his captain. A note of jealousy creeps into the following passage in Lamb's letter:

> When we got to sea and I saw your partiality for the young man, I gave him every advice and information in my power, though he went about every point of duty with a degree of indifference that to me was truly unpleasant; but you were blind to his faults and had him to dine and sup every other day in the cabin, and treated him like a brother in giving him every information.

Another quotation from Lamb's letter is frequently made as bearing on the accusation by Bligh that Christian was motivated to mutiny by his desire to return, not only to the delights of Tahiti in general, but to the arms of his one true love, presumably the dusky Isabella. Said Lamb:

> In the Appendix [the publication in which brother Edward attacked Bligh] it is said that Mr. Fletcher Christian had no attachment amongst the women at Otaheite; if that was the case he must have been much altered since he was with you in the "Britannia," he was then one of the most foolish young men I ever knew in regard to these. . . .

Apparently Lamb equated foolishness with fixity on a single female.

This is perhaps the appropriate place to note that Christian was down on the V.D. list for fifteen shillings.

Christian ran away to sea at the age of sixteen, dashing parental hopes that he would remain to operate the family estate. Early in his naval career (1782–1783) he shipped on H.M.S. "Cambridge." Bligh was sixth lieutenant on this first class ship of the line. He subsequently took two trips to Jamaica with Bligh on the "Britannia." This was the basis for his judgment that, though Bligh was "very passionate" (the inevitable adjective!), he knew how to humor him.

Christian has been described as having "a bright, pleasing countenance, and tall commanding figure, well adapted to those feats of strength and agility which he so frequently exhibited on the passage to Otaheite.''

Captain Bligh's description was less kind: ''Master's Mate, aged 24 years, five feet nine inches high, blackish or very dark brown complexion, dark brown hair, strong made; a star tatowed on his left breast, tatowed on his backside; his knees stand a little out, and he may be called rather bowlegged. He is subject to violent perspiration, and particularly in his hands, so that he soils anything he handles.''

This last detail noted by the sharp-eyed Bligh has inevitably provided material for the diagnosticians, with or without shingles. One draws therefrom the suggestion of ''hyperidrosis, a disease often associated with mental instability.''[4] It takes no medical analysis, but only reference to his conduct, to arrive at the conclusion that Fletcher Christian might be described as thin-skinned, mercurial, spirited, and emotional. Or, in the apt words of his schoolmate, the poet Wilkinson:

. . . quick of spirit as the electric beam
When from the darkling clouds its lightnings gleam.

Indications of a playful, if odd, streak of humor in Christian are his transmutation of his consort's name, Maituiti, into ''Mainmast,'' and his christening of his first born as ''Thursday October'' in honor of the date of his birth. He was survived by three children of his amorata: Thursday (sometimes Friday) October, Charles, and Mary.

William McCoy, A.B. William McCoy, variously spelled M'Koy, M'Coy, Mickoy, Mackay, was born in Ross-shire. He is distinguished by being one of the two ''bad men'' (the other being Quintal) among the nine, and by a skill which was to prove fateful in the annals of the Colony. Prior employment in a Scottish distillery and admiration for its product powered an experiment with the ti-root in April of 1795 which was successful enough to induce ''his companion, Matthew Quintal, to alter his kettle into a still,'' with the result that the ''Demon Rum'' (the ship's stores having presumably been exhausted) was reintroduced to the ''imperfect Eden'' of Pitcairn, with consequences to fuel a thousand temperance lectures. (McCoy thus became a precursor of the American soldiers who invaded the South Pacific in the Second World War and tested their skill and ingenuity in a gallant struggle against dehydration.)

Bligh thus described McCoy: ''aged 25 years, five feet six inches high, fair complexion, light-brown hair, strong made; a scar where he has been stabbed in the belly, and a small scar under the chin, is tatowed in different parts of his body.''

McCoy's ''Bounty'' history includes no flogging, and he was not on the V.D. list. Morrison's account fixes him as an active mutineer and indicates that two days before the mutiny he came under the whip of his captain's tongue in connection with the theft of the grapnel at Annamooka. Bligh ''passed the compliment on officers and men to tell them that they were a parcel of lubberly rascals and that he would be one of five who with good sticks would disarm the whole of them and presenting a pistol at Wm. McCoy threatn'd to shoot him for not paying attention.''

McCoy's progeny by Teio were Sam and Kate. Teio had arrived at Pitcairn with the infant girl, Sally, product of an unidentified union.

Isaac Martin, A.B. Isaac Martin is another member of the crew without much ascertainable history. He was born in Philadelphia.* He was not on the V.D. list. Bligh's description is brief: ''aged 30 years, five feet eleven inches high, sallow complexion, short brown hair, rawboned; tatowed with a star on his left breast.''

Martin's ''Bounty'' record includes nineteen lashes, reduced from twenty-four on the plea of Tinah and Iddeah. His offense was that he struck a Tahitian ''without any real cause but a supposition that the native had stolen a piece of iron hoop from him.'' McKee suggests that his anxiety to recover the article was caused by fear of punishment for allowing it to be stolen.

Martin's role in the mutiny was an equivocal one. According to Adams' story to Beechey, when Christian broached mutiny to Quintal, he refused to participate, thinking it too dangerous. Taxed with cowardice, Quintal denied it, saying, in effect, ''try someone else.'' Whereupon Christian turned to Martin, who immediately said, ''I'm for it; it is the very thing.''

Unless we postulate a change of heart in midstream, this is difficult to square with the statement of Bligh, in his *Narrative*, that

---

* Martin has frequently been called an American on the basis of the muster book designation of his birthplace. However, no one has excluded the possibility that the Philadelphia in question was a community near Durham, England, known by that name.

Isaac Martin, one of the guard over me, I saw, had an inclination to assist me, and as he fed me with shaddock (my lips being quite parched) we explained our wishes to each other by our looks; but this being observed, Martin was removed from me. He then attempted to leave the ship, for which purpose he got into the boat; but with many threats they obliged him to return.

This statement probably accounts for Montgomerie's conclusion that Martin, if brought to trial, "would have stood an even better chance than the four who were acquitted." However, there is no record of Bligh having given Martin absolution, and Martin, like Brown, threw in his lot with the Christian contingent and met his destiny at Pitcairn.

Martin's Pitcairn mate was Jenny. He left behind no children, and this circumstance has been given as a reason for Jenny's strong desire for repatriation.

John Mills, Gunner's Mate. John Mills was one of the duo (Brown the other) whose grog was "stop't" for refusal to dance. He was born in Aberdeen. He was not on the V.D. list. Bligh describes him as one who "assisted under arms on the outside in the mutiny" and as "aged 40 years [making him the senior of the Pitcairn contingent], five feet ten inches high, fair complexion, light brown hair, strong made, and raw-boned; a scar in his right armpit occasioned by an abscess [sic]."

The few scraps of his pre-"Bounty" history gleaned from the record suggest a sadistic bully-boy. On the "Mediator," under Collingwood, Mills was known to send midshipmen on fools' errands in order to steal their food. Once he exacted tribute for retrieving a midshipman's cap from the pump well where he had got the mess boy to hide it.

Mills had two children by Vahineatua: Elizabeth and John, Jr. Because the boy died in his youth, the Mills name did not become one of the "Bounty" patronymics on Pitcairn. These were confined to Adams, Christian, McCoy, Quintal, and Young.

Mills' daughter, Elizabeth, lived until 1883 and was the last survivor of the first generation born on the Island. If we accept Rosalind Young's designation of Elizabeth's age at death as ninety-three (the Register indicates 1791 as the earliest date for her birth), she could not have been much over three at the time her father was killed, according to the most plausible chronology. This fosters skepticism on learning that she "never wearied of telling how her father sorrowed over the destruction of the "Bounty," as it was his hope one day to return to England, even at the risk of his life."

The story draws some support, however, from indications that, while Christian and a small party were making their original inspection of Pitcairn, Mills proposed to those left aboard to make sail for Tahiti "and leave their companions on shore to their fate."[5]

Matthew Quintal, (Quintall, Quintrell, Quintral), A.B. Matthew Quintal, a Cornishman from Padstow, was easily the outstanding "heavy" in the Pitcairn cast, despite no inconsiderable competition. His comradeship at arms (and bottle) with McCoy apparently antedated their "Bounty" experience. Quintal was the very prototype of the "hard cases," typical of Royal Navy crews of the time, for whose control the lash had been sanctioned. He was the first aboard the "Bounty" to taste it; early in the voyage Bligh had ordered twenty-four applications of that sovereign remedy applied to Quintal's back for what Bligh variously described as "insolence and mutinous behavior" and "insolence and contempt to the master."

Quintal was down for thirty shillings on the V.D. list. His participation in the mutiny, despite Adams' story of Quintal's initial refusal of Christian's first bid, is attested by Bligh and Morrison.

Quintal appears on Bligh's list as "aged 21 years, five feet five inches high, fair complexion, light-brown hair, strong made [no exaggeration], very much tatowed on the back side, and several other places."

Quintal's pre-"Bounty" life is recorded in a book presented by Adams in 1819 to Captain Reynolds of the "Sultan." From it, it appears that his mother died when he was young, that he went to school, lived with an uncle for two years, and after two years at Plymouth with his father, shipped aboard the sloop-of-war "Nymphas" as servant to his uncle, a gunner. After his uncle's death he was "appointed" servant to the captain of a man-of-war, serving three years, "when he applied to be put before the mast."[6]

Quintal was the leader in the maltreatment of the Polynesians. "Asserted as a fact" by Rosalind Young is the story "handed down that one day his wife went out fishing, and, not succeeding in obtaining enough to satisfy Quintall, he punished her by biting off her ear."[7]

Another indication of his character is the incident at Tubuai in which Quintal took unauthorized shore leave. Charged with his dereliction, Quintal asserted, "We are now our own masters," sounding a note to be recurrent in Pitcairn history. Christian's response of clapping Quintal in irons was only a temporary curb on this ungovernable insurgent.

The Quintal name was passed into Pitcairn history by the following offspring of Tevarua: Matt, Jenny, Arthur, and Sarah. One child was lost at the age of seven days. In addition, Quintal was survived by a posthumous child, Edward, born to Teraura, Young's original consort.

Edward Young, Midshipman. Most enigmatic of the nine men was Edward Young, one of the two "official" midshipmen allowed by the ship's table of organization. The other three or four were *pro forma* ranked as A.B.s, although they did regular duty as, and were considered, officers. Young was the only officer besides Christian in the Pitcairn contingent.

Bligh's description of Young makes one wonder how he could have been "a great favourite with the women." He appears to have been anything but handsome. "Aged 22 years, five feet eight inches high, dark complexion, and rather a bad look; dark brown hair, strong made, has lost several of his fore teeth, and those that remain are all rotten; a small mole on the left side of the throat, and on the right arm is tatowed a heart and a dart through it, with E.Y. underneath, and the date of the year 1788 or 1789."

Young was recommended to Bligh by his uncle, Navy Captain Sir George Young, Bart., and is said to have been a half-caste West Indian, born in St. Kitts. Young was not on the V.D. list, and his name does not appear in any account of friction on the "Bounty."

The record raises many puzzling and largely unanswered questions about Young. Why did he join Christian? Though called an "active mutineer" by Mackaness, no support is offered for the charge, and Montgomerie says that "he seems to have taken no active part during the mutiny."* He offers the suggestion that Christian may

---

* The only suggestion found in the record of Young's connection with the mutiny is in a footnote of Edward Christian's *Appendix*. "Captain Bligh said to Mr. Young 'This is a serious affair Mr. Young.' Mr. Young replied, 'Yes, it is a serious affair to be starved, I hope this day to get a belly full.'" In the same

have needed someone else who could navigate, but this does not explain why Young went along. The only suggestion from the record is that it was out of friendship for or loyalty to Christian: "We shall never leave you, Mr. Christian, go where you will."

Several accounts indicate that Young was popular with the women on Pitcairn, but no explanation is proffered. There are also indications of gentleness, as in his efforts in his last days to aid in the religious and secular education of the Pitcairn children, but these are offset by evidence that he was ready to assume a part in any "needful" butchery, such as his brutal slaying of Nihau.

And there are suggestions that it was Young, rather than McCoy, who was the father of Pitcairn distilling, as in the statement in Jenny(1): "Neddy taught them to distil spirits from the tea root." This is corroborated by Brodie.

Most puzzling of all, however, is a story indicating that Young was the Island Machiavelli, involved in what the Islanders always called the "massacre," that is, the slaughter of five of the mutineers by the Polynesian men. The story comes from Buffett, who has it:

"Adams has told me that he believed Young was aware of the massacre, as the Tahitians, told him when he came back, that they had forgot that Young told them not to hurt Adams."* This story, if true, suggests a depth of villainy notable even in this group of outlaws. Other versions of the story have Young being hidden by the women to preserve him from harm at the time of the massacre.

Young arrived at Pitcairn paired with Teraura, but the progeny he left behind when he died circa 1800 was the product of two other women. He was the most fecund of the "Bounty" sires, bringing wonderment to Sir Charles Lucas at a Pitcairn Register entry indicating the birth of seven Youngs between 1794 and 1799. The mystery would have been cleared by attribution of four of them, Nancy, George, Robert, and William, to Toofaiti, and the other three, Edward, Polly, and Dorothea, to Isabella, widow of Fletcher Christian.

Appendix appears a statement of somewhat ambiguous purport. Arguing that the unpremeditated nature of the mutiny was indicated by the number of alleged mutineers in bed at the time the insurrection began, Edward Christian says, ". . . it is remarkable that Mr. Young was the only person among Christian's messmates, who was concerned in it, and he was in bed when it broke out."
* This story is corroborated by the version Brodie derived from Arthur Quintal, son of Matthew Quintal, in 1850.

John Williams, A.B. John Williams, born in Stepney, was the subject of the lightest punishment with the cat ordered by Bligh: "Six lashes for neglect of duty in heaving the lead" at Capetown. He was the man who bolstered the crew's anger and resistance in the affair of the missing cheeses by reporting that he had carried them to Bligh's house. He was clearly active in the mutiny. We know nothing of his earlier history. He was not on the V.D. list.

Williams' rating of A.B. gives no clue to the fact that he probably assisted Joseph Coleman, armourer of the "Bounty," and was the closest approximation of an artisan or mechanic in the Pitcairn group. Because his fellow mutineers placed high value on his skills, they aided him in the wife-snatching which was the genesis of the carnage that almost obliterated the adult males on Pitcairn.

Williams appears on Bligh's list as "Aged 25, five feet five inches high, dark complexion, black hair, slender made; has a scar on the back part of his head; is tatowed and a native of Guernsey; speaks French."

Despite his deuterogamy, Williams left behind no children by either Faahotu, the first wife, who predeceased him, or by Toofaiti, whom he took away from Tararo to replace her.

THE "BOUNTY" MEN AS A GROUP

While the nine men who landed at Pitcairn could hardly be characterized as God-fearing or law-abiding, it would be an oversimplification to regard them simply as outlaws or "bad men." They were fairly representative of the original "Bounty" roster of forty-six; and, perhaps to a lesser extent, of their country. The accidents of history tended to bring their worst qualities to the fore. It is quite possible that in other circumstances little might have developed to distinguish them from the multitude.

Indeed, the Marquis of Ruvigny found in 1911 that, "The most concentrated area of descendants of early kings, extraordinarily enough, is probably Pitcairn Island in the Pacific. This happened because Fletcher Christian, the chief mutineer of the "Bounty," was descended from Edward III." (As were a hundred thousand others.)

Leaving aside these traces of nobility, the group of nine may be characterized as having a brisk lacing of the gentry (Christian and

Young) and a dash of the artisan class (Brown and Williams), plus a base of unskilled or semi-skilled workers in the other five. This mixture contained a strong streak of violence (particularly Quintal and McCoy), a trickle of perspicacity (Adams), and a full measure of racial prejudice and obtuseness.

In assessing the quality of the Pitcairn lineage, it should be remembered that only six of the nine mutineers contributed progeny: Adams, Christian, McCoy, Mills, Quintal, and Young. Numerically, the descendants of Christian and Young were to predominate, so that blood lines were heavily weighted with what many might consider the bluest variety offered by the English settlers.

THE POLYNESIANS IN GENERAL

The Polynesian members of the cast of the Island mystery drama are particularized by the record in regrettably fragmentary fashion. The most lengthy account, Beechey's, names all six of the males, but only three of the twelve adult women. Only Jenny's first account and the Pitcairn Island clerical register name all the Polynesians. The numerous accounts published in the first half of the nineteenth century evidence a maddening (to a later investigator) reluctance to interview the surviving women who had witnessed the carnage of the first decade or even to identify them otherwise than as "a Tahitian woman" or "a native wife." One, Teraura, original consort of Young, survived until 1850.

This failure to tap such an obvious source of information possibly resulted from Adams' tendency to monopolize visitors and from the difficulties of communication with the Polynesian women, whose English was less than fluent. Moreover, Polynesian names offered special traps for Westerners. There was the whimsical custom of changing names for various or no apparent reasons, as Bligh and others had occasion to note. Add to this the uncertainties of ear and orthography, and the prevalence of nicknames and mutations, and it is less surprising that one of the Polynesian men emerges from the literature variously as Oher, Oopee, Hu, Ohoo, Oohu, Ohuhu, Oha, and Heiaho. This appellative anarchy may account for some obvious mistakes in the literature and may suggest supposititious ones, such as the number of women whose deaths were attributed to falling from cliffs while gathering eggs.

The scarcity of what modern journalists call "hard news" about the Polynesians has inevitably led to speculation. One of the most interesting is that of James Norman Hall, in *The Tale of a Shipwreck* containing elements of plausibility.

> What sort of women were those who came here with the mutineers? It is likely that two of them—the consorts of Christian and Young—were women of distinguished Polynesian blood. Probably both men availed themselves, during their long sojourn at Tahiti, of their opportunities to choose from the ranks of women of good birth. Captain Wallis and his officers had done so, Captain Bougainville and his, Captain Cook and his; and there is no reason to suppose that Captain Bligh and the "Bounty" officers failed to follow so pleasant and so well established a precedent. The "Bounty's" sojourn had been the longest of that of any vessel from Wallis's day on; and I imagine that both Christian and Young had formed attachments which it cost them dear to break when they sailed for home, as they then believed. Upon their return, after the mutiny, what more likely than that these attachments should have been resumed? Or that, upon the departure for Pitcairn, their women had been persuaded to go with them?
>
> There is also the likelihood that the wife of Taaro, the young chief from Tubuai (Tetahiti, the Transplanted One, he later called himself), was herself of the kindred of chiefs. This would make three women to gift the children of the mutineers with strains of the best Polynesian blood. The women of the other men were, probably, of the *oeré*, or landless class. Wholesome vigorous blood theirs would be, but not that from which the rulers and leaders came.

Dr. Shapiro, less convinced that "the best blood is concentrated in the upper classes," after noting that little is known of the Polynesian women, says:

> One or two had excellent connections, and all of them were raised in favorable conditions and belonged to a stock famous for its physical beauty. The fact that these women readily formed liaisons with the "Bounty's" crew does not argue their depravity or socially inferior status. The more than liberal ideas of the Tahitians and the almost divine repute of the white men were sufficient to account for the ease with which the sailors established these connections.

H. E. Maude(4) notes that the Tahitian men, Teimua, Manarii, and Niau, seem to have been of the *manahune* or commoner class, and that there is reason to believe that Mauatua and Teraura were at least of *raatira* stock (landed gentry), but dismisses the remaining women as "nondescripts of the Polynesian lower classes, who alone were normally permitted to consort with the crews of visiting ships."

The indications from the record are that the Polynesians, like the mutineers, were young and venturesome; as a group they were probably as representative of their culture as the haphazard nature of their selection would suggest. Or as the English were of their country.

THE POLYNESIAN MEN

Titahiti (variously Taroamiva, Taheiti, Tetahita, Tetihiti). Titahiti was the younger brother of the Tubuaian chieftain Taroatohoa. On Tubuai he had been known as Taroamiva. He had appealed to Christian for asylum from the wrath of his compatriots kindled by his friendship with the leader of the mutineers. He shared Tinafornea as spouse with his fellow Tubuaian, Oher. As indicated, Titahiti was the Polynesian male whose privileged status in his homeland is best authenticated.

Oher. Oher was the follower or hanger-on of Titahiti, and joined his compatriot in exile. It may be of some interest that the apparent difference in their status did not preclude the sharing of Tinafornea, who may have also been a Tubuaian.

Tararo (variously Taralow, Talaloo, Talalo). Tararo was apparently a Raiatean who happened to be in Tahiti at the vessel's last departure. There is a suggestion in the record that he, too, was of a privileged class, which may draw some support from the fact that he was the only Polynesian to enjoy, if only for a while, a woman for his exclusive own. Her name was Toofaiti.

Niau (variously Nehow, Nehou). Niau is described by Jenny(1) as "a boy," which could mean that he was in his early or mid-teens at the time of the Pitcairn landing. From the fact that Jenny assigns him no woman, but says that his two fellow Tahitians, Teirnua and Manarii, shared the favors of Mareva, it could be inferred that he was too young for the exercise of marital privileges or, in any event, too young to assert a claim thereto. He was not too young, some three years later, to be marked for slaughter. While "looking at Young loading his gun, which he supposed was for the purpose of shooting hogs, and requested him to put in a good charge, . . . he received the deadly contents."

Teirnua (variously Teimua, Temua, Te Moa, Timua, Tenina, Timoa, Taimor). Teirnua was a Tahitian. He shared with his country-man, Manarii, the attentions of Mareva.

Manarii (variously Menalee, Manale, Manali, Manody). Manarii was one of the three Tahitian males. His *ménage à trois* included Mareva and Teirnua.

THE POLYNESIAN WOMEN

Jenny (in her native Tahiti Teehuteatuaonoa). About Jenny we know more than we do about most of the Polynesian women, and she is easily the historians' favorite, because of the three interviews with her reported after her repatriation to Tahiti.

Her first interviewer, the anonymous author of the account in the Sydney *Gazette* for July 17, 1819, says of her: "She has been apparently a good looking woman in her time, but now begins to bear the marks of age. She is marked on the left arm 'AS 1789,' which was done by Adam Smith, to whom she attached herself at first, and sailed with him both before and after the ship was taken." However, it was as the consort of Isaac Martin that she arrived at Pitcairn.

Whether by reason of her childlessness, homesickness, or unhap-piness with Pitcairn life, Jenny was a leader in the unsuccessful attempt of the Pitcairn women to leave the Island, as shall appear. Many years later she was able to effect her desire by departing on the whaler "Sultan" in 1817, becoming Pitcairn's first emigrant. If we can trust Von Kotzebue's account, she was anxious to return to Pitcairn, but this desire was never realized.

Isabella (variously Maimiti, Mauatea, Mauatua, Mainmast, Mai Mast, Mi Mitti). Isabella occupies a special position in the story by reason of being Christian's consort. There are suggestions in the record that it was love for her which inspired Christian to mutiny, so that their pairing was merely the continuation of a relationship which had developed before the "Bounty" first left Tahiti. This indication was, of course, eagerly seized upon by poets, novelists, and movie script writers. The record neither establishes nor disproves it, nor does it confirm the suggestion that Isabella was a member of the Tahitian aristocracy.

Isabella bore Fletcher Christian three children before he was

50

shot: Thursday (Jenny(1) says Friday) October, Charles, and Mary. After Fletcher's death, she bore Edward Young three more: Edward, Polly, and Dorothea. She lived until 1841, survived only by Teraura of the original settlers. The Register Book noted that she had frequently said she remembered the arrival of Captain Cook at Tahiti.

Toofaiti (variously Nancy, Tohaiti, Hutia). Toofaiti arrived at Pitcairn as consort of Tararo, the only Polynesian to have a woman to himself. Toofaiti was literally cast in the role of *femme fatale,* for which she seemed to have a natural predisposition. Her appropriation (apparently she was not too unwilling) by Williams to replace his deceased wife precipitated deadly interracial strife. After the death of Williams, Toofaiti bore Edward Young three sons, George, Robert, and William, and one daughter, Nancy.

Teraura (variously Ta-ou-piti, Sussanah, Doubit, Mataohu). Teraura was the original mate of Young and achieved a number of distinctions in Pitcairn history. She bore Young no children, but gave birth to a son, Edward, after the death of his father, Matthew Quintal. Several versions of Island history fix her as the one who cut off Tetahiti's head with an axe while he was sleeping with Brown's widow, Teatuahitea.

She was the apparent bone of contention between Quintal and Young which led to the axing of Quintal by Young and Adams. After the death of both Quintal and Young, she became the spouse of Fletcher Christian's eldest son, Thursday October, when he was of a tender age, seventeen or younger, and she presumably past thirty. She bore him six children, Charles, Joseph, Thursday, Mary, Polly, and Peggy. She was the longest lived of the Pitcairn settlers, and died in 1850, almost twenty years after Thursday October succumbed to the infections of Tahiti in 1831.

Obuarei (variously Opuole). Obuarei arrived on the Island as consort of Adams. She bore him no children. Jenny(1) says she fell from a precipice "when getting birds"; hence, her death must have been no later than 1817. She left no children.

Teio (variously Te'o, Mary, Sore Mummy). Teio bore McCoy two children, Daniel and Kate. After his death, she lived with Adams, to whom she bore his only son, George. She is the partially blind and ailing woman whom Beechey formally married to Adams, at his request, in 1825, sanctioning a tie of long standing. She followed Adams in death in 1829.

Vahineatua (variously Wahineatua, Bal 'hadi). Vahineatua bore John Mills two children, Betsy (Elizabeth) and John, Jr. The boy died in a fall. After the death of the senior Mills, she bore Adams three daughters, Dina, Rachel, and Hannah. According to Jenny(1) Vahineatua "was killed, being pierced in her bowels when she was with child."

Faahotu (variously Fahutu, Fasto). Faahotu, consort of Williams, died within "about a year after their arrival" on Pitcairn, the first fatality on the Island. According to Jenny(1) her death resulted from "A scrophulous [sic] disease, which broke out in her neck," but Beechey has her falling from a precipice while seeking birds' eggs. In any event, her death was a double tragedy, because it resulted in Williams' demand for a replacement and the ensuing holocaust. It is interesting to speculate on whether the warfare which broke out would have been averted or merely delayed if Faahotu had remained alive. She died without offspring.

Tevarua (variously Te Walua, Sarah, Big Sullee). Tevarua bore to Quintal five children, Matt, Jenny, Arthur, Sarah, and an unnamed child who died at the age of seven days, before falling from a precipice circa 1799. In view of Quintal's brutal nature, she was probably the most abused of the women on the Island.

Teatuahitea (variously Te Lahu, Sarah). Teatuahitea bore no children to gardener Brown. She died of "the dropsy" before Jenny left Pitcairn in 1817.

Mareva (variously Malewa). Mareva, consort of both Teirnua and Manarii, had no children by either.

Tinafornea (variously Toholomota). Although "common to the two Tubuaians," Oher and Titahiti, Tinafornea likewise left no descendants.

Sarah, Teio's daughter (variously Sally, Sully). A ten-month-old infant on arrival at Pitcairn, Sarah grew up to become the wife of Charles Christian, Fletcher Christian's second son. The issue of their union was numerous: Fletcher, Edward, Charles, Jr., Isaac, Sarah, Maria, Mary, and Margaret.

☙ THE DRAMA ☙

The drama or "argument," as the narrative thread of a play was once designated, does not follow any neat pattern of dramaturgy. It is a maze of tortuous and confused plots and counterplots. The story is best approached, as the first visitors to Pitcairn seem to have done, by attacking the question of what happened to those members of the cast missing when Mayhew Folger lifted the curtain in 1808, eighteen years after it had been pulled down.

WHAT HAPPENED TO CHRISTIAN?

What most concerned the first visitors was: "What happened to Fletcher Christian?" Their special curiosity on this score was natural. Christian was Bligh's chief antagonist and leader of the mutiny, the man of highest social position among the mutineers, and the one about whose pre-"Bounty" life most was known. Christian was also the focal point of the controversy between his brother, Edward, and Captain Bligh.

The simple question of Christian's fate produced five different answers:

1. Christian died a "natural" death after becoming ill (Delano).

2. Christian became insane and threw himself into the sea. (Attributed to the second mate of Folger's ship by Lt. Fitzmaurice.)

3. Christian was killed by the Polynesians in reprisal for appropriating one of their women to replace his deceased wife (Shillibeer, Pipon, Staines).

4. Christian was killed by the Polynesians in the "massacre" of five mutineers which developed out of the appropriation of the consort of Tararo, named Toofaiti, to replace the deceased spouse of Williams (Jenny (1), (3), Beechey).

5. Christian left Pitcairn and returned to England. (Suggested in a Barrow footnote and developed by C. S. Wilkinson in his *Wake of the Bounty*.)

53

Captain Mayhew Folger's visit of itself produced three different stories. Folger's own statement was, "About six years after they landed at this place, their servants (the male Polynesians) attacked and killed all the English, excepting the informant (Adams), and he was severely wounded."

According to the report of Lt. Wm. Fitzmaurice, transmitted to the Admiralty via Rio de Janeiro, Captain Folger related that, "About four years after their arrival (a great jealousy existing), the Otaheitans secretly revolted, and killed every Englishman except himself [Adams] whom they severely wounded in the neck with a pistol ball." Fitzmaurice went on to note that the second mate of the "Topaz" (Folger's ship) "asserts that Christian, the ringleader, became insane shortly after their arrival on the island, and threw himself off the rocks into the sea; another died of a fever before the massacre of the remaining six took place." (This version apparently results from a confusion of the fate of Christian with that of McCoy.)

Amasa Delano's version, purportedly based on what he was told by Mayhew Folger, gives yet another story of Christian's end. "Smith said, and upon this point Captain Folgar [*sic*] was very explicit in his enquiry at the time, as well as in his account of it to me, that they lived under Christian's government several years after they landed; that during the whole period they enjoyed tolerable harmony; that Christian became sick and died a natural death; and that it was after this when the Otaheitan men joined in a conspiracy and killed the English husbands of the Otaheitan women, and were by the widows killed in turn on the following night."

Considering that Folger's visit did not involve more than four or five hours, a good part of which he spent in bringing Adams up to date on world history, it is remarkable how much confusion it was able to generate.

None of the versions emanating from Folger's discovery of Pitcairn square with the indications that Young lived until approximately the turn of the nineteenth century and died in bed. The three versions, including discrepancies of time as well as the manner of Christian's death, illustrate clearly what is true of practically all the voyagers' stories; we have to contend not only with the unreliability of Adams, but with dubious reporting of what he said.

The Pipon-Staines visit also resulted in plural accounts by the two captains and by Lt. Shillibeer (*A Narrative of the Briton's*

Voyage to Pitcairn Island; London, 1818). The discrepancies in these accounts were not very large, except in fixing the time of events. According to Staines, ''Christian fell a sacrifice to the jealousy of an Otaheitan man, within three or four years after their arrival on the island. [The Polynesian males] were all swept away by desperate contentions between them and the Englishmen, and five of the latter died at different periods (all the mutineers also died, or were killed with the exception of Adams).''

Pipon reported, ''from what we could learn [Christian] was shot by a black man whilst digging in his field & almost instantaneously expired. This happened about eleven months after they were settled in the island, but the exact dates I could not learn.''

Pipon attributes to Adams the statement that the killing of Christian resulted from his ''cruelty & oppression towards the people . . . in consequence they divided into parties which ran very high, seeking every opportunity on both sides to put each other to death.'' A further cause, which aroused the fury of the Polynesian men ''to a degree not to be pacified'' was Christian's forcible seizure of one of their wives to replace his own wife, who had died.

Lt. Shillibeer of the ''Tagus,'' although not granted shore leave, had the presence of mind to subject to ''cross-examination'' some of the younger generation who visited his ship. But he thereby added little to the results obtained by his superiors, whether by reason of his lack of forensic skill or because his witnesses had no more than hearsay acquaintance with the facts. They, too, told the story that Christian was shot in the back by an Otaheitan while he was at work in his yam plantation, ''about two years after his arrival at the island'' and that the chief cause was his forcible appropriation of one of the wives ''of the black followers'' to replace his own, who died soon after his son was born.

The references to the death of Christian's wife create an enigma within the mystery. According to Jenny, Christian ''left his wife and three children; she had more children by another husband.'' According to all available records, Christian's one and only wife was Isabella, mother of Thursday October Christian, whom the Pitcairn Island Register describes as ''relict'' of Christian, giving the date of her death as September 19, 1841.

It seems clear that Isabella was alive and on Pitcairn at the time of the Pipon-Staines visit in 1814. It is implausible to believe that a demonstrable lie was told the visitors. The more reasonable inference is that we are confronted with another piece of garbled reporting. Just as the second mate of the "Topaz" apparently confused Christian and McCoy, the later visitors may have substituted Christian for Williams in relaying the story of the lost wife and her replacement.

Beechey's report, based on his 1825 visit of several weeks, is the most completely circumstantial. It is the only one, besides Jenny's and Captain King's, which gives a complete necrology; each death has a name and date, is clothed with a circumstantial description and assigned a cause. Beechey's account is the only one which quotes Young's journal.

According to Beechey, "everything went on peaceably and prosperously for about two years" until Williams, "who had the misfortune to lose his wife about a month after his arrival, by a fall from a precipice while collecting birds' eggs, became dissatisfied." He "threatened to leave the island in one of the boats of the 'Bounty,' unless he had another wife." The Europeans, "not willing to part with him on account of his usefulness as an armourer, constrained on one of the blacks [Talaloo] to bestow his wife upon the applicant."

This resulted in a plan by the "blacks" for revenge, which was imparted to the women and relayed to the mutineers. Thus warned, Christian blackmailed the other Polynesians into killing Talaloo and Ohoo to win absolution for themselves. Two years of peace followed, when ill treatment of the remaining four Polynesian men by McCoy and Quintal produced a new plot for revenge. Temua and Niau agreed to steal arms, desert and hide in the woods, but to keep in touch with Titahiti and Manarii. On a given day they were to slay all the Englishmen at work.

Titahiti borrowed a gun "to shoot wild hogs," joined his accomplices and shot Williams. The party proceeded to Christian's house, near which Manarii was working with Mills and McCoy, and asked for Manarii's help to bring in the hog which they pretended to have killed. "The four, being united, proceeded to Christian, who was working at his yam-plot, and shot him."

This story of Christian's fate, disregarding variances in background, is essentially in agreement with that of Moerenhout, and, even more importantly, with that of Jenny. Her account adds some gruesome detail which enhances its credibility, if not its flavor.

"Williams was the first man shot, while putting up a fence round

56

his garden. The natives next proceeded to shoot Christian: they found him clearing ground for a garden, and while in the act of carrying away some roots, they went behind him and shot him between the shoulders—he fell. They then disfigured him with an axe about the head, and left him dead on the ground.''

There remains for discussion a version of Christian's fate which adds a seeming excess of ''romance'' to a story already sufficiently bizarre. According to this account, Christian returned to his native Cumberland from Pitcairn by some means or other and prowled its purlieus with the connivance of friendly countrymen and a purposely oblivious Admiralty. It derives from a footnote in Barrow's book which must set a record for fruitfulness.

According to the Barrow footnote,

> About the years 1808 and 1809, a very general opinion was prevalent in the neighborhood of the lakes of Cumberland and Westmoreland, that Christian was in that part of the country. . . . This, however, might be passed over as mere gossip, had not another circumstance happened just about the same time. . . . In Fore Street, Plymouth Dock, Captain Heywood found himself one day walking behind a man, whose shape had so much the appearance of Christian's, that he involuntarily quickened his pace. Both were walking very fast, and the rapid steps behind him having roused the stranger's attention, he suddenly turned his face, looked at Heywood, and immediately ran off. But the face was as much like Christian's as the back, and Heywood, exceedingly excited, ran also.

The man eluded Heywood, and Heywood decided to let the matter drop as a ''more prudent'' course, but was deeply impressed and frequently recalled the incident.

This casual footnote was the genesis of a wide train of speculation in the Bounty-Pitcairn literature. It was even dignified by acceptance in the *Dictionary of National Biography* account of Fletcher Christian. The most elaborate edifice built on this peg is C. S. Wilkinson's *Wake of the Bounty* (London, 1953).

Using a large number of literary clues and a wealth of ingenuity, the author supports a belief in the validity of the story of Christian's return to England. Commentators have offered a variety of explanations of how Christian could have effected his repatriation. One involves sailing in a small boat to South America, another has him rowing out to a passing vessel and ''hitching'' a ride, and it has even been suggested that he left with Folger in 1808. Two circumstances bulwarked the tale: Adams' inability or unwillingness to point out Christian's grave* to inquiring visitors, and the failure to account for a number of gold ducats thought to have been on the "Bounty." A desire to cover up for Christian was offered as the explanation for Adams' discrepant stories.

In the light of the fantastic nature of the whole Pitcairn story and the almost incredible Pacific voyages of which we have documented accounts, it is hardly impossible that Christian could have made his way back to England. What argues convincingly against the fact of his return is the overwhelming weight of the circumstantial and direct evidence that he died on Pitcairn.

On the circumstantial side, there is the fact that Christian had shown keen awareness of, and sensitivity to, the possibility of capture and death on the yardarm, and disgrace of his family. He had emphasized secrecy and inaccessibility in the search for an island home. He was the one of his company who would be most easily recognized and identified if he returned to England. It is implausible that news of such a sensational event as Christian's departure from Pitcairn could have been completely suppressed, even with the connivance of Adams.

Paramount, however, is the corroboration of the essential fact of the death of Christian on Pitcairn at the hands of the Polynesian men by *every* version Adams gave the early visitors, by Island tradition, and by Jenny, however the stories may differ as to time, background, and motivations. The reluctance of Adams to point out Christian's grave may have been the result of the failure to properly bury him—a possibility suggested by Young's journal. The missing gold ducats could have been purloined, lost, or gone down with the "Bounty," or Christian could have buried them on Pitcairn and carried to his death the secret of their hiding place. There can be little doubt that his remains rest in the island he rediscovered.

WHAT HAPPENED TO THE BOUNTY?

After learning of Christian's fate, the interest of the ship-conscious captains who first visited Pitcairn was centered on what happened to the "Bounty." All accounts agreed that she had been

---

* Bennett reported being shown Christian's grave in 1834, but this is the only indication of its existence.

destroyed, but there were considerable variances as to the circumstances of her destruction.

Folger's account had it that the "Bounty" was run on the rockstrewn shore of Bounty Bay to prevent desertion, and that the surf completed her dismemberment. Adams told Captains Pipon and Staines that, finding no good anchorage close to Pitcairn, and the ship being too weakly manned to entrust themselves in her, Christian determined to run her into a small creek against the cliff, in order to remove more conveniently anything of use, and to land the hogs, goats, and poultry brought from Tahiti. Having accomplished this, Christian ordered the vessel set on fire to prevent escape and possible discovery.

According to the Beechey version, the crew

> . . . brought the ship to anchor in a small bay on the northern side of the island, which I have in consequence named "Bounty Bay," where everything that could be of utility was landed, and where it was agreed to destroy the ship, whether by running her on shore, or burning her. Christian, Adams, and the majority, were for the former expedient but while they went to the forepart of the ship to execute this business, Matthew Quintal set fire to the carpenter's storeroom. The vessel burnt to the water's edge, and then drifted upon the rocks, where the remainder of the wreck was burnt for fear of discovery. This occurred on the 23rd of January, 1790.

The most graphic and plausible account is again that of Jenny (3).

> Christian got the vessel under a rocky point and came to anchor. The mutineers began to discharge the ship, by means of the boat and a raft made out of the hatches. The property from the ship was landed principally on the raft, by means of a rope fastened to the rocks. When all they wanted was brought on shore, they began to consider what they should do with the vessel. Christian wished to save her for a while. The others insisted on destroying her, and one of them went off and set fire to her in the fore part. Shortly after two others went on board and set fire to her in different places. Some regretted exceedingly they had not confined Captain Bligh and returned to their native country, instead of acting as they had done.

In 1933 the rudder of the "Bounty" was fished up from six fathoms of water in Bounty Bay by one of Fletcher Christian's descendants, Parkin Christian. This discovery and others inspired the 1956 expedition by Luis Marden, a man skilled in diving and marine photography. The Marden expedition resulted in the recovery of a rudder pintle, hull fittings, and oarlock, and sheathing nails from the wrecked "Bounty."[8]

CHRISTIAN'S ROLE ON PITCAIRN

As the leader of the mutiny, an officer, and one of the two men on the last journey of the "Bounty" who could navigate her, Christian retained some measure of authority while she was afloat. Its limited nature is indicated by the incidents at Tubuai, where the men broke into the spirit room without punishment after Christian denied them more grog, and where Christian reluctantly yielded to the vote of the majority for a return to Tahiti and a split-up. The further deterioration of his authority after the split-up is eloquently attested by Jenny's report of an episode in the vessel's wanderings, when it touched on an island Jenny called Purutea and Maude believes may have been Rarotonga in the Cook group. A native who had come out to the "Bounty," on exhibiting the jacket given him by Christian, was shot dead by one of the mutineers. "Christian was highly indignant at this. He could do nothing more, having lost all authority, than reprimand the murderer severely. . . ."

Another instance of the feebleness of Christian's command was the burning of the "Bounty" at Pitcairn over his expressed desire to "save her for a while."

Once the ship was resting on the bottom of Bounty Bay and the mutineers were now all landsmen, are there any indications that Christian retained any special position in the new community? Yes, but they are highly inconclusive and, on close scrutiny, seem to derive more from the natural assumption of the early writers that such would be the case than from any actual facts.

Delano refers to the Colony as living "under Christian's government several years." And Beechey has Adams saying that Christian "won the good opinion and respect of all who served under him; which cannot be better exemplified than by his maintaining, under circumstances of great perplexity, the respect and regard of all who were associated with him up to the hour of his death; and even at the period of our visit, Adams, in speaking of him, never omitted to say, 'Mr. Christian.' " One cannot but suspect, on the basis of the insubstantiality of the item of supporting evidence, that both the language and gist of this passage are more Beechey than Adams; it reads like something the author might have thought would sound well.

Buffett has a story that is interesting in this connection:

> It has been said by some, that after the mutiny Christian became sullen, and that he was not respected by his fellow mutineers, this was not the case. After landing on Pitcairn's Island, he devoted most of his time to cultivating the ground; was never idle, and genarally [*sic*] respected, and always called "Mr. Christian." [Echoes of Beechey.] John Adams informed me that on one occasion he found the consequence of not showing him respect! The case was this; having allowed the hogs to run at large, it became necessary to fence in the cultivated land, and each man had his portion to keep in repair. Adams' part being out of order he was called upon to put it into repair which he refused to do. Christian told Adams that if he caught his hogs coming through the fence he would shoot them. —Adams replied, "Then I will shoot you." He had no sooner made this reply than they seized and bound him, and sentenced him to be set adrift on a plank in the ocean, which sentence would have been put into execution had it not been for Christian.

The story fails to support Buffett's claim that Christian was "respected," especially if it were intended to imply thereby that he enjoyed authority. Though clearly in the wrong, Able Seaman Adams defies Master's Mate and Acting Lieutenant Fletcher; he answers a threat against his hogs with a threat to kill the ranking man; he is subdued and sentenced by "they," signifying action by the group rather than Christian alone. Even assuming that the sentence was intended seriously rather than to frighten Adams into conformity, its remission at Christian's request would be a natural deference to the complainant in the case before the court, rather than a bowing to the will of the leader. If Christian had established real authority, this case would probably never have arisen.

Other facts indicate that any special status Christian may have retained after the mutiny did not survive the landing on Pitcairn. "The island was divided into equal portions, but to the exclusion of the poor blacks. . . ." "Equal" division indicated lack of any recognition of leadership; "equal" was not the share of a prize which would have been awarded the captain of a fortunate vessel. Further, on the matter of land division, there is a suggestion that Christian knew, or should have known, of the dangers incipient in the exclusion of the Polynesian men, especially any of the land-owning class, and that it was effected against his will. Further, Jenny's accounts of the Pitcairn Colony place no special emphasis on Christian, although her interviewers were likely to do so.

Finally, it seems clear that any attempt by Christian to play "captain" with this hard shell crew would have run a course as rocky as Pitcairn's "iron-bound" shores. His shipmates were fiercely insistent on being their "own men." The mutiny and its aftermath had brought out in them all the rugged individualism which their characters and actions indicated; it was not fondness for authority or orders that had brought them to Pitcairn Island.

The captains who first visited Pitcairn and the early commentators were keenly conscious of the "moral" issue (and betrayal of class?) involved in the "Bounty" mutiny and were eager to learn of Christian's reactions after his subversive conduct and his self-imposed exile. Failing satisfactory information, some were all too eager to project themselves into his situation and provide him with a proper remorsefulness.

This is particularly evident in the never fully published account of Captain Pipon:

> It appears that this unfortunate and ill fated young man was never happy after the rash and inconsiderate step he had taken, but always sullen and morose, a circumstance which will not surprize any one; this moroseness however led him to many acts of cruelty and inhumanity, which soon was the cause of his incurring the hatred and detestation of his companions.

A considerably different picture emerges from Beechey, although subject to the same suspicions:

> As Christian and Young were descended from respectable parents, and had received educations suitable to their birth, it might be supposed that they felt their altered and degraded situation much more than the seamen who were comparatively well off; but if so, Adams says, they had the good sense to conceal it, as not a single murmur or regret escaped them; on the contrary Christian was always cheerful, and his example was of the greatest service in exciting his companions to labour. He was naturally of a happy, ingenuous disposition, and won the good opinion and respect of all who served under him. . . .

Barrow was skeptical of Beechey's picture of a cheerful Christian. He states:

On the contrary [Christian was] always uneasy in his mind about his own safety . . . proved by his having selected a cave at the extremity of the high ridge of craggy hills that runs across the island, as his intended place of refuge, in the event of any ship of war discovering the retreat of the mutineers, in which cave he resolved to sell his life as dearly as he could. In this recess he always kept a store of provisions, and near it erected a small hut, well concealed by trees, which served the purpose of a watch-house. "So difficult," says Captain Beechey, "was the approach to this cave, that even if a party were successful in crossing the ridge, he might have bid defiance, as long as his ammunition lasted, to any force." The reflection alone of his having sent adrift, to perish on the wide ocean, for he could entertain no other idea, no less than nineteen persons, all of whom, one only excepted, were innocent of any offence towards him, must have constantly haunted his mind, and left him little disposed to be happy and cheerful.

The assurance with which the captains and writers were able to read Christian's mind and mood inhibits any desire to excel them. One is timid even about suggesting the ambivalences which permeate mortals, so that the gay man is as likely as the next to be melancholy on a different occasion, and the troubled man to alternate between self-accusation and self-justification. Forced to guess, one could speculate that, on the basis of Christian's history, the odds would favor continued mercurial moods, running the gamut indicated by his volatile temperament. It pleased many who told the story to have Christian brooding and repentant; it may have pleased Christian himself to concentrate on the demands and pleasures of the moment.

WHAT HAPPENED TO THE "BLACKS" AND WILLIAMS, MILLS, BROWN, AND MARTIN?

The death of Williams, Mills, Brown, and Martin, and the wounding of Adams in the "massacre" by the Polynesian men are established by the most complete accounts, although there are variations in the descriptions of circumstances, which will be discussed later. The manner in which the "blacks" were dispatched is more obscure and is the subject of many discrepancies and legends.

Strife originated with the death of Williams' wife (whether by a fall, as Beechey says, or "a scrophulous disease, which broke out in her neck," as Jenny(1) says) and his demand for a replacement. If we are to believe Buffett, his fellow mutineers sensed trouble in this

63

situation: "... at first the others were not agreeable, but proposed he should wait and have the daughter of M'Coy's wife when she should be of age, she being but an infant when they left Tahiti. To this he would not consent ..."

The dramatic upshot is described by Jenny(1) and (3): "The Europeans took the three women belonging to the natives, Toofaiti, Mareva, and Tinafornea, and cast lots for them, and the lot falling upon Toofaiti, she was taken from Tararo and given to Jack Williams. —Tararo wept at parting with his wife, and was very angry ... betook himself to the hills. After three days, he returned and got his wife away, and took her to the mountains with him. The native men now proposed to kill the English ..."

"Fortunately," as Beechey relates it, "the secret was imparted to the women, who ingeniously communicated it to the white men in a song, of which the words were, 'Why does black man sharpen axe? to kill white man.'"

The instant Christian became aware of the plot, he seized his gun and went in search of the conspirators, with a view to showing them that their scheme was discovered and thereby to prevent its execution.

> He met one of them [Ohoo] at a little distance from the village, taxed him with the conspiracy, and in order to intimidate him, discharged his gun, which he had humanely loaded with powder only. Ohoo, however, imagining otherwise, and that the bullet had missed its object, derided his unskilfulness, and fled into the woods, followed by his accomplice, Talaloo [Tararo], who had been deprived of his wife. The remaining blacks, finding their plot discovered, purchased pardon by promising to murder their accomplices, who had fled, which they afterwards performed by an act of the most odious treachery. Ohoo was betrayed and murdered by his own nephew;* and Talaloo, after an ineffectual attempt made upon him by poison, fell by the hands of his friend and his wife, the very woman on whose account all the disturbance began, and whose injuries Talaloo felt he was revenging in common with his own.

A somewhat variant version of this phase of the plots and counterplots is derived from Jenny:

> ... The English ... were, however, upon their guard; three of the principals in the plot thought proper to seek refuge in the mountains. One of the natives† who remained with the English, was sent by Christian to

---

* There is no other indication in the record of any relationship between Ohoo, Tubuaian, and Manarii, Tahitian, presumably the nephew referred to.
† It is fairly certain Manarii is referred to here, but there is a strange reluctance in all the accounts to name him.

the mountains, for the purpose of shooting the principal conspirator, whose name was Oopee, promising to reward him handsomely if he succeeded, but, if he did not, he was to lose his own life. This man took a pistol with him as directed: he found Oopee among the craggy precipices and killed him. Tararo, who had taken his wife from Williams, and was still in the mountains, was shot by order of the Europeans; his wife now returned to Williams.

Buffett's version incorporates an Island tradition:

To prevent quarrels among the whites it was at last agreed to destroy [Tararo] the husband of the woman called Nancy [Toofaiti]. He suspecting it secreted himself on the west side of the island. Having found his hiding place they sent him food by his wife in which they had put poison, but he would not eat of it unless his wife would also. She of course would not. She next went with a Tahitian who was armed with a pistol. Having found him, he presented the pistol but it missed fire. A scuffle ensued, and the husband of Nancy fell. She took a stick to beat him with, on seeing which he said, "I shall contend no longer since you are against me." He was killed and Nancy became the wife of Williams.

Apparently Titahiti had been involved in the plot for revenge against the whites. He "was put in irons for some time, and afterwards released; when he and his wife lived with Martin, and wrought for him."

An interval of "tranquillity" now ensued for about two years, "at the expiration of which dissatisfaction was again manifested by the blacks, in consequence of oppression and ill treatment, principally by Quintal and M'Coy." (Beechey)

And Buffett adds: "Quintal and M'Coy were very cruel to their servants, Quintal in particular. —Sometimes after coming home late at evening with sea fowl, he would make his servant clean and cook them, and if not done to please him he would severely flog him, sometimes putting brine on his back!"

The picture is fleshed out by Jenny (3), who relates that Manarii "stole a pig belonging to M'Koy, for which offence the English beat him severely. Teimua afterwards stole some yams, and one of the women informed of him. He was also severely chastised."

The day of reckoning was to more than even the score for the murder of the two "blacks." The toll of the "massacre" would be five whites dead, one wounded.

The natives again concerted among themselves to murder the English, and went about from day to day with their muskets, on a pretence of shooting wildfowl. The mutineers did not suspect their intentions; Williams was the first man shot, while putting up a fence round his garden. The natives next proceeded to shoot Christian . . . they found Miles [sic] and M'Koy [in another enclosure]: the former was shot dead, but M'Koy saved himself by flight. They now went to Martin's house and shot him: he did not fall immediately, but ran to Brown's house, which was not far off. He was there shot a second time, when he fell; they beat him on the head with a hammer till he was quite dead. Brown at the same time was knocked on the head with stones, and left for dead. As the murderers were going away, he rose up and ran. One of them pursued and overtook him. He begged hard for mercy, or that they would not kill him until he had seen his wife. They promised they would spare his life; however, one with a musket got behind him and shot him dead.

Further details are included in Beechey's version of the "massacre":

Tetaheite . . . borrowed a gun and ammunition of his master, under the pretence of shooting hogs . . . he joined his accomplices, and with them fell upon Williams and shot him. Martin, who was at no great distance, heard the report of the musket, and exclaimed, "Well done. We shall have a glorious feast today," supposing that a hog had been shot. The party proceeded from Williams' towards Christian's plantation, where Menalee, the other black, was at work with Mills and M'Coy; and, in order that the suspicions of the whites might not be excited by the report they had heard, requested Mills to allow him [Menalee] to assist them in bringing home the hog they pretended to have killed. Mills agreed; and the four, being united, proceeded to Christian, who was working at his yam-plot, and shot him.

M'Coy, hearing his groans, observed to Mills, "There was surely some person dying," but Mills replied, "It's only Mainmast [Christian's wife] calling her children to dinner." The white men being yet too strong for the blacks to risk a conflict with them, it was necessary to concert a plan, in order to separate Mills and M'Coy. Two of them accordingly secreted themselves in M'Coy's house, and Tetaheite ran and told him that the two blacks who had deserted [Timoa and Nehow] were stealing things out of his house. M'Coy instantly hastened to detect them, and on entering was fired at; but the ball passed him. M'Coy immediately communicated the alarm to Mills, and advised him to seek shelter in the woods; but Mills, being quite satisfied that one of the blacks whom he had made his friend would not suffer him to be killed, determined to remain.

Mills had scarcely been left alone, when the two blacks fell upon him, and he became a victim of his misplaced confidence in the fidelity of his friend. Martin and Brown were next separately murdered by Menalee and Tenina; Menalee effecting with a maul what the musket had left unfinished. Tenina, it is said, wished to save the life of Brown, and fired at him with powder only, desiring him, at the same time, to fall as if killed; but, unfortunately, rising too soon, the other black, Menalee, shot him.

The count of adult males now stood at two "blacks" murdered, five whites murdered; four "blacks" alive, four whites alive. McCoy and Quintal had fled to the woods, Adams had been wounded, but his life spared, and Young had hidden out during the butchery. The next killing, like the first two, was to be of "black" by "black," and again like the first, was the result of a dispute over a woman.

The party in the village lived in tolerable tranquility for about a week; at the expiration of which, the men of colour began to quarrel about the right of choosing the women whose husbands had been killed: which ended in Menalee's shooting Timoa as he sat by the side of Young's wife, accompanying her song with his flute. Timoa not dying immediately, Menalee reloaded, and deliberately despatched him by a second discharge. He afterwards attacked Tetaheite, who was condoling with Young's wife for the loss of her favourite black, and would have murdered him also, but for the interference of the women. Afraid to remain longer in the village, he escaped to the mountains and joined Quintal and M'Coy, who, though glad of his services, at first received him with suspicion.

Adams or the women managed to convey to Quintal and McCoy the message that "if they would kill the black man, Menalee, and return to the village, they would all be friends again. The terms were so far complied with that Menalee was shot; but, apprehensive of the sincerity of the remaining blacks, they refused to return while they were alive."

The not overly subtle suggestion of Quintal and McCoy was soon put in effect. Beechey, from whom we have been quoting, tells us:

Adams says it was not long before the widows of the white men so deeply deplored their loss, that they determined to revenge their death, and concerted a plan to murder the only two remaining men of colour. . . . The arrangement was, that Susan should murder one of them, Tetaheite, while he was sleeping by the side of his favourite; and that Young should at the same instant, upon a signal being given, shoot the other, Nehow. The unsuspecting Tetaheite retired as usual, and fell by the blow of an axe; the other was looking at Young loading his gun, which he supposed was for the purpose of shooting hogs, and requested him to put in a good charge, when he received the deadly contents.

Jenny (3) has a slightly variant version of this savory episode.

> Next day [after the killing of Menalee] the women agreed with Smith and Young to kill the two Otaheitans. About noon, while one of the Otaheitan men was sitting outside of the house, and the other was lying on his back on the floor, one of the women took a hatchet and cleft the skull of the latter; at the same instance calling out to Young to fire, which he did, and shot the other native dead.

WHAT HAPPENED TO McCOY, QUINTAL, YOUNG, AND ADAMS?

There were now left on Pitcairn, of the original twenty-eight settlers, only McCoy, Quintal, Young, and Adams, ten women, and the child Sally. We return to Jenny's account of the "massacre" to pick up the story of what happened to Adams and Young before it ended. After the shooting of Brown, Adams

> . . . was next fired at in his own house; the ball grazed his neck and broke two of his fingers. He was saved by the women, who were at this time assembled. The murderers, after wounding him, permitted him to take farewell of his wife. The women threw themselves on his body, and at their entreaties his life was spared. . . . One of the mutineers [obviously Young] was spared by the murderers, and lived with Smith and the woman ["women" apparently was intended here.]

This accords with Beechey's statement that, "Young . . . a great favorite with the women . . . had, during this attack, been secreted by them." However, Beechey's and other accounts contain considerable deviations in the story of the wounding of Adams and how he escaped the wrath of the Polynesians.

As Adams told the story to Beechey, he was

> . . . first apprised of his danger by Quintal's wife, who, in hurrying through his plantation, asked why he was working at such a time? Not understanding the question, but seeing her alarmed, he followed her, and was almost immediately met by the blacks, whose appearance exciting suspicion, he made his escape into the woods. After remaining three or four hours, Adams, thinking all was quiet, stole to his yam-plot for a supply of provisions; his movements, however, did not escape the vigilance of the blacks, who attacked and shot him through the body, the ball entering at his right shoulder and passing out through his throat. He fell upon his side, and was instantly assailed by one of them with the butt end of the gun; but he parried the blows at the expense

of a broken finger. Tetaheite then placed his gun to his side, but it fortunately missed fire twice. Adams, recovering a little from the shock of his wound, sprang on his legs, and ran off with as much speed as he was able, and fortunately outstripped his pursuers, who seeing him likely to escape, offered him protection if he would stop. Adams, much exhausted by his wound, readily accepted their terms, and was conducted to Christian's house, where he was kindly treated.*

Other versions confirm the story of Adams' wounding and escape, albeit with further variances of detail.

Adams now tried to get McCoy and Quintal back to the village from the mountains; these understandably suspicious characters refused until "the hands and heads of the deceased were produced" to confirm Adams' story of the death of the Polynesian men. The date of their return is given as October 3, 1793. The ten Polynesian women were divided up, three each to Adams and Young, and two each to Quintal and McCoy.

Jenny(3) makes short work of the subsequent necrology.

They soon began to distill a spirituous liquor from the tea-root. In a drunken affray, Matthew Quintal was killed by his three countrymen, M'Koy came to his death through drinking spirits, which brought on derangement, and caused him to leap into the sea, after having tied his own hands and feet. Young died a natural death on Christmas day.

In her earlier story, Jenny (1) has it,

Old Matt, in a drunken fit, declaring that he would kill F. Christian's children, and all the English that remained, was put to death in his turn. Old M'Koy, mad with drink, plunged into the sea and drowned himself; and Ned Young died of a disease that broke out in his breast.

Jenny adds,

Several of the women also are dead. Obuarei and Tevarua fell from the precipices when getting birds. Teatuahitea died of the dropsy, and Nahineatua [sic] was killed, being pierced in her bowels when she was with child.

No dates are given for these deaths, but obviously all must have preceded Jenny's departure in 1817.

A fuller account of the demise of Quintal, McCoy, and Young appears in Beechey, partly based on Young's journal:

---

* Adam's suggestion to Buffett that Young knew of or was in on the plot of the "blacks," and had requested Adams be spared, was previously mentioned.

It unfortunately happened that M'Coy had been employed in a distillery in Scotland; and being very much addicted to liquor, he tried an experiment with the tee-root, and on the 20th April, 1798, succeeded in producing a bottle of ardent spirit. This success induced his companion, Matthew Quintal, to "alter his kettle into a still," a contrivance which unfortunately succeeded too well, as frequent intoxication was the consequence, with M'Coy in particular, upon whom at length it produced fits of delirium, in one of which, he threw himself from a cliff and was killed.

. . . about 1799 Quintal lost his wife by a fall from the cliff while in search of bird's eggs . . . he grew discontented, and, though there were several disposable women on the island, and he had already experienced the fatal effects of a similar demand, nothing would satisfy him but the wife of one of his companions. Of course, neither of them felt inclined to accede to this unreasonable indulgence; and he sought an opportunity of putting them both to death. He was fortunately foiled in his first attempt, but swore he would repeat it. Adams and Young having no doubt he would follow up his resolution, and fearing he might be more successful in the next attempt, came to the conclusion that their own lives were not safe while he was in existence, and that they were justified in putting him to death, which they did with an axe.

This final bit of butchery brought to a temporary end the intramural warfare on Pitcairn. The next man to die was the first whose end was not the result of violence. ''An asthmatic complaint, under which he [Young] had for some time labored, terminated his existence about a year after the death of Quintal, and Adams was left the sole survivor of the misguided and unfortunate mutineers of the 'Bounty.' ''

THE REVOLT OF THE HAREM

While it is possible to glean from the record a fairly coherent picture of the slaughter that marked the first decade of the Pitcairn community, what defies complete comprehension is the role and actions of the Pitcairn women, especially after the killing of the Polynesian men, as it appears in Beechey's account, and solely in Beechey's account.

It is not surprising that this story of the war between the sexes which replaced the racial warfare does not appear in the accounts of the other visitors, incomplete and garbled as most of them were. What is difficult to understand is why Jenny's accounts make no mention thereof, especially as she played a leading role in the drama reported by Beechey.

He states that about December 1793, when there was left "Adams, Young, M'Coy, and Quintal, ten women, and some children . . . Young commenced a manuscript journal." (There is no other evidence of the existence of this journal, but there is no reason to believe Beechey invented it.) "From it we learn that they lived peaceably together, building their houses, fencing in and cultivating their grounds, fishing, and catching birds, and constructing pits for the purpose of entrapping hogs, which had become very numerous and wild, as well as injurious to the yam-crops." This idyllic picture is shattered by the next sentence: "The only discontent appears to have been among the women, who lived promiscuously with the men, frequently changing their abode." If Beechey intended to suggest a relationship between promiscuity and discontent, it may be said his account provides other reasons for the women's unhappiness.

Young says, March 12, 1794, "Going over to borrow a rake, to rake the dust off my ground, I saw Jenny having a skull in her hand: I asked her whose it was? and was told it was Jack Williams'. I desired it might be buried: the women who were with Jenny gave me for answer, it should not. I said it should; and demanded it accordingly. I was asked the reason why I, in particular, should insist on such a thing, when the rest of the white men did not? I said, if they gave them leave to keep the skulls above ground, I did not. Accordingly, when I saw M'Coy, Smith, and Mat. Quintal, I acquainted them with it, and said, I thought that if the girls did not agree to give up the heads of the five white men in a peaceable manner, they ought to be taken by force, and buried." About this time the women appear to have been much dissatisfied; and Young's journal declares that, "since the massacre, it has been the desire of the greater part of them to get some conveyance, to enable them to leave the island." This feeling continued, and on the 14th of April, 1794, was so strongly urged, that the men began to build a boat; but wanting planks and nails, Jenny, who now resides at Otaheite, in her zeal tore up the boards of her house, and endeavoured, though without success, to persuade some others to follow her example.*

On the 13th of August following, the vessel was finished, and on the 15th she was launched: but, as Young says, "according to expectation

---

* The only other version of this episode discovered comes from Buffett . . . "When the 'Bounty' left Tahiti, some of the females were taken against their will, and after their arrival at Pitcairn's Island, they wished to return home. For this purpose the white men constructed a raft to satisfy their desire to return. They appointed one of the females captain, and directed them how to steer, etc. The raft was launched and upset, and their visionary voyage ended."

she upset," and it was most fortunate for them that she did so; for had they launched out upon the ocean, where could they have gone? or what could a few ignorant women have done by themselves, drifting upon the waves, but ultimately have fallen a sacrifice to their folly? However, the fate of the vessel was a great disappointment, and they continued much dissatisfied with their condition; probably not without some reason, as they were kept in great subordination and were frequently beaten by M'Coy and Quintal, who appear to have been of very quarrelsome dispositions; Quintal in particular, who proposed "not to laugh, joke, or give anything to any of the girls."

On the 16th of August they dug a grave, and buried the bones of the murdered people; and on October 3rd, 1794, they celebrated the murder of the black men at Quintal's house. On the 11th November, a conspiracy of the women to kill the white men in their sleep was discovered; upon which they were all seized, and a disclosure ensued; but no punishment appears to have been inflicted upon them, in consequence of their promising to conduct themselves properly, and never again to give any cause "even to suspect their behavior." However, though they were pardoned, Young observed, "We did not forget their conduct; and it was agreed among us, that the first female who misbehaved should be put to death; and this punishment was to be repeated on each offence until we could discover the real intentions of the women." Young appears to have suffered much from mental perturbation in consequence of these disturbances; and observes of himself on the two following days, that "he was bothered and idle."

The suspicions of the men induced them, on the 15th, to conceal two muskets in the bush, for the use of any person who might be so fortunate as to escape, in the event of an attack being made. On the 30th November, the women again collected and attacked them: but no lives were lost, and they returned on being once more pardoned, but were again threatened with death the next time they misbehaved. Threats thus repeatedly made, and as often unexecuted, soon lost their effect, and the women formed a party whenever their displeasure was excited, and hid themselves in the unfrequented parts of the island, carefully providing themselves with fire-arms. In this manner the men were kept in continual suspense, dreading the result of each disturbance, as the numerical strength of the women was greater than their own.

Young's journal raises many perplexing questions impossible to answer satisfactorily. Why were the women so eager to risk almost certain death to escape from Pitcairn? Why were the men willing to build a boat (no light task) to carry from them the women and their children? Why were the women, who apparently had sided with the Europeans in the confrontation of "black" against white, now grown so hostile to them that they planned their destruction? Why were the women able to plot against and attack the men, but unable to defend themselves against beatings by McCoy and Quintal? What really prevented them from exterminating any or all of the men if they so desired?

An inescapable desire to make sense of what seems senseless suggests that the picture must be distorted, whether by omission of pertinent facts (most likely) or false emphasis on the facts given. The only explanation encountered attributes the conflict to "sex antagonism. The women's movement may perhaps be interpreted as a very primitive affair—a revolt of the harem."[9] This is not very helpful, nor is resort to such pejoratives as "anarchy," "degeneration," or "bestiality."

PEACE DESCENDS

But matters now improved. Coming to the year 1796, Beechey says that the men "appear to have been more sociable; dining frequently at each other's houses, and contributing more to the comfort of the women, who, on their part, gave no ground for uneasiness." After the death of the pot-valiant McCoy, the execution of the brutal Quintal, and the demise of Young, peace, religion, and government came to Pitcairn, pulling the community back from the edge of extinction on which it had teetered. The nineteenth century ushered in what many were to call the "Golden Age of Pitcairn."

❧ NOTES: PART TWO ❧

1. *Gentlemen's Magazine,* 1818, part 2, p. 37.
2. Newell, G., *New-England Galaxy,* vol. 4, January 12, 1821.
3. Wilkinson, C. S., *Wake of the Bounty* (London, 1953).
4. Montgomerie, H. S., *William Bligh of the Bounty in Fact and in Fable,* London, 1937.
5. Bennett.
6. Newell.
7. Young.
8. The story of this expedition is well told and beautifully illustrated in the

December 1957 issue of the *National Geographic Magazine,* vol. 112, pp. 725–729.

9. Hancock, Prof. W. K., "Politics in Pitcairn," *Nineteenth Century,* May 1931, vol. 109, pp. 575–587, incorporated in a book of the same title, London, 1947.

Part Three

THE WORLD OF PITCAIRN

❧ THUMBNAIL HISTORY ❧ OF PITCAIRN TO DATE

Because it is the scheme of this book to treat separately from the beginning to the present each aspect of the Pitcairn experience, rather than attempt to juggle contemporalities, the reader is offered the following bare-bones sketch of Island history for the purpose of general background.

Neither Mayhew Folger's discovery of the settlement in 1808 nor the 1814 visit of Captains Pipon and Staines had a marked effect on the Pitcairn way of life, although the latter initiated an entente with the British Navy. The community was largely agricultural and entirely self-supporting, but very much subject to vagaries of the weather, most cruelly evidenced in occasional droughts. The important staple of the Island economy and one that required much labor was the yam. The yam was supplemented by fruits and other vegetables, pigs, fowl, goats, fish, and arboreal products such as coconuts and breadfruit.

Adams, lone survivor of the fifteen males who had landed on Pitcairn in 1790, after undergoing a "conversion," fostered religious instruction and observances about the turn of the century, and schooling of a rudimentary type. He was later aided in these endeavors by seaman John Buffett, who became Pitcairn's first immigrant in 1823. The early visitors reported Pitcairn a bountiful Arcadia, peopled by a devout, hospitable, ingenuous, and frictionless family, and headed by the universal "father," John Adams.

Beechey's epochal visit in 1825, at the instigation of the British Admiralty, had more dramatic and definite results than those of his predecessors and ultimately resulted in a *rapprochement* which made Pitcairn part of the British Empire. Beechey, prompted by Adams, took note of the rapidly increasing population of the two-square-mile island, sixty-six at the time, and the threat of water shortage. Misgivings on this score prompted the reluctant emigration of the total Pitcairn Colony of eighty-six to Tahiti in 1831. The transplantation soon proved disastrous; seventeen Pitcairners died of infections acquired during this period. Within less than six months all survivors returned to the hazards of Pitcairn, vowing never again to leave.

Adams died in 1829. His successor as leader of the community was an erstwhile sailor of fortune with a religious cast of mind, George Hunn Nobbs. He had arrived in 1828—the consummation of a long-cherished dream—and was to be a dominant figure for many years. Nobbs became Island pastor, teacher, doctor, recorder, publicist, and ambassador-at-large.

Nobb's ascendancy was temporarily interrupted in 1832 by the advent of one Joshua Hill, a pretender of megalomaniac tendencies, who claimed authority to govern Pitcairn and succeeded in exiling Nobbs. Hill made himself complete dictator until he overreached himself and was put down, literally and figuratively, by an aroused parent, Arthur Quintal. Hill had insisted on dire punishment for Quintal's daughter. After exposure of the falsity of his pretensions, Hill was expelled in 1837. Nobbs resumed his previous status.

Two new elements entered the Pitcairn economy in the first thirty years of the nineteenth century. Whaling in the Pacific, largely by ships from New England, became a large industry and Pitcairn became a supplier of fruits, vegetables, and water, which were traded for whatever goods the whalers could offer and, sometimes, for money. Religious societies, exhilarated by the story of redemption on Pitcairn, interested themselves in the welfare of the Islanders and sent them books and other supplies. (They also praised them for their piety, with the result that some of the Pitcairners may have been induced to preen themselves a bit on this point.)

The British Government, too, supplemented the Island economy with occasional contributions of various goods, and other windfalls arrived intermittently from admirers enchanted by the Pitcairn story.

Despite these spasmodic accretions to the simple agricultural economy of Pitcairn, drought and crop failures reduced the community at intervals to desperate straits and there was much talk (mostly by outlanders) of removing the Colony to another location. It took more than a little arm-twisting to persuade the Pitcairners, devoted as they were to their native soil even beyond most islanders and ruefully recollectful as they were of the unhappy Tahiti migration, but in the end, afraid of being marked ingrates and of being abandoned by a paternal British Government, all 194 agreed to go to Norfolk Island. The move was made in 1856, leaving Pitcairn unoccupied for the third time in some sixty-six years.

The pull of that "special island" brought back "home" one-fourth of the emigrants within eight years after the exodus, and the Pitcairn community was "back in business," albeit faced with the necessity of repairing the ravages of time and the depredations of shipwrecked sailors who had used Pitcairn houses to build a ship with which to reach Tahiti. A few years of bumper crops were followed by seedy times when rainfall failed. The whalers were fading from the seas, communications with passing ships became infrequent, and world interest, fickle as always, was at a low level.

School and religious services were resumed after the return. A notable change in religious affiliation occurred in 1886, when the entire community transferred allegiance from the Church of England to the then new sect of the Seventh Day Adventists. The Adventists, proud of their triumph, now took a special interest in the Pitcairners, sending them teachers, missionaries, and supplies, as well as naming their missionary ship the "Pitcairn." This interest was to wane at intervals, but its evidences were to be an important part of Island life thenceforward.

The last twenty years of the nineteenth century were also marked by a series of shipwrecks, some of which resulted in new immigrants and a variety of substantial gifts reflecting gratitude for the Islanders' hospitality. It was also distinguished by increasing ship traffic and abortive attempts, continuing into the twentieth century, to establish a merchant marine. This period, and the following several decades, witnessed a deterioration of Island life in morals, energy, and material achievements.

Pitcairn Island

After the opening of the Panama Canal in 1914, passenger steamers on the New Zealand run began to make brief stops off Pitcairn to introduce a bit of diversion into the lengthy passage. The Islanders rushed on board to trade fruits, vegetables, and curios of growing quality with passengers and ships. The manufacture of curios, long a subsidiary occupation, was to become the principal Island industry, breaking the predominantly agricultural pattern. It developed to the point (sales on board ships being supplemented by exports) where Islanders were able to afford such twentieth century luxuries as electricity, refrigerators, and even telephones.

A new source of public income developed from the implementation in 1940 by Mr. Maude, representing the British High Commissioner in Fiji, of a long suggested scheme for the issuance of Pitcairn postage stamps. The "phenomenal" results of this enterprise financed the building of a new post office and school, and the procurement of professional teachers.

Other amenities of the western world arrived in Pitcairn, either as a result of individual or governmental efforts, including a nurse-attended dispensary, a sea wall and jetty to improve landing facilities at Bounty Bay, power winches for the slipways, motors for the publicly-owned boats, and a power hoist to enable the Pitcairners to get freight from the landing place to the village of Adamstown above it without carrying it on their backs up the notorious "Hill of Difficulty."

But an irony not without parallels in the western world marks these revolutionary changes; the nearer the material luxuries of the Island approached mainland standards, the more pronounced became the drift to emigration, particularly to New Zealand. Today (1966) Pitcairn has less than 90 residents. Today the fear raised by the hazard watchers is not overpopulation, but depopulation, of Pitcairn.

The way of life on Pitcairn and the problems of the Colony have changed in the course of its 175-year history, but danger to the continued existence of the community has been a constant.

⚜ THE PITCAIRN ECONOMY ⚜

INTRODUCTORY

Were Pitcairn Island a person, one might describe it as "charismatic." The lure of Pitcairn for both natives and outsiders is dramatically underlined by many events in its history. A mass exodus to Tahiti in 1831 was followed by the return of all survivors within six months. A later total emigration of the Pitcairners to Norfolk Island in 1856 was followed by the return of two families in 1859 and four families in 1864 (forty-three people in all, about one-fourth of those who left). In both cases, seemingly brighter economic prospects were abandoned for that special island.*

Outsiders who succumbed to the call of Pitcairn included men of wide worldly experience and no mean ability and intelligence, such as Nobbs and Buffett. By the 1820s visitors were coming in astonishing numbers, considering the remoteness and inaccessibility of the Island. Whalers began to call, not only for "fresh provisions in unusual variety . . . at moderate prices, but occasionally, it seems evident, out of sheer curiosity."[1] Pitcairn was "loaded with glamor."

Though ultimately to become the chief support of the Colony, glamor provided no calories to the twenty-eight settlers who came ashore from the "Bounty" in 1790. They were faced with the problem of utilizing the limited resources of this tiny "pimple on the ocean" and their own ingenuity to survive. As the prolific early generations multiplied, the threat of overpopulation became vivid.

If this did not accord with the standard lotus-land picture of South Sea economics, it may have been because that picture, capsuled by Byron as "the feasts without a toil," was based on the tales of early voyagers to Tahiti—Wallis, Cook, Bougainville, and Bligh. The

---

* Even Jenny, the most anxious to leave of the settlers and the first emigrant from Pitcairn in 1817, pined for this magic island after her return to Tahiti, if we can trust Captain Kotzebue's account. "The Tahitians, she assured me, were by no means so virtuous as the natives of the little Paradise to which she was now all impatience to return."

81

enticing scenario of a land of plenty without labor, though not entirely baseless, was subject to caveat. No statistics offered a clue to the population and economic standards of Tahiti, although the voyagers made many wild guesses as to the former. Circumstantial evidence indicates that the rich natural resources of Tahiti, possibly the most favored of the South Sea Islands, were constantly pressed by the needs of the population.

Otherwise, how account for the fear of overpopulation openly expressed to visitors and dramatized by the practice of infanticide among a child-loving people? If fish were so abundant and easily caught, how explain the seeming insatiability of the Tahitian appetite for this favorite food? If exertion were superfluous in this inexhaustible cornucopia, where food dropped into the lap while the Tahitian took an afternoon siesta in the shade, why the prodigious labor that went into such pursuits as tapa-making, fishing, and building fleets of elaborate canoes and *marae?*

Moreover, thousands of other South Sea islands were inhabited by peoples of less advanced cultures and more stringent circumstances, and the available evidence indicates that many of them existed, when not totally submerged, barely above the level of starvation. The discovery of the skeletons of shipwrecked European sailors on barren atolls demonstrated the distinct possibility of starving to death in this bountiful terrain.*

We are afforded a vivid insight into the low level at which it was possible for men to survive in this "paradise" area from the travels of Pitcairn's own Pastor Nobbs. During his exile in the Gambier Islands in the 1830s, he had occasion to visit a

> small lagoon sand-bank, called Crescent Island . . . some forty or fifty miles from Gambier. . . . to our surprise we found about forty persons, meagre and wretched in appearance, inhabiting it. . . . we learned that, fifty or sixty years previous, their progenitors were forced to quit Mangareva on a raft, and that after having been some time at sea they succeeded in landing here. . . . They seemed quite satisfied with their lot, although the only articles of food they could obtain were squid, and small fish taken in the holes of the coral reef, and the kernels of the nut of the pandanus or screw-palm, which is the only tree or vegetable growing on their sand bank.

---

* One such discovery was made by the Pitcairners themselves in 1851 on their first trip to Henderson (Elizabeth) Island, an atoll 105 miles from Pitcairn.

After Nobbs related the "plight" of this group to the chiefs of Mangareva,

> They were all brought to Mangareva . . . and so plied . . . with bread-fruit that one actually died from repletion, and several others would have shared the same fate if I had not dosed them with emetics and cathartics. What became of them after I left I never heard, but was told that most of them pined for their coral home.

This little excursion suggests the subjective and elastic nature of "standard of living." To the "Bounty" men, fed on salt pork and biscuits that would test the teeth of a shark, the Tahitian bill of fare must have been as savory as dinner *chez* Escoffier, and the Pitcairn diet would not be too unsatisfactory, barring the absence of grog. We can only guess as to how the Pitcairn standard measured up for the Polynesians, or how it would compare with, say, Calcutta or Naples or Cairo or the back country of Appalachia in our own day.

These ruminations are preliminary to a consideration of the Pitcairn economy, the story of how the Colony managed to feed, clothe, and shelter itself, to cope with the intermittent threat of overpopulation, to develop commerce—to survive. Christian's variation on the *Swiss Family Robinson* began life on Pitcairn with definitely circumscribed assets.

⚜ PHYSICAL RESOURCES ⚜

LAND

Pitcairn is roughly two miles long by one mile wide, giving it a land area of two square miles. But only a fraction, on the order of four hundred acres, can be used for growing such crops as the indispensable yam, because of the mountainous and rocky terrain. Captain Waldegrave's estimate that Pitcairn, supporting eighty-one people in 1830, could ultimately support a thousand, since eleven-twelfths was uncultivated, drew the derision of Barrow as a triumph of arithmetic over fact. (It may also serve to indicate the quality of some of the reportage which emanated from visitors.) "Flat or flattish land forms only eight per cent (eighty-eight acres) of the total surface of Pitcairn; rolling land thirty-one per cent (352 acres) ; steeply sloping land thirty-four per cent (385 acres) ; and cliffs the remaining twenty-seven per cent (293 acres)."[2]

Waldegrave's prediction was never put to the test because the population of the Pitcairn community never exceeded 233 (1937)* in its 175-year history. However, it is quite possible that, at the level of the Crescent Islanders described by Nobbs, it could have provided for one thousand or more, barring disastrous weather. The fertility of the reddish-brown volcanic soil, twenty inches deep in some places, was eulogized by natives and visitors alike. Two crops were sometimes grown in a year, but Island experience indicated that letting land lie fallow was the best substitute for fertilizer, the only other supplement being inadequate amounts of seaweed.

WATER

Like all mariners, the "Bounty" men were keenly sensitive to the importance of a supply of fresh water. Their preliminary inspection of the Island must have satisfied them on this score, although it is not clear that it revealed "Brown's Well" or "Brown's Water," a spring of "intermittent flow" which seldom failed, about a half mile from Bounty Bay. After rains, cascades of water streamed down the Pitcairn slopes and the settlers "cut large tanks in the rocks" to take advantage thereof soon after landing, indicating that fresh water was an immediate concern. It continued to be a perpetual concern; what no preliminary survey could have disclosed was the fickleness of Pitcairn weather. Despite the general abundance of rainfall (81 inches per annum on the average in 1956–60), occasional drought proved to be one of the severest hazards of life on Pitcairn.

CLIMATE

The climate of Pitcairn was generally benign in the subtropical manner, but with relative humidity "usually upwards of eighty per cent and cloud averages six-tenths." East to north-east winds are

---

* Population figures are made somewhat questionable in later times, when traveling became easier, by failure to specify whether wandering Pitcairners and semi-permanent residents were included.

predominant; westerly winds increase in frequency in winter. East to south-east brief gales may occur some dozen times a year; hurricanes are rare. Mean temperatures run from 66°F. in August to 75°F. in February, with a recorded range of 51° to 93°F.

This statistical picture of moderation does not prepare us for the claim that it has been known to snow, nor the complaint of Hall that he had not been so cold, since a trip to Iceland, as he was on Pitcairn. In addition to occasional "unusual" extremes of temperature and cruel droughts, devastating storms sometimes attacked the sea-girt rock, hurling land, trees, buildings, and boats into the angry Pacific.[3]

FISH

The generous supply of salt water surrounding and isolating Pitcairn was a potential source of that favorite Polynesian food—fish. Fishing was practiced, with varying results, from the inception of the Colony, when rough weather did not preclude it. The most common catches were rock-cod, grey mullet, red snapper, and a species of mackerel. Barracuda, tuna, and kingfish were caught at certain times of the year. Squid and crawfish rewarded hazardous expeditions among the rocks which ringed the Island.

LIVESTOCK AND FAUNA

The "Bounty" brought to Pitcairn hogs, goats, and fowl. There are indications that it also brought rats, but this department was already provided for by the Polynesian rat (*Rattus exulans*), Pitcairn's only native mammal. Some early accounts note the presence of only a single land bird, a species of warbler. Sea birds of several varieties were occasionally shot as game and their eggs were purloined by dangerous and sometimes fatal expeditions among the Pitcairn cliffs. A modern list states that the best-known birds breeding on Pitcairn are the Fairy Tern (*Gyis alba pacifica*), the Common Noddy (*Anous stolidus pileatus*), and the Red-tailed Tropic Bird (*Phaethon rubicauda*). The Pitcairn Island Warbler (*Acrocephalus vaughani vaughani*) or "sparrow" is a native subspecies, dark brown above and yellowish to buff below.[4]

TREES

When discovered by the men of the "Bounty," Pitcairn was an intensely green and heavily-forested island. Increasing deforestation was yet in the future, when use of trees for houses, boats, furniture, and firewood, plus the depredations of wild-running goats, were to create problems. The stands of precious miro (*thespesia populnea correa*), tuny-nut (*hernandia peltata*), doodoe or candlenut (*aleurites tricoba*), paw paws, breadfruit (*artocarpus incisa*), coconut palm (*cocos nucifera*), and aute or paper mulberry (*broussonetia papyrifera ventenat*)* indicated the previous habitation of the Island. Banyan trees spread their outreaching earth-seeking branches, dramatically picturesque even in this richly-treed landscape.

The mutineers had saved a few of Bligh's precious breadfruit plants for the contingency of their settlement; not only were they superfluous, but the existing breadfruit trees did not thrive and never became important in the Island economy. At every turn, the role of the much-eulogized breadfruit in the Bligh-Bounty-Pitcairn saga was destined largely to evoke the ironical laughter which greets repeated frustration.†

PLANTS

The settlers brought with them plantains and yams, sweet potatoes, taro, and yappa. They found on Pitcairn yams of an inferior strain, bananas, taro (*arum esculentum*), plantains (*Musa Paradisiaca*), sugar cane, and the ubiquitous ti root (*Cordyline terminalis*), destined for a dramatic role in Island history, among a variety of flowering bushes, plants, and ferns. Introduced after settlement, with

---

* This tree was so highly valued that it almost precipitated dissension when the mutineers divided the Island into nine parts. According to Jenny (3), "The cloth plant . . . was discovered growing upon one of the lots, about which some squabbling took place, but they afterwards agreed to divide it equally among them."

† Though scorned as a source of food by the West Indian slaves, some of the breadfruit trees, brought to Jamaica by Bligh after his second expedition, survive to provide a "tourist attraction."

varying success, were melons, pumpkins, potatoes, tobacco, lemons, peas, beans, onions, ginger, pepper, turmeric, and oranges. The last achieved a considerable position as a leading export for a period during the twentieth century.

Special mention must be given to the yam, staple and main support of the Pitcairn diet, to which the largest share of agricultural space and labor was devoted. The yam (genus *Dioscorea,* species *alata*) is not to be confused with the sweet potato (genus *Ipomea,* species *batata*), although it has thick roots like the latter.

SALT

Salt was obtained in the early days from the rocks along the coast. ". . . the sea being hove into the cavities during the blowing weather, is left there, and by the rays of the sun produces salt, a circumstance very common in warm climates."[5] In later years, sea water was let into pans and heated with wood fires, evaporation leaving behind a deposit of salt.

TOOLS

The mutineers brought to Pitcairn tools of high value in the metal-hungry South Pacific. Perhaps most notable were an anvil and forge, and, presumably, the appropriate blacksmith's tools. Copper and steel nails, bolts, and other items essential to the operation of a ship, with its carpentry and armorer's activities, probably came ashore, though we are provided with no catalogue. We have cogent evidence, however, of the importation of tools of destruction in the form of muskets which were used to kill off many of the male settlers.

BOATS

Whether the settlers preserved any of the boats (originally three) in the "Bounty" complement is not clear from the record. (See p. 193.) By 1795, according to the Register, there were built "the two first canoes . . . for the purpose of fishing." These were of the dugout type. The Pitcairners' desire for a whaleboat, stimulated by their first contacts with the whalers, was gratified by whaler Captain King in 1819. The whaleboat was best adapted to the rough Pitcairn waters and the purposes of the Islanders and has survived as the Pitcairn workhorse, even though engines have been added in latter days.

SHELTER AND FURNITURE

The first Pitcairn shelters of the settlers, according to Jenny(1), were "temporary houses of the leaves of the tea, and afterwards more durable ones thatched with palm, as at Taheiti." Buffett indicates that the settlers used the "Bounty" sails as tents before they were turned over to the women for clothing.

But the mutineers had in mind, and gradually built, shelters more in keeping with English notions of proper housing. To this end they used timber salvaged from the "Bounty," supplemented by wood from the native miro (*thespesia populnea correa*) and the tuny-nut (*hernandia peltata*) trees, both excellent for the purpose.

The house which resulted was typically two-storied, with ladder and trap door in the center leading to an upper floor used as a bedroom, with bunks built into corners. The lower floor held the eating and living quarters and sometimes additional bunks. Sliding wall planks could be adjusted to admit air. The house was raised off the ground on wooden sleepers resting on large stones. Tongue and groove construction was used for walls and shutters. Roofs were thatched, first with coconut leaves, then with pandanus, until much later replaced by corrugated iron roofs designed to capture rainfall.

While the houses would seem impressive for the locale, both from many of the early descriptions and from Dr. Shapiro's statement that a few survived at least until 1934, Maude(4) assesses them as "such as one would expect sailor-handymen to build ashore (many similar types were erected by beachcomber-settlers on other islands of the South Seas)." In any event, their English cast was accentuated by their situation in a village built around a common, fenced to include chickens and exclude pigs and goats. But un-Englishlike, they lacked chimneys and fireplaces.

Cooking was done in an outhouse, generally attached, which

featured a stone-lined oven, the Polynesian "umu." Other outhouses served to house poultry and for workshops.

Furniture was crude and sparse. The principal items were bunks, tables, chairs, and stools. Mattresses were made of palm leaves and layers of tapa cloth. Sea chests were used for storage.

In succeeding years, the standard of housebuilding and house-keeping, like the supply of suitable timber trees, deteriorated and was criticized by visitors who failed to grasp that the casual Tahitian attitude toward housing was more natural in view of the terrain and the Pitcairn emphasis on outdoor living. With the increase of prosperity in the middle of the twentieth century, money became available to pay for imported building materials and some houses were built closer to Western notions.

CLOTHING

The Pitcairn settlers brought with them whatever clothing they wore and whatever clothing might have been left on the "Bounty" after the Tahiti split-up, plus whatever tapa cloth remained of the Tahitians' gift to Bligh. Sailcloth from the ship, after use as a tenting material, supplemented the wardrobe of the women. But the jagged Pitcairn topography and the strenuous activities of men and women in farming, fishing, and climbing the steep inclines must have reduced their resources in short order, even though the amount of clothing worn was minimal. It could not have been long before the women fell back on the ancient Polynesian craft of tapa-making, as the cloth-tree and other suitable trees were at hand. The fact that tapa-making involved strenuous labor did not absolve the women from this traditional chore.

The Pitcairn costume, before its "corruption" or "improvement" by contact with westerners, was the essence of Polynesian simplicity. The men, including Patriarch John Adams, wore a piece of tapa passed around the waist, with one end drawn between the legs and tucked in at the waist—the "maro." The women wore a skirt (dyed with pigment obtained by steeping the "doodoee" nut in water) reaching from waist to the ankle, wrapped around the hips and secured by rolling down the top—the "pareu." The women sometimes added a loose mantle reaching to the ankle, and sometimes a sort of poncho, the "obidah."

Beechey reported that in 1825 the women were "always careful to conceal . . . the bust," but Pipon had noted in 1814 that "the upper part of the body is entirely exposed." And Captain King refers to the Pitcairn women of 1819 as "naked," but the context suggests that he intended to indicate they wore no clothes to cover the breasts.

The changes wrought by increasing commerce with Western ships is indicated by Beechey's oft-quoted description of Island fashion as he encountered it: "Their dress, made up of the presents which had been given them by the masters and seamen of merchant ships, was a perfect caricature. Some had long black coats, without any other article of dress, except trowsers; some shirts without coats; and others, waistcoats without either; none had shoes or stockings, and only two possessed hats, neither of which seemed likely to hang long together."

The strictly extempore nature of the Pitcairn costume was destined to disappoint for generations to come both those who mourned the absence of the traditional Polynesian costumes and those distressed at the failure of the Pitcairners to hit the mark of Western sartorial elegance.

The clothing windfalls, unfortunately for the women, were largely masculine in nature. With the advent of an occasional whaler's wife on Pitcairn, the women tried to catch up with Western modes of dress, but it was an uphill battle and they were always somewhat behind the trend, a handicap only partially remedied by gifts from abroad.

In the twentieth century, cloth and ready-made dresses were more frequently ordered by mail, but as recently as 1934 one Pitcairner confided that she had never had a new dress. Today, with money and communication more available, it is possible for Pitcairn women and men to move closer to the Western norm in dress. The housedress seems to be the most favored feminine costume on Pitcairn, while the men are inclined to wear pants, sometimes cut off at the knees and, frequently, a shirt. A variety of hats is worn by both sexes, but not by everyone. The trite apparel of the Pitcairners does not diminish their highly individual appearance.

𝕎 HUMAN RESOURCES 𝕎

SKILLS OF THE MUTINEERS

The limited resources of Pitcairn dramatized what many urban dwellers never consciously recognize—skills of the members of a community are an important part of its capital. "Know-how," as well as physical resources, determines how a society is fed, clothed, and sheltered. To say nothing of such less tangible matters as its education, amusement, and worship.

All of the "Bounty" men who landed on Pitcairn had seafaring experience of greater or lesser extent. In the case of the two officers, Christian and Young, it encompassed the art of navigation. The houses and furniture that were first built on the Island evidence considerable, if limited, knowledge and skill in carpentry, although the source can not be identified.

Brown's post of "Botanist Assistant" on the "Bounty" indicates a horticultural background of great utility. This "landlubber" must have come into his own as the emphasis shifted from sailing to agriculture with the burning of the ship.

Williams' craft as armorer, roughly equivalent to a blacksmith's, was held in such esteem that it proved a pivotal point in Pitcairn history. When he threatened to leave Pitcairn unless his deceased wife was replaced, the Europeans "constrained one of the blacks to bestow his wife upon" Williams. This was the genesis of the "massacre."

Demonstrating that not all crafts are necessarily beneficial, McCoy's distilling skill proved to be one of the community's greatest hazards.

Christian and Young were formally educated and definitely literate. Adams's marginal literacy was to prove the most important by reason of his survival.

SKILLS OF THE POLYNESIANS

No specific information exists on the individual skills of the Polynesians. The circumstantial evidence indicates that, as a group, they brought to the cultural stew some knowledge of South Seas agriculture and of the utilization of indigenous trees and plants, some experience in boat handling, and their own fishing lore. This knowledge was evidenced in roof-thatching, tapa-making, fish-spearing, the underground oven, clothing styles, "linens," and lighting with doo-doee nuts.

⚜ THE POPULATION PROBLEM ⚜

Had Malthus waited thirty years to publish his *Essay on the Principle of Population,* issued in 1798, he could plausibly have offered Pitcairn as a dramatic proof of his thesis that population tends to multiply faster than its means of subsistence.

The 1790 settlement was made by fifteen men, twelve women, and an infant girl, twenty-eight in all. When Mayhew Folger discovered the Colony in 1808, the population was thirty-five, inclusive of twenty-five children. The wholesale intramural slaughter of males in the first decade had achieved one of the products of international warfare—a checking of population growth, but the number of Pitcairners had increased nonetheless.

What the economy of Pitcairn was like in the period from 1790 to 1808 must be gathered largely from Adams's statements and from the inferences to be drawn from conditions existing when Folger and later visitors reached the Island. Adams told Folger that Pitcairn produced "plenty for all," but he did not define "plenty." However, the strapping physique of seventeen-year-old Thursday October Christian, as well as other youths, provided tangible evidence that caloric intake had been adequate.

Captain Folger further noted that "the ground . . . now produces plenty of yams, cocoa-nuts, bananas and plantains; hogs and poultry in abundance." But he sounded a note frequently to be echoed

92

when he stated, "The island is badly supplied with water, sufficient only for the present inhabitants."

By 1814, the population had reached forty, by 1819 it was forty-four, by 1825 it was sixty-six, and in 1830 Captain Waldegrave counted eighty-one. The most complete description of the Pitcairn economy, way of life, and bill of fare is derived from the lengthy stay of Captain Beechey in 1825. In assessing the Pitcairn larder described by Beechey, as well as other visitors, we must allow for the fact that guests, especially on hospitable Pitcairn, generally fared better than their hosts ordinarily did. Yams constituted the staple of the Pitcairn cuisine; yams baked, yams boiled, yams mixed with coconut, yams made into cakes and eaten with molasses extracted from the ti root, yams "cooked in so many different ways that a stranger would be puzzled to find out the yam at all." Typically the guests were fed baked pig, yams, and taro, and sometimes sweet potatoes.

The hosts' preferences had a vegetarian cast. They did not relish the flesh of the numerous goats on the Island, nor even their milk. (Why they continued to raise them into the twentieth century is still a puzzle.) Nor did the Islanders often kill a pig for themselves, living mostly on fruits and vegetables. The fruits included bananas, plantains, and appoi. Taro-root was used as a bread substitute. Water was the common beverage, supplemented by tea made from the ti plant, flavored with ginger, and sweetened with the juice of the sugar cane.

Adams interrupted his bragging about the assets of Pitcairn long enough to voice to Beechey his fear that Pitcairn might become overpopulated and to plead for assistance from the British Government. The ultimate result of this plea was that Britain added Pitcairn to its Empire and forever after had the Islanders as one of its concerns. Beechey's consequent representations to his Government were also the genesis of the reluctant and short-lived exodus of the entire Colony of eighty-six to Tahiti in 1831.

The Pitcairners returned to their Island within six months, reduced in numbers as a result of deaths from infection, before and after the return, said to total seventeen. But the population curve turned upwards again. By 1855, it had reached the number of 187, and the cry of imminent overpopulation was again sounded, mostly by outlanders. It was sharpened by intermittent droughts, which were a source of keen hardship. Again reluctant, and again overwhelmed by the insistence of the British Government that it was for their own good, all 194 Pitcairners left for Norfolk in 1856.

Pitcairn Island

Sixteen returned in 1859, joined by twenty-seven more in 1864. By 1894 the population increased to 115, by 1914 to 164, and by 1937 to a peak of 233. The birth rate, prodigious in the early days, with some interruptions, followed a declining tendency. But even more significant was a trend to emigration developed in the twentieth century, accelerated after the Second World War, which changed the threat from that of overpopulation to new expressions of doubt about the continued existence of the Colony. As the economy of the English-speaking countries expanded, and as travel and contacts with the outside world became more common, improved conditions at home failed to check the urge of the younger Pitcairners to try their luck elsewhere, particularly in New Zealand. The pioneers made it easier for others to follow.

By 1961 there were only nineteen men under sixty; the total population was 126. Figures for 1965 show a population of 88. Fluctuations in birth rate and population on Pitcairn are indicated in the following table of Population Statistics which appears as Appendix I on page 47 of *A Guide to Pitcairn*.* (Other valuable statistical material will be found in Shapiro.)

POPULATION AND STATISTICS

BIRTHS AND DEATHS

Years	Births	Deaths	Increase
1864–1933 (average per decade)	43	16	27
1934–1943	36	21	15
1944–1953	26	24	2
1954–1963	30	17	13

COMPOSITION OF POPULATION

Year	Men	Women	Boys	Girls	Total
			(under 16)		
1936	81	67	29	23	200
1954	52	45	14	25	136
1955	55	46	18	24	143
1956	60	50	25	26	161
1957	56	46	22	28	152
1958	50	39	21	26	136
1959	49	40	24	33	146
1960	47	40	24	33	144
1961	38	36	21	31	126
1962	39	41	20	28	128
1963	28	31	15	11	86
1964	34	29	14	13	90
1965	34	31	14	9	88

* Extensions made after publication of the *Guide* are included.

The Pitcairn experience with the population problem, with its ironical reversal from fear of overpopulation to fear of underpopulation, offers little applicable to the general question. The smallness of the community prevented catastrophe because it made possible mass and individual emigration not available to most explosive populations. It would have provided a neater case if Pitcairn had been sealed from ingress and egress after its settlement. We then should have been able to observe how long it took before population growth pressed severely on available resources, and whether the pressure was met by birth control, infanticide, intramural warfare, constant lowering of living standards, ingenuity, or some combination of these factors.

As long ago as 1936, Dr. Shapiro estimated that the six mutineers who left offspring on Pitcairn were represented by a progeny which hovered close to the thousand mark. Had emigration been precluded, the result might have paralleled the experience of Tikopia, as reported by Raymond Firth.*

☙ THE MEANS OF LIVELIHOOD ☙

AGRICULTURE

The basic economy of Pitcairn before discovery of the Colony in 1808 was agricultural. Hand tools, chiefly hoes and spades, were used to turn the earth, twenty inches deep in places, but not to any great depth. The staple crop was yams, which was to Pitcairn as the potato to Ireland and rice to the Orient.

The best description of yam culture on Pitcairn comes from John Buffett, Pitcairn's first immigrant in 1823:

---

* In 1929, with a population estimated at 1281 and a land area of less than three square miles, Tikopia was again facing the Malthusian dilemma. Speaking of "former times," Firth indicates that the recurrent problem of overpopulation had been attacked with "four direct checks: contraception of a crude kind (coitus interruptus); infanticide; celibacy of junior males in large families; and in the last resort slaughter or expulsion of whole sections of the people by others" (Chapter II, "*Primitive Polynesian Economy,*" London 1939). From the *Pacific Islands Year Book* (ninth edition, 1963), we learn that some of the Tikopians, estimated to number 1378 in 1963, had been resettled in the Russell Islands "due to overcrowding."

A great deal of labor is required to cultivate them, they are generally planted in October and November, the Harvest time is August. Each family plants according to their numbers, that is, a family of eight persons generally plant 8000. They are generally cut up into pieces, a common sized yam making 8 or 10 plants, and spread on the ground and covered with earth, where they remain till they have budded, which is in about six weeks, the ground for planting being dug up, the plants are taken from the bed and the weaker shoots or buds broken off, leaving one or two, they are then planted at the distance of two feet each way, and are kept weeded till digging time. . . . Each family fattens one or two hogs (before digging the yams) and salt them down, so that we may have meat while working and not be obliged to leave it and go for fish. At such time we have more meat than at any other season. . . . The yams being dug are laid by in a shady place where they will keep eight or nine months, if the buds are kept broken off.

Yams were supplemented by plantains, sweet potatoes, taro and yappa, sugar cane, the ti root, and post-discovery importations. Trees and bushes were highly important in the Pitcairn economy; the miro for lumber, the cloth tree for tapa, the coconut for food, the doodoe for lighting, the pandanus for thatching, the "porou" and "fowtoo" for rope, cord, and fishing twine—in the "make-do" world of Pitcairn, little grew that was not put to use. Bananas were plentiful and of high quality. Pitcairn pineapples won many accolades.

Meat was derived from pigs, goats, and fowl, all brought to Pitcairn on the "Bounty," but it played a comparatively minor role in the Pitcairn diet. The pigs and goats were allowed to roam at large and were "harvested" in an operation half husbandry and half sport—by shooting them with muskets as though they were wild game.

FISH

Fishing was an important activity of the Pitcairn settlement. The first fishhooks used were fashioned from "Bounty" iron, and the only Polynesian influence appears to have been spear-fishing and use of the accompanying torch. The Pitcairners did not employ the Polynesian lunar piscatorial calendar, the stone fish-trap, or nets. Fishing line made from dried tree bark, stripped while the sap was circulating, was used and, later, preferred over imported line because it did not twist as easily in deep water.

Cod, grey mullet, kingfish, red snapper, and occasional tuna were among the fish caught. Squid were caught along the shoreline, but snatching them from the powerful surf along the rocky shore was a hazardous pursuit. Fishing was "difficult and precarious, as they have to seek the fish in very deep water, often at the depth of 150 or 200 fathoms." Moreover, the frequent turbulence of the water surrounding Pitcairn made fishing a sometime thing.

Some of the reports create the impression that this favorite Polynesian food was to be had practically for the taking, but the weight of the evidence indicates that it was fortunate for the Pitcairners that, unlike residents of some atolls, they were not forced to rely on the products of the sea for sustenance. As Adams told Captain King in 1819, ". . . when they first settled on the island . . . there were plenty of fish; but for some time before my touching at this place, they could not catch any, and they thought the copper of the 'Bounty' had poisoned them all." A later excuse for poor catches was the landslide of 1845.

And Buffett, describing his experience on Pitcairn from 1823 to 1845, says: "Generally in fine weather when we have not much work, we go a fishing, and as we sometimes fish in 150 or 180 fathoms, we lose many hooks and lines by their getting entangled among the rocks, and by the sharks. So that hooks and lines are always in demand."

Fish were a lucky supplement to the Pitcairn table, rather than a staple of the diet. This is borne out by the infrequency with which fish are mentioned in the many visitors' reports of feasts tendered by the Islanders. Even more striking is the failure to refer to fish in the descriptions by Islanders of periods of famine. Writing of one such time in 1853, which "reduced them to great straits," Rev. Nobbs speaks of their only resource for some weeks as some "half-grown pumpkins."

But, as any fisherman knows, the uncertainty of reward is what makes fishing a sport. Pitcairners have remained devoted to fishing to this day. Like their fellows the world over, when mortified by the indifference of their quarry to the allurements offered them, Pitcairn fishermen today are prepared to open a can of "something" when they return empty-handed.

TRADE—SUPPLIER TO WHALERS

Beginning in the 1800s, the whalers and sealers, having nearly exhausted the Atlantic, sought happier hunting grounds in the Pacific. Pitcairn was discovered by a wandering Nantucket sealer, Captain Folger, in 1808. The Island attracted an increasing number of these ships by reason of its nearness to one of the whaling grounds. Their number swelled into thousands until the influx peaked out in the middle of the century. By the 1820s (there had been previous contacts) each year saw from one to seven arrivals; in the 1830s it was two to thirteen; and in the peak period of the forties from nine to forty-eight (1846.)

Pitcairn was anything but ideal for the purpose of resupplying and refreshing the whalers. It had no harbor and the amount of water, fruits, vegetables, and meat it was able to provide was limited and undependable. The Pitcairn women were ''off limits''* and liquor was likewise unavailable. What kept the Island in business as a supplier to whalers and a stop for refreshment was the absence of nearby competition, the desire of some of the predominantly New England captains, frequently Quakers, to bypass the gamier ports, the Pitcairn reputation for fair-dealing and prices which did not fluctuate with the captains' needs, and, to a lesser extent, curiosity about this much-publicized community.

The Islanders were happy to have company and whatever the whalers could offer in trade, and the whalers developed an admiration for and generally paternal attitude toward the community. Some of them visited Pitcairn repeatedly, and their encomiums created an Island reputation for hospitality and honesty, as well as piety. On voyages typically lasting two to four years, Pitcairn was an ideal spot to leave a captain's wife for a badly needed shore rest or for assistance in childbirth.

What the Pitcairners derived from the whaling trade is unverifiable by statistics. Benefits varied with the particular captain; many

---

* In 1904, Deputy Commissioner Simons found it ''an alleged fact that, on suitable occasions, women will accompany men on board of passing ships, ostensibly to sell curios, but in reality for immoral purposes.'' The admittedly hearsay nature of this evidence, like that relied on in many of the official reports, renders it suspect.

ABOVE. *Hauling a longboat in from Bounty Bay in the 1930's.*
BELOW. *Thatched boathouses at Bounty Bay.*

CAPTAIN and MRS. IRVING JOHNSON.

ABOVE. *Pitcairn faces.*

BELOW. *Courthouse and Church (LEFT) made of unpainted boards cut by handsaws over a sawpit (1930's).*

TOP RIGHT. *Pitcairn longboat pulling up to greet Captain and Mrs. Irving Johnson and crew of ''Yankee.''*

MIDDLE RIGHT. *Pitcairners in one of the boats they made, rowed, and sailed.*

BOTTOM RIGHT. *A tough Pitcairn chore—getting a longboat out of water to shelter.*

CAPTAIN and MRS. IRVING JOHNSON.

CAPTAIN and MRS. IRVING JOHNSON.

CAPTAIN and MRS. IRVING JOHNSON.

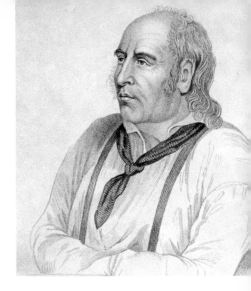

TOP LEFT. *"The Chapel" in the late nineteenth century.*

TOP RIGHT. *John Adams, for thirty years sole survivor of the mutineers on Pitcairn and patriarch of the Colony. He was responsible for the establishment of the Christian religion and the perpetuation of English. Drawn by Captain Beechey in 1825.*

MIDDLE LEFT. *Pitcairn family group in the late nineteenth century.*

MIDDLE RIGHT. *Thursday (sometimes Friday) October Christian, first born of the Pitcairn community, son of mutiny leader Fletcher Christian and Isabella.*

BOTTOM LEFT. *The Mission House, late nineteenth century, after establishment of Seventh Day Adventism.*

BOTTOM RIGHT. *George Hunn Nobbs, successor to John Adams as Pitcairn leader, pastor, teacher, doctor, and recorder until and after emigration of the Colony to Norfolk Island in 1856.*

The mutineers turn Captain Bligh and the "loyalists" adrift.

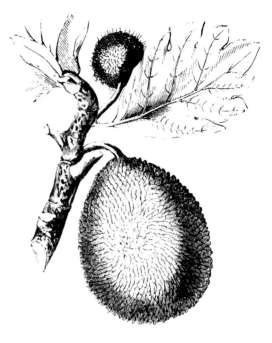

TOP. *The breadfruit, with which it all began.*

BOTTOM. *Pitcairners say thanks to their good friends, the Johnsons, with two tons of their choice fruits, including eighty watermelons.*

CAPTAIN and MRS. IRVING JOHNSON.

Captain William Bligh, as painted by J. A. Russell, R. A. Painting in the possession of W. Bligh Nutting, Esquire.

Bounty Bay and the Village of Adamstown.

TOP. *John Adams' house.* BOTTOM. *Church and schoolhouse on Pitcairn in the time of Nobbs.*

TOP. *Longboats dare the Pitcairn surf.*
MIDDLE. *Parkin Christian and retrieved ''Bounty'' rudder.*
BOTTOM. *Pitcairn longboat carried on the ''Yankee.''*

were generous, some were hard-fisted. The trade, however, did bring the Islanders substantial increments of clothing, tools, nails, needles, and so on. In some cases the Islanders accepted cash and, as most of the whalers were Yankees, American dollars entered the Pitcairn economy.

One of the more generous captains was Henry King of the "Elizabeth," who visited Pitcairn in 1819. He was regaled with a dinner of

> a sucking pig, cooked after the Otaheitian manner, two brace of fowls, plenty of yams and plantains. After dinner, were served up bananas and a species of apple (pineapple) peculiar to the island, which we found very good. . . . we were shewn to . . . a good feather-bed and clean sheets, made from the bark of a tree, where we slept very comfortably all night. In the morning, we breakfasted on fowls and a beverage like tea, made from a root similar to the gentian, but which they called ginger. . . . Each family gathered together some poultry, hogs, goats, plantains, and every thing the island produced.

Water had already been collected.

Now for the payoff:

> I now gave them a whaleboat, in return for their refreshments, some books, razors, combs, and, in short, every thing they stood in need of; but nothing pleased them so well as the books: as they wished much to read and write. I offered Auther Quintral [sic] two claw hammers, which he refused; and Adams, who was present, told him, that it was very improper to refuse any thing their countrymen offered: Auther replied, it was much more improper to take things they do not want.[5]

The whaling trade diminished after reaching its peak in 1846, and this was one of the strong considerations offered in support of the proposal to remove the Pitcairners, which eventuated in their migration to Norfolk Island in 1856. The Pitcairners feared being restored to the isolation of the early days. At Norfolk, offshore whaling became an important industry.

CHARITY

It was frequently difficult to distinguish trade from charity in the Pitcairn economy, as can be seen from Captain King's account, quoted above. Possibly the exchange was simply *quid pro quo,* although one is susceptible to the suggestion from the account that the "quid" was enlarged by the captain's kindly feelings towards his friendly hosts.

Sometimes the Islanders got the worst of the bargain. In the case of the very first visitor, Captain Folger,* the Islanders presented him with a time-piece (chronometer)[6] and an azimuth compass from the "Bounty." (A precedent to be followed by scores of gifts of "souvenirs" to subsequent visitors.) In addition they furnished him with water and provisions. In return, Folger, unable to fill a request for agricultural tools, gave Adams "a silk pocket handkerchief which he seemed to prize and kept many years in memory of the donor."[7]

But unmistakable charity did become a constituent element of the Pitcairn economy. In 1819 the "Hercules," with Captain Henderson in command, came laden with gifts purchased with 3500 rupees raised by the Calcutta *Journal*. These included a 22-foot cutter, carpenter and agricultural tools, ironmongery, cooking utensils, cutlery, crockery, cloth, guns, fishing gear, razors, mirrors, writing materials, and a large British ensign. Individuals had added plants, cuttings, and seeds. The Society for Promoting Christian Knowledge included fifty books, largely of a religious nature.

As a result of Captain Beechey's "representation . . . of the distressed state of this little society, with regard to the want of certain necessary articles," Captain Waldegrave brought them in H.M.S. "Seringapatam" in 1830. The British Government had previously shipped these to Valparaiso: ". . . a proportion for sixty persons of . . . sailors' blue jackets and trousers, flannel waistcoats, pairs of stockings and shoes, women's dresses, spades, mattocks, shovels, pickaxes, trowels, rakes. . . ."

These were among the first of a long series of gifts which were to be showered on these distant "cousins" of Britain and were to saddle them with the title, "beggars of the Pacific." This epithet was more than a little unfair. It suggested that the donations were the result solely of importunity, whereas the facts admitted of a kinder interpretation. Practically every visitor was seized by admiration for the Pitcairn community. The combination of its romantic history and aura and the unaffected and eager hospitality accorded visitors, plus the simplicity and piety of the Islanders, activated whatever glands of

---

* In 1958, on a visit to the United States to attend a Seventh Day Adventist convention, Parkin Christian, great-great grandson of the mutineer, visited Folger's grave in Massillon, Ohio.

benevolence the ships' captains (and frequently the crews) might possess.

In the circumstances, giving and getting others to give, seemed as natural as a thank-you note, accompanied by a small present, from a departed guest who has been genuinely entertained. There was the added satisfaction of helping the truly worthy and kinsmen to boot. Religious institutions, eager to seize on the obvious inspiration of the Pitcairn experience, added to the flow of charitable contributions, frequently larded with their literature.

The Islanders soon became a sort of ward of the British Navy, looking to its visiting captains for the settlement of disputes, and greeting each approach of His Majesty's ships with especial fervor. This entente was reinforced by the visit in 1852 of Rear Admiral Fairfax Moresby of the Pacific Station in H.M.S. "Portland." The Admiral and his son and secretary, M. Fortescue Moresby, had previously evinced interest in Pitcairn and, on making this and a subsequent visit in 1853, became the particular patrons of the community.

As a result of Admiral Moresby's efforts, there was formed a Pitcairn Fund Committee to which he contributed a hundred pounds. The Society for Promoting Christian Knowledge added another hundred pounds. Part of the money realized from these and other donors was used to supply agricultural implements and a whale boat.

In addition to organized charitable contributions to the Pitcairn economy, sporadic contributions from individuals, of clothing and other articles, were not infrequent. But, lest this concentrated listing give the misleading picture of an ever-flowing cornucopia of charity, it must be pointed out that these donations were erratic and undependable, in contrast to needs which were constant and unending. They were a welcome and frequently comforting addition; but the continued existence of the Colony was not dependent on charity.

TRADE—SUPPLIER TO PASSENGER SHIPS

Pitcairn was one of the most ship-conscious communities in the world. Life turned on the hope or expectation of the next vessel to cross the horizon. A graphic manifestation of ship hunger occurred in 1911, when eighteen Pitcairners, including one woman, rowed out sixteen miles "just to intercept and exchange greetings" with the

Glasgow bark "Wendur." They told Captain Blackstock that on the average they saw only twenty vessels a year and were visited by a trading schooner once a year. The whalers were gone, and the British Navy had ceased patrolling the Pacific. In the interval between the return to Pitcairn in 1859 and the opening of the Panama Canal in 1914, trade had at intervals fallen on seedy times, and the reports of visiting officers and officials during this period are critical of the Island economy, as well as other matters.

Hard times were undergone when the vagaries of the weather produced insufficient rain or cruel drought. The results of the drought of 1874 are described by one who suffered them, Rosalind Amelia Young: "Yam crops, in some instances, almost totally failed. The Irish potato and the sweet-potato yielded but poorly . . . Brown's water . . . was dry, and there seemed but small prospect of rain . . . the plants all suffered."

Efforts of the Islanders to develop their own fleet (see p. 195) ended in disaster. Before that a scheme in 1878 by a Liverpool firm which contemplated the production of cotton, arrowroot, copra, and candlenut oil on a commercial scale had failed. Sales of arrowroot and edible fungus to Tahiti in the early part of the twentieth century were chilled by a discriminatory tariff. A like fate met later exportation of oranges to New Zealand. Ships touched the Island with varying frequency after the return from Norfolk; in considerable numbers around the turn of the century, but the resulting trade was not greatly productive. The period from 1870 to 1920 was not a lustrous epoch in Island economics, especially as the tendency was to compare with Western rather than Polynesian standards.

The opening of the Panama Canal in 1914 inaugurated a new commercial era for the Pitcairners, although the effect was not visible for some years. These erstwhile suppliers to whalers became suppliers to the passenger ships of the Shaw-Savill, Albion, and New Zealand Shipping lines. These carriers were so anxious to break the monotony of the 7500-mile run between the Canal and New Zealand by some colorful interlude that they were willing to deviate slightly from a straight course and stand hove to for an hour or two to give passengers a look at the storied Islanders, and a chance to buy their excellent pineapples, oranges, and bananas, and originally crude curios. Foodstuffs were also sold to the ships for use in their kitchens.

TRADE—SOUVENIRS AND CURIOS

It was not fruit, however, but souvenirs and curios which developed into the mainstay of the trade with steamers and became the leading industry of Pitcairn, translating glamor into calories and twentieth century luxuries.

The original commerce was in what might be called true, as distinguished from fabricated, souvenirs—generally something derived from the "Bounty" or the Polynesian settlement of the mutineers' predecessors on Pitcairn. Thus, as noted, the very first visit to the Colony resulted in Captain Folger's carrying away the "Bounty" chronometer and compass. In 1817 Adams presented Captain Reynolds of the "Sultan" with the "Bounty" spyglass. Almost every visitor took away some memento of the vessel (one in 1837 carried away the ship's Bible and prayer book),* leading George Adams to complain circa 1845 that even the stump to which the "Bounty" had been moored before being burned had been taken away.

Dubious equivalents were sometimes exchanged for souvenirs by the visitors, although there was no schedule of prices for them, as in the case of yams and other commodities, and the hit or miss basis of the exchange could hardly be characterized as "trade." Pitcairn was a "natural" for souvenir hunters; in any game of one-upmanship played by travelers, a trip to the remote and inaccessible Island was a very blue chip, and its verification a natural impulse. But the supply of "Bounty" relics was not inexhaustible. Moreover, many travelers preferred more conventional types of mementoes, true or fabricated.

John Buffett, Pitcairn's first immigrant in 1823, had been a Bristol shipwright and joiner before becoming a seaman. His woodworking skills, in which he instructed his fellow Islanders, and the weaving arts of the Polynesian women were to provide the basis of the Pitcairn curio industry, although its peak was not reached until more than a century later.

When Brodie was marooned on Pitcairn in 1850, the curio industry had developed to the point where he could describe the

---

* See *The Bounty Bible*, Bulletin of the Connecticut Historical Society, vol. 19, no. 2, pp. 63 and 64, and *The Pitcairn Bible*, Bulletin of the New York Public Library, vol. 28, pp. 443 to 452, and p. 682.

Pitcairners as "very ingenious cabinetmakers" and note the ready sale to visitors of

> neat workboxes and dressing cases, of a reddish streaked wood . . . for 20s. to 30s. each. . . . They also make very handsome walking-canes of the same wood, as well as of the cocoa-nut and palm trees. The women make hats and baskets from the leaves of this same palm [the Pandanus], which leaves are likewise used in thatching their houses. They sell as many of all the above as they can make, every person coming on shore wishing to carry away some memorial from this interesting island.

The state of the art of curio manufacture on Pitcairn apparently deteriorated after the Norfolk exodus in 1856, which permanently absorbed Buffett and three-fourths of the community, although it is difficult to follow its course in detail. A steamship passenger's* eye view circa 1920 indicates that at that date the curios offered were more distinguished by their origin than their craftsmanship. "Empty cocoanuts with some typical carving on them, strings of sea shells, or of vegetable beads—'Job's tears'—mats and simple needlework were all they had to offer as mementoes."[8]

The arrival of an Austrian wood carver on Pitcairn inspired a marked improvement in curio manufacture. The development reached the point in the 1960s where work of Pitcairners was offered for sale in the pretentious art galleries of New York City. As the potentialities of the curio trade became more obvious, the Islanders polished their skills, imported machinery, and enlarged their stock. Popular items carved were flying fish, tortoises, vases, walking sticks, inlaid boxes and models of clippers and of the "Bounty."

The exact monetary rewards of the curio trade, doubtless substantial, are difficult to arrive at. Some clue can be derived from one episode in the mid-1950s when the Pitcairners realized $5000 from sales to passengers on the "Caronia"—"the biggest day in Pitcairn's business life. Few families took in less than $100, and the Seventh Day Adventist pastor gave a little talk, showed color slides, and collected

---

* This same passenger offers a view of the "payoff" of the curio trade: "Their stock being in the way of disposal, there was a raid on the barber's shop to purchase such things as he could supply. The demand was chiefly for children's boots, ribbons, hairpins, scent, brilliantine and soap! I heard of an umbrella and a cloak being bartered by one of the passengers for oranges: a rascal on board attempted to exchange one of the ship's blankets for fruit; he got the fruit, but the blanket was discovered by one of the officers as the luckless and innocent islander was just about to depart, and he was compelled to restore it, without having time even to identify the thief who had secured his fruit."

$600 for the new church."[9] The impressiveness of this figure is enhanced when it is compared with an estimate of 180 pounds per annum as the total Island income for the 1902–1903 period, when the Pitcairners were exporting produce to Mangareva on their cutter "Pitcairn."

Originally confined to touching ships, the curio trade has grown to include mail orders, largely to the United States, in a growing proportion. This has become a necessary development since the liners of the New Zealand Shipping Company ceased to call in 1962. An official souvenir agency on quasi-cooperative lines has been established.

The leading position of the curio industry, although it has not escaped criticism from those outlanders who favor a subsistence economy in which the Islanders raise their own food rather than buy it, is now established. Nearly every household is a small factory, with bench, lathe, gouges, chisels, and planes, but work is not confined to this locale. "Going to and from work, even while standing talking, most of the men will be whittling or sanding a wooden bird, fish or other souvenir. With their day's cooking completed, the women usually gather under the shade of a tree to weave their baskets, hats or fans, with their tongues moving at an even speed with their adept fingers."[10]

The position of curio making in Pitcairn life is focused by a description of the pattern of Island activities:

> On an average a man will spend about one day a week in his garden; one day fishing; one day visiting ships and trading aboard them, or getting fruit and vegetables for sale or exchange or attending the boats; part of a day on public work; two days making souvenirs for sale; and the Sabbath at Church and at rest. Occasionally there is the chance of paid labour on government jobs, but it usually provides work only for a small number of men for a few days or weeks at a time. All the women do some form of weaving in addition to their household duties.[11]

STAMPS—CAPITALIZING ON GLAMOR

The issuance of stamps by Pitcairn had been more than once suggested. Until 1926 letters from Pitcairn franked, "Posted on Pitcairn: no stamps available," were delivered free of charge in New Zealand and elsewhere. For the next fourteen years, New Zealand stamps and rates were used. It remained for Mr. H. E. Maude, representing the British High Commissioner in Fiji, during an eight-month stay in 1940 with the mission of preparing a revision of the Constitution, government and laws, to establish a new post office and bring out the first stamp issue, in eight denominations, on October 15.

The financial results of this simple device are described by its promulgator as "phenomenal." The combination of Pitcairn glamor and philatelic frenzy proved a "natural"; the proceeds enabled the Islanders to build a modern new school and pay professional teachers, as well as provide a school teacher's residence. Special issues of Pitcairn stamps, designed and printed in England and featuring distinctive Pitcairn insignia, are the object of orders from all over the world, including Russia. Customers are dealers and individual collectors. Especially prized are "first-day covers," envelopes with a stamp cancelled the first day of issue.

Supplementary income is derived by individual Pitcairners.

Envelopes, specially printed with a Pitcairn-Bounty device in the upper left hand corner and four Pitcairn-issue stamps of different denominations in the upper right hand corner, are sold to boat passengers for the equivalent of one dollar. The difference between the sale price and the cost of envelope and stamps is pocketed as income. Glossy colored postcards made from original Kodachromes and bearing a single Pitcairn-issue stamp sell for the same amount. The purchaser addresses the cards, and the islanders take them to the post office in Adamstown, where they are cancelled with a Pitcairn seal and thus become of philatelic value to the recipient.[12]

While the results of the curio trade are difficult to ascertain, and have perhaps been affected most recently by diminution in the number of touching passenger ships, public records reveal the extent of stamp revenue for the period from 1957 to 1965. In the banner year 1957, distinguished by a new stamp issue, the bonanza reached 20,349 pounds. In a fifteen-month period, 1958–1959, the take was 9,087 pounds; 1959–1960, 2,614 pounds; 1960–1961, 2,852 pounds; and 1961–1962, 10,424 pounds. The most recent figures show 3,886 pounds for 1962–1963; 16,391 for 1963–1964, and 29,063 for 1964–1965.

On November 15, 1961, three stamps were released to commemorate the centenary of the return from Norfolk in 1859 and 1864. Other special issues have been "Peace" (1947), "Silver Wedding" (1949), "Universal Postal Union" (1949), and "Coronation" (1953). The public revenues from stamps have obviated the need for taxes, which have never gone beyond trifling firearms license fees and payment of tuition fees.

While no single component, from yams to stamps, is without its counterpart elsewhere, the blend and history of the Pitcairn economy are unique.

Ferdon, who estimated that Pitcairn could comfortably support no more than two hundred on a "subsistence basis," observed in 1958, "In the past 22 years the Pitcairner has raised himself from what was basically a subsistence-and-barter economy, supplemented by church and other aid from abroad, to a position of economic independence in public administration and welfare. . . . Its [Pitcairn's] economic resource is not its natural environment but its history."

It should not be forgotten, however, that the Pitcairn community survived a number of lean years with nothing but the natural resources of the Island to fall back on. There were periods of severe undernourishment, largely owing to droughts, but no record exists of anyone starving to death on the Island chosen from thousands by Fletcher Christian for his motley entourage.

❧ NOTES: PART THREE ❧

1. Maude(4).
2. *A Guide to Pitcairn.*
3. A vivid description of a notable Pitcairn storm and the havoc it created appears in Nobbs' entry of April 16, 1845 in the Pitcairn Register Book, quoted in Shapiro. Destruction included three hundred uprooted coconut trees, 4000 plantain trees, fishing boats, and a massive landslide.
4. "The Birds of Pitcairn Islands, Central South Pacific Ocean," *Ibis,* vol. 102, pp. 58–70.
   See also Nicoll, Michael John, *Three Voyages of a Naturalist,* London, 1908.
5. King.
6. For the character and adventures of this chronometer, see *Horological Journal,* December 1957, vol. 99, p. 760.
7. Letter of Captain Folger's wife, Massillon Library and Historical Museum, Massillon, Ohio.
8. Fullerton, W. Y., *The Romance of Pitcairn Island.*

  9. Johnson, Captain and Mrs. Irving, *Yankee's People and Places.*
10. Schubert, E., "Pitcairn Island Today" (a chapter in *The Pitcairnese Language*, New York, 1964).
11. *A Guide to Pitcairn.*
12. Ferdon.

Part Four

EMIGRANTS, IMMIGRANTS, AND VISITORS

✤ FIRST EMIGRANTS ✤

Study of the Bounty-Pitcairn story raises the question of whether its seemingly high quotient of remarkable characters demonstrates its romantic superiority or simply evidences that intense scrutiny, like a highly lighted, closeup photograph, will develop the unique nature of a subject indistinguishable in a long shot of a crowd.

On the "Bounty" we have encountered such noteworthies as Bligh himself, Morrison, who would merit a biography of his own, and Heywood, who, at the age of sixteen, compiled a useful Tahitian lexicon. And such lesser lights as Fryer, Purcell, and Christian, who, whatever might be said in their disfavor, were all "character." To say nothing of founding father John Adams, born for anonymity, but to whom fate gave the chance to demonstrate that all he lacked of kingship was the proper stage. Despite the fact that tiny Pitcairn had no crown jewels or hint of gold, and that its remoteness and inaccessibility were hardly surpassed short of the polar regions, it was to attract other men worthy of a place in the roster of "characters."

The first transfer was the emigration of the erstwhile spouse of Isaac Martin, Jenny, who departed Pitcairn in 1817 on the whaler "Sultan" (Captain Reynolds) and eventually reached her native Tahiti. Jenny was childless and had early evidenced eagerness to leave Pitcairn by her leadership in the fruitless attempt of the women to sail away. She alone of those who landed on Pitcairn from the "Bounty"

111

did not die on the island. In 1826 Jane Quintal, daughter of Matthew Quintal, left on the "Lovely" (Captain Blythe) in pursuit of a liaison with an English ship officer and wound up on Rurutu as bride of a native.

☙ FIRST IMMIGRANTS ☙

Buffett and Evans. The first immigrant to arrive at Pitcairn was John Buffett of Bristol, in 1823. Buffett had succumbed to the lure of the sea, having been trained as a shipwright and joiner. His career as a sailor had been marked by hairbreadth escapes from shipwrecks. He had read about Pitcairn and, in his own words, thought it "the most eligible place in the world, a place free from temptation, and with no hindrance to prevent a man becoming a christian. . . . I had escaped many dangers, and those dangers were the means of causing me to think of a future state, or, if I should express my desires at that time to become religious."

When his boat, the whaleship "Cyrus" of London, touched at Pitcairn for refreshments, the "inhabitants being in want of some person to teach them to read, and write, the Captain asked me if I should like to remain there. I told him I should, and was discharged and went on shore."[1]

Along with Buffett, but unbargained for by either the captain of the "Cyrus" or the people of Pitcairn, came undersized John Evans, son of a Longacre watchmaker, who jumped ship and hid in a tree trunk (as legend has it) until the "Cyrus" departed. He was accepted into the community and married Rachel Adams in 1824, but never played an important role in Island affairs.

Buffett, however, became schoolmaster and took over the main burden of religious services, assisted by Adams, as well as initiating the Pitcairn Island Register book. He married Dorothy Young in 1824, and demonstrated the fallacy of his vision of Pitcairn as "free from temptation" by himself fathering two children out of wedlock. Until the advent of the next immigrant to Pitcairn, George Hunn Nobbs, in 1828, he occupied a leading position in the community.

Buffett emerges from the record a curiously appealing figure—a man whose reach for virtue exceeded his grasp. Despite his fall from grace, he was popular among the Islanders. This resulted in part from his lack of aggressiveness, his good nature, and his willingness to use and teach the woodworking skills which were eventually to become the basis for Pitcairn's chief industry.

George Hunn Nobbs. A settler destined to become leader of the community and symbol of Pitcairn for decades, Nobbs, if we are to accept his own story of his previous history, more properly belongs in a Dumas tale than on the unsophisticated Pitcairn scene in the role of pastor and schoolmaster.

His career began

> unfortunately [as] the unacknowledged son of the Marquis ——,* and my mother was the daughter of an Irish baronet, who, becoming implicated in the Irish rebellion, left his country. . . . on her death-bed [my beloved mother] extracted from me a solemn promise that I would never accept of any favor at the hands of my father's family. . . . Moreover my mother was anxious that I should quit England, and take up my abode in some distant part of the world, where her wrongs and mine might be buried in oblivion. I mentioned Pitcairn Island to her, and as much of its history as had come to my knowledge. . . . almost her last words were, "Go to Pitcairn."[2]

Nobbs' career in the British and Chilean navies is replete with escapes from shipwrecks, capture by the enemy, and near disasters, further dramatized by the deaths of many of his shipmates. His history as a sailor of fortune, as he relates it, is filled with enough incidents to enliven three Hentys and four Rider Haggards.[3]

As if this were not a surfeit of romance, Nobbs arrived at Pitcairn in 1828, aged 28, under highly curious circumstances, accompanied by a mysterious American shipmate, "Captain" Noah Bunker. They came from Calloa in an eighteen-ton cutter after a six-week voyage. Nobbs was never very explicit about this voyage; as nearly as can be gathered, he had entered into an arrangement whereby Nobbs supplied the money to fit out Bunker's boat and they agreed to make the 3500-mile trip to Pitcairn.

We are indebted to Moerenhout, who arrived at Pitcairn some three months after the two outlanders, for some light on their advent.

---

* H. E. Maude, in a sketch of Nobbs written for the *Australian Dictionary of Biography,* identifies the parents of Nobbs as the Marquis of Hastings and Jemima French on the basis of Nobbs' own statements.

Moerenhout was highly suspicious of the two *mysterieux* strangers, and indicates a similar attitude on the part of the Islanders. They were apparently undecided about granting the request of Bunker and Nobbs for admittance to Pitcairn, but were swayed by the fact that Bunker was seriously ill.

Bunker claimed to be sole owner of the cutter. Nobbs claimed ownership in common. The Pitcairners suspected the claims of both, and several years later voiced a dark suspicion that the crew of the cutter, which had been employed in sealing, was done away with.

Bunker was so ill that the Pitcairners posted a guard over him, but he escaped observation long enough to pursue a bent for suicide by jumping over a precipice. He was discovered at its bottom, still alive, but in very bad shape, and his pleas to be put to death were ignored.

Moerenhout was naturally much puzzled over the reasons why Bunker and Nobbs had left Peru in such a flimsy craft on such a long voyage; why Nobbs seemingly paid no attention to his sick shipmate; and why Bunker was so stubbornly determined to end his life and had traveled so far to consummate his suicide. Direct inquiry of Bunker on the last point failed to elicit a satisfactory explanation. Bunker refused to specify the "very strong" reasons* and spoke of his death as a matter of indifference, saying that it must come sooner or later. It came between the end of Moerenhout's initial stay on Pitcairn, February 25, 1829, and his return on March 25. Using the laudanum that he had cadged from Moerenhout for his relief, Bunker had poisoned himself.

Moerenhout's examination of the papers left by Bunker reinforced his suspicion that neither Bunker nor Nobbs had any good title to the ship. (Some of the Pitcairners subsequently charged that Nobbs destroyed these papers.) If the title to the ship were not sufficiently dubious, Quintal put in a claim that Bunker had left him in particular and the community in general Bunker's share of the boat. One account indicates that the boat, which was lent to Buffett, Evans, and Young for an abortive trip to Elizabeth (Henderson) Island, was broken up and used to build a house for Nobbs.

Moerenhout was not only the first outlander to report Nobbs' presence on Pitcairn, he was the first of a long line who viewed him

---

* Rosalind Young's suggestion that it was because "Peggy Christian would not listen to his suit" draws no corroboration from the record.

with marked distaste. He describes Nobbs as saying grace with closed eyes and a tone of lamentation which he found affected and pharisaic. But apparently Nobbs had used his time on the Island to win over an effective majority. Moerenhout notes that the Pitcairners believed him a saint and invokes Heaven that they be not mistaken.

Nobbs achieved a position of leadership in Pitcairn in a relatively short time, but not without struggle. Apparently Buffett was not happy about being superseded, and for a period two rival schools were being conducted. After Adams' death in 1829, his expressed wish that the community select a head was ignored. Nobbs took over by force of his genuine talents and determined will. As Buffett put it,[4] many years later, "Mr. Nobbs being a good scholar, and my family increasing, I gave up school teaching and he succeeded me."

Nobbs' coming did not escape overseas criticism. The speed with which news from Pitcairn got back to England, albeit frequently garbled, almost passes understanding.

Thus Barrow, whose book was published in 1831, is found complaining therein of

> . . . George Hunn Nobbs, who calls himself pastor, registrar, and schoolmaster, thus infringing on the privileges of John Buffett; and being a person of superior talents, and of exceeding great impudence, has deprived Buffett of a great number of his scholars; and hence a sufficient cause exists of division and dissension. . . . this Nobbs not only claims exemption from labour as being their pastor, but also as being entitled to maintenance at the expense of the community. . . . The only chance for the continuance of peace is the general dislike in which this Nobbs is held, and the gradual intellectual improvement of the rising generation. . . . This Nobbs is probably one of those half-witted persons who fancy they have received a *call* to preach nonsense—some cobbler escaped from his stall, or tailor from his shopboard. . . . Whoever this pastoral drone may be, it is but too evident that the preservation of the innocence, simplicity, and happiness of these amiable people, is intimately connected with his speedy removal from the island."

This criticism was echoed by Hall a century later. It seems that it was not necessary to know Nobbs personally to dislike him.

Despite the strictures of Barrow and other detractors, at home and abroad, Nobbs was destined to survive as leader of the Pitcairn community for more than half a century, long after its removal to Norfolk in 1856, just as he had survived shipwrecks and three captures by the enemy. Though he did not lower the quotient of controversy

115

which hovers over many characters and situations in the "Bounty"-Pitcairn story, every aspersion on his character can be at least matched by encomiums from his flock and from outlanders. There can be little doubt of his genuine abilities or of his general devotion to his duties, frequently arduous. He became the voice of Pitcairn to the outside world. He was a tireless correspondent and could drop in the right places humble suggestions as to what would most benefit his charges with seemingly artless inoffensiveness. His activities as public relations officer without portfolio undoubtedly stimulated many of the growing list of friends of Pitcairn, such as Admiral Moresby. His many letters and Register entries testify to a considerable gift for expression, and only occasionally descend to the bathos of Dickens at his worst. If he frequently verges on religiosity, much of the literature of his time was subject to like criticism. The flavor of his personality was highly individual and difficult to assess; in view of his history, even with generous allowance for coloration, this is hardly surprising.

TOTAL EMIGRATION

In 1831, the score stood at two emigrants, four immigrants, one of them (Bunker) dead soon after arrival. In that year, the balance was more than redressed; the entire community of eighty-six left Pitcairn for Tahiti.[5]

This hegira, ever after to be considered a sorry mistake, had its genesis in Beechey's representations to the British Government that the Pitcairn community was in danger because of lack of water and a fast-growing population, a notion he derived from Adams. These representations were underlined by a severe drought and crop failure in 1830, but when it came to the sticking point in 1831, the Islanders evidenced a reluctance to leave their little "rock" which almost aborted the venture.

The British Government sent Captain Sandilands, H.M. Sloop "Comet," together with the transport bark "Lucy Anne," to effect the migration. Captain Sandilands assembled the family heads on his arrival and explained that Pomare, King of Tahiti, had generously offered to set aside a tract of fertile land for the Pitcairn Colony. He reiterated the hazards of continued existence on the Island. Although the proposal had been on the fire for a considerable period before

Captain Sandilands arrived at the end of February, only half signed up for the exodus. The rest capitulated by morning. It seems clear that they were convinced against their will. More impelling than the drought was the fear of offending the awesome government of His Majesty and being forever after abandoned to their own resources.

The Colony departed Pitcairn on March 7th and arrived at Tahiti on March 23rd, having added one to its number with the birth of Lucy Anne Quintal en route. Pomare was dead and civil war was in the offing. Nevertheless, Queen Pomare, his sister, honored the King's commitment and the genial Tahitians gave the immigrants a hearty welcome, albeit marred by a lavish display of their notoriously uninhibited sexual activities.* Captain Sandilands arranged for the provisioning of the Pitcairners until their crops matured. Before he departed, he had already received some requests to be returned to Pitcairn, which he could not choose but to ignore.

Homesickness, a particularly virulent disease among Pitcairners, set in from the beginning, despite the geniality of the Tahitians and the discovery of a sister by one of the women who had arrived at Pitcairn with the "Bounty." This could have been cured in time, perhaps, but an attack of some infection which the underexposed Pitcairners found difficult to resist soon made Pitcairn look even better.

On April 21, Thursday October Christian, firstborn child of the Colony, died. Other deaths followed to the number of seventeen, if there be included those deaths following repatriation which were attributed to infection at Tahiti. Further, it became apparent that the vaunted moral standards of Pitcairn were endangered by the same "blandishments" to which Bligh attributed the mutiny.

Within a month of landing, a handful of the Colony had departed for home. The remainder returned September 2 on a chartered American brig, "Charles Dogget," using the copper bolts of the "Bounty" and contributions of the kind-hearted to pay for their passage. They had apparently not so much as turned a spadeful of earth in further-

---

* According to Moerenhout, devoted friend of the Pitcairners, who happened to be in Tahiti at the time of their arrival, on their very first night the newcomers witnessed Tahitian girls offering themselves to sailors and being prostituted without shame by their fathers, brothers or husbands. Taking the Pitcairners to Tahiti, as Moerenhout viewed it, was the equivalent of introducing convent girls into a brothel.

117

ance of the Tahiti project; their eyes were set on return practically from the moment they landed. Their joy in being home was voiced in resolutions never to leave again, and was only slightly dampened by the necessity of repairing damage to plantings and buildings from wild-running livestock and the passage of time. "Malthus be damned!" could have been their cry, or "Sufficient unto the day"—to choose a more likely thought.

Immigrant Hill. The Pitcairners had not recovered from the Tahitian debacle when, in 1832, there arrived on the Island one of those plausible paranoids who punctuate the pages of history with blood. This "very tall" gentleman in his sixties bore the name of Joshua Hill and had come most recently from Tahiti. His credentials authorized him, in his interpretation, to assume command of the Island. His many claims of eminence[6] included one of kinship to the Duke of Bedford. He oozed authority and grandeur, and could employ very impressive language.

Hill's career at Tahiti, which followed a similar ploy in the Sandwich Islands (Hawaii), presaged and was of a piece with the Pitcairn drama which followed his coming. He arrived at Tahiti in 1831, totally unknown, but was shortly ensconced in the house of the English consul for a four-month period, during which he "said nothing but ill of him, as a return, apparently for the hospitality extended him." Next he took possession of a chamber in the house of the missionary Pritchard while his unwitting host was absent.

> The man gave himself airs of importance, and pretended to have been sent by the British Government to arrange for the transportation of the Pitcairners to some other island, and let it be understood that he was in charge of some secret mission, concerning the state of all the islands. The missionaries, Pritchard more than the rest, believed him to be a person of importance. He was presented to the queen, and, with the missionaries as interpreters, questioned her concerning her government with all the gravity of a diplomatic envoy. . . . This man, during his residence at Tahiti, showed a childlike vanity, a boundless pride, a dangerous fanaticism, and an implacable hatred for whosoever dared to oppose him. As he never gave the least proof concerning his pretended mission, people came to realize he was an impostor; but for more than a year, he lived wholly at Pritchard's expence, who was even obliged to pay his laundress. At last he got rid of the man when an English captain offered to take him to Pitcairn where Hill had long wanted to go."[7]

Here indeed must be the original of the man who came to dinner.

What attracted an eccentric con man like Hill to the impecunious Pitcairn shore can only be conjectured; most likely it was the notion that on this untutored isle he could play the absolute ruler, imposing his dream life on the Islanders as reality, thereby making it so.

It did not take Hill long to realize that the chief obstacle to his dominance of Pitcairn was Nobbs. With Nobbs he included the other immigrants, Buffett and Evans, possibly because he regarded the outlanders, with their greater sophistication, as the strongest threat to his claims and authority. The epithet with which this newest comer to Pitcairn chose to denigrate his predecessors was, curiously enough, "lousy foreigners."

Hill had Buffett publicly flogged in church because, according to Buffett, he had made known Hill's plan to send Buffett's wife and family off the Island. After ejecting his host, Nobbs, from Nobbs' own house, because Nobbs did not quickly accept his pedagogical directions, Hill took over the teaching and conducted religious services.

The Island was soon in a turmoil, split among the pro- and anti-Hill factions. When Captain Freemantle arrived on H.M.S. "Challenger" in 1833, he was apparently of half a mind to remove Hill. He informed the Pitcairners that Hill was not acting on the authority of the British Government. But when Hill charged that Nobbs had "partaken of the spirits distilled by the natives," Freemantle refused to reinstate him "in the situation of which Mr. Hill had deprived him" and contented himself with admonishing Hill not to "interfere with the laws" and to be better behaved. This admonition was disregarded as soon as Freemantle sailed away.

According to Evans, Hill

> . . . still asserted he was sent out by the British Government, that Captain F. was no gentleman, and denounced vengeance on every native that did not join with him in oppressing the lousy foreigners. Whenever a ship appeared in sight, two confidential men were dispatched on board to forbid the captain and officers holding any communication with foreigners. . . . In May last a prison was built, for the avowed purpose of confining the Englishmen and their friends, and a law passed [by force] depriving our children of their mothers' inheritance . . . your petitioner received one dozen lashes. . . . Mr. Hill and his colleagues were continually threatening the life of someone or other. . . .

Hill finally achieved the departure of the three Englishmen on the "Tuscan" (Captain Stavers), which touched on Pitcairn in March

119

of 1834, on its way to Tahiti. Buffett became mate of a trading vessel, and Nobbs went to Mangareva as a missionary, accompanied by Evans. They were later reunited with their families, but still hungered for Pitcairn, peppering the British authorities with petitions for the removal of Hill and their restoration to their Island homes.

Downfall of a Dictator. Exiling of the "lousy foreigners" marked the peak of Hill's sway. A reaction set in which was to bring it to a dramatic end. Meanwhile Hill had a field day. He appointed elders, subelders, and cadets and played with the reins of power with as much passion as Napoleon at the summit of his conquests. The beginning of the end of the melodrama was marked by mutiny, a resort not without precedent among Pitcairners.

Arthur Quintal's daughter

> . . . had been charged with stealing some yams, and was proved guilty. The father was summoned before Hill, to hear what his daughter's sentence would be. Hill declared that the offender ought to be executed, or, at least be made to suffer very severely for her fault. The father strongly opposed. . . . Aroused to fury . . . Hill rushed into his bedroom, and, grasping his sword . . . presented it to the breast of Q., saying "confess your faults, or you are a dead man." Q. replied "I do not know that I have to confess."
>
> Hill then pricked him with the point of the sword still urging him to confess. . . . Fixing his eye steadfastly on Hill, he grasped the sword blade, and pushed H. down on to the floor. Hill said to him, "If he would let him get up he would treat on christian principles." Quintal then allowed him to rise, and Hill being up tried to get hold of a sword cane, but Q. prevented him. Some young men hearing the noise entered the house and secured Hill. He requested to be allowed to live in the school house until he could leave the island, which was granted him.[8]

A letter from Pitcairn asking Nobbs to resume teaching was followed by the return of the exiles to resume their erstwhile positions in October of 1834. Hill's opposition was overruled by a "majority of the people." The record contains little description of the life of Hill for the considerable period in which he remained on Pitcairn in limbo, so to speak.

In 1837 His Lordship, Edward Russell, arrived in H.M.S. "Actaeon" to hold a public inquiry. By one of those coincidences permissible only to ten-twenty-thirty melodrama, His Lordship was the son of that very Duke of Bedford with whom Hill had claimed close relationship.

The inquiry was marked by humor, in strange contrast to the grim history that preceded it. Hill retained sufficient spirit to thrust and parry insults with his opponents. His Lordship was much amused by such tidbits as Hill's interpretation of the abbreviation "P.S.M." in Nobbs' signature, which was intended to represent "Pastor and Spiritual Master," but, "in *his* estimation," more properly rendered as "Public Miscreant and Scoundrel." Lord Edward prolonged the show for two days and then decreed banishment, a sentence not carried out until the arrival of H.M.S. "Imogene" in December, 1837.

With departure of the protagonist, the Hill episode passed into the long history of megalomaniac persecution. In attempting to explain it, some twenty years afterwards, Buffett said: "It may appear strange how such a person could gain such an ascendancy over the people. It was through fear partly, and hopes of gain. He said to them, if they did not obey him he would write to *government* and a ship of war would be sent to chastise them. If on the other hand they would obey him, whatever they wanted he would write for and it would be sent them." The stick and the carrot; it neither began nor ended with Hill.

Removal to Norfolk. In the 1840s, removal of the Pitcairn colony again became a live issue, although the necessity for it again seemed much more obvious to outlanders than to the Pitcairners themselves, who remembered vividly the Tahitian disaster. Captain Wood of H.M.S. "Pandora" reported in 1849 that "it was evident that none of them had yet made up their minds to the necessary evil of a removal." Wood stated: "There is no necessity for any of them leaving the island at present, they allow that there is much land uncultivated, and a more equal distribution of it [Wood had noted how the Island system of land inheritance had resulted in the less prolific families holding larger pieces] would make what they have go much farther."

But this was the minority view among the outlanders. Baron de Thierry, who was stranded on Pitcairn in 1850, represented the prevailing view. He set forth,

> . . . in vivid colors, the calamities which appeared too surely to impend over the island, with an increasing population [156 in 1850], a diminishing quantity of food, and a precarious supply of indifferent

121

water, which another landslide might cut off altogether. What a helpless condition, humanly speaking, with nothing to attract shipping out of its usual course, no trade, no harbour, no means of repair, nothing but exposure and danger.

And even Nobbs, who had been quoted as saying that he would stay at Pitcairn as long as two families remained, indicated the seemingly inexorable drift in a letter on June 29, 1855: "Whaleships do not come, because they rarely can obtain such an amount of vegetable refreshments as they require. . . . I want your opinion as to what I ought to do, if some families remain here, in preference to removing. . . . I hold myself in readiness to go if desired to do so."

Doubts about the adequacy of Pitcairn had been reinforced by a punishing drought in 1853, which reduced the Islanders to "pumpkins, berries, cocoanuts, and beans for their existence."

Before a decision was reached, the focus of discussion turned from "whether" to "where." Suggestions for resettlement at Juan Fernandez and Huahine [where one of the Tahitian women had a land claim] and other places were rejected because of impracticality or undesirability. Like their mutineer forebears before the settlement on Pitcairn, the Islanders had very special requirements in view in their search for a home. Foremost was the desire for the seclusion which had enabled the Colony to develop the attributes which had won such heart-warming praise, and to follow its own bent. There was also a preference for a climate similar to Pitcairn's. And the choice was limited; there were few available places unclaimed and unpopulated.

A solution appeared in the form of Norfolk Island, the penal colony which was abandoned by Great Britain in 1855. In response to a feeler, the Chief Magistrate and councillors of Pitcairn responded that "the inhabitants do unanimously agree in soliciting the aid of the British Government in transferring them to Norfolk Island, or some other appropriate place." In consequence, the Governor of Norfolk was told to exclude squatters and to hold Norfolk for the Pitcairners.

The claim of unanimity proved grossly exaggerated when Captain Freemantle arrived in 1855 on H.M.S. "Juno" to prepare the Pitcairners for removal. The Pitcairners persisted in recalling the "Tahitian tragedy," some predicting that this would be a "second edition." The waverers expressed "much anxiety to know what succour or protection those that remained behind might expect hereafter," a point on which the captain "was unable to afford positive informa-

122

tion. . . . The discussion, however, ended by 153 out of a population of 187 declaring for Norfolk Island; the rest I will not say determined to remain on Pitcairn, but they would not then acquiesce in the voice of the majority.''

Further persuasion was required when Lieutenant Gregorie of H.M.S. ''Juno,'' appointed to superintend the removal of the Pitcairners on the emigrant ship ''Morayshire'' (Captain Mathers), arrived in April of 1856. By the time the ''Morayshire'' departed in early May, it ''brought away every soul,'' 194 in all. For the third time in 66 years, Pitcairn lay deserted.

After a passage of some five weeks, the emigrants arrived at Norfolk on June 8, with all their most prized possessions, some much the worse for attacks of seasickness.

Norfolk Island, the newly promised land of the Pitcairners, is situated at 29° S. latitude and longitude 167° 50′, over 4000 miles west of Pitcairn. Despite its larger area (thirteen as against less than two square miles), sturdy and commodious government buildings, and the livestock left behind for the new settlers' use, the Pitcairners found cause for grousing.

Complaints included ''the paucity of wood and water. There is scarcely a tree in sight from the settlement . . . and, with one exception, all water has to be raised from a few dangerous wells, sixty or seventy feet deep.'' Another disappointment was the necessity of sharing the island with a Melanesian Mission which Dr. Selwyn, Bishop of Melanesia, had been given permission to establish at one corner of the island.

But the die was cast for most of the Colony. Dr. Shapiro, who spent five months on Norfolk in 1923, in lieu of a frustrated trip to Pitcairn, says: ''. . . the new life of the Pitcairn colony was established auspiciously on Norfolk. The land was divided into fifty-acre allotments, one for each family. A thriving trade was commenced with the whalers, dripstones were manufactured from a suitable rock discovered on the island, and offshore whaling became a possibility where beaches were accessible.''[9]

The Second Return. If most of the Pitcairners had adjusted, this was not true of ''some simpletons,'' as Nobbs characterized them; Moses Young, whose family included a wife and five young children, and Mayhew Young, whose wife had seven children, six by a former marriage to a deceased McCoy. After nearly two years on Norfolk, despite entreaties and admonitions, they returned "home" on the "Mary Ann" in January of 1859, in the nick of time to save Pitcairn for the British Empire, for a French man-of-war had appeared intent on claiming it for France.

But they were too late to prevent depredations by part of the crew of an American vessel shipwrecked on nearby Oeno. They had reached deserted Pitcairn in search of succor, not knowing it had been abandoned, and had appropriated the planks and nails of Island houses for the building of a ship in which to reach Tahiti.* In addition to these human depredations, wind, weather, and time had altered the plantations for the worse, although the subsequent crops were improved by the rest given the land.

Five years after the initial resettlement, four more families returned from Norfolk, including one "stranger," as the Pitcairners designated anyone not born on the Island. The stranger was a sailor from Rhode Island, Samuel Warren, who had joined the Norfolk colony and married Pitcairner Agnes Christian. They were accompanied by Thursday October Christian, 2d, his wife and nine children, as well as his mother-in-law; Simon Young, wife, mother, and eight children, and Robert Buffett and wife.

Strong dissuasion had not prevailed over the call of Pitcairn. And repeated subsequent appeals from Norfolk, including an offer to pay for the charter of a transport, failed to dislodge the reestablished community.

Naturally, subsequent visitors to Pitcairn quizzed the Islanders on why they had left a seemingly more promising situation to return to the abandoned Island. As reported by Captain Montresor of H.M.S. "Calypso" in 1860, the men gave the health of their wives and a "strong desire to revisit their native country" as the reasons.

> . . . to the officers with whom they were more confidential, they admitted that they did not consider Norfolk Island as their own . . . a school-master and a miller had been placed among them, who were not of them, the school-master having charge of the sheep. . . which they had been

---

* This episode is memorialized in Josiah N. Knowles' *Crusoes of Pitcairn Island*, Los Angeles, 1957. It is interesting to learn from the afterword to this little volume that the men from the shipwrecked clipper "Wild Wave," left on Oeno by the Captain, Knowles, and the small part of the crew which headed for Pitcairn, quarreled among themselves and "set up separate camps." Apparently women were not an essential ingredient for dissension.

led to believe would have been their own property; and that some sappers and miners, with their wives and families, had also been quartered on the island; that their own magistrates, formerly only responsible to the people themselves, were now held responsible by Government for the performance of certain obligations by the people; and that altogether they found it was different from the life of freedom and irresponsibility, to all but themselves and their elected magistrates, they had led at Pitcairn, that they had a longing to be back to the island, where nobody could interfere with them, however good and kind the intention, and however necessary, perhaps, the interference. . . . whatever justice there may be in these arguments, the first and great reason for their return, and which could not veil itself from our observation, was evidently the longing for the land of their birth. . . .

This analysis is quite close to the mark; the attachment of islanders for their own way and habitat is more marked than that of mainlanders, even when that habitat may strike outsiders as unappealing. A recent dramatic example was the eager return of the inhabitants of Tristan da Cunha from the green fields of England to the dubious attractions of their island home. In the case of the Pitcairners, the usual considerations were perhaps accentuated by their peculiar history. No reminder is needed that Pitcairn was settled by outlaws; even before their arrival at the Island their battle cry was sounded by Sumner and Quintal at Tubuai. When reprimanded by Fletcher Christian for taking unauthorized shore leave, they had replied, "We are now our own masters." This cry was to reecho time and again in Pitcairn history; even when they recognized that something was being done without ulterior motive "for their own good," Pitcairners clung tenaciously to the right to follow their own grain. Frequently they were ready to accept half a loaf of their own kind of bread rather than a full loaf of a superior but uncongenial product. It was not that the Pitcairners were not as other men; rather it was that they were more so.

Immigration by Shipwreck. Pitcairn's next immigrants, the first since Hill, were acquired as a result of shipwreck. When the "Khandeish" was wrecked on Oeno in 1875, the crew made for Pitcairn in their gig and launch, and remained for fifty-one days before they could secure passage from the Island. One of the crew, Butler, married a Pitcairn woman, Alice McCoy, whom he deserted after she presented him with twin daughters. The Islanders' generosity to the sailors was acknowledged by a cargo of gifts, including an organ, being sent to Pitcairn from citizens of San Francisco as a mark of gratitude.

In 1881 the shipwreck of the "Acadia" on Ducie Island created a problem for the Pitcairners. The crew, like others in like circumstances, made for Pitcairn, and three remained after the "Edward O'Brien" arrived to pick them up. Two of them, Albert J. Volk and Phillip Coffin, married Island girls, Mary Ann Young and Mary Florence Warren. The third, Albert Knight, found favor over a home-grown rival (a Christian at that) and the banns for his marriage to Maria Jane Young were published, when protests raised by the girl's family resulted in his removal from the Island by the next British man-of-war to arrive, the "Sappho" (Commander Clark), and in an interdiction of further settlement by strangers. When James Russell McCoy, Chief Magistrate, absent at the time of this imbroglio, returned, he berated the Islanders for ejecting Knight, who possessed useful carpentering skills, rather than the other two "useless interlopers." Volk eventually returned to his native Wales with his wife, leaving Coffin as the sole "Acadian" on Pitcairn, until Lincoln Clark rejoined him many years later. Clark, a mere youth on the "Acadia," had returned to the United States and married. He brought his sixteen-year-old son, Roy, back to Pitcairn with him in 1906 to share his remembered dream of paradise. Clark remarried and founded a new family. Roy eventually became Elder and schoolmaster and, later, Pitcairn's first postmaster.

In addition to permanent emigration and immigration, the mobility of the Pitcairners increased with the passing years from the time when Moerenhout employed them in 1829 to assist his pearl-diving expedition. The early visitors were frequently importuned for a "ride" to faraway places, requests which were overruled by parental objections or the inconvenience envisioned by the ships' captains. (Likewise, the captains overruled requests from crew members to be allowed to stay on Pitcairn.)

Nobbs, Evans, and Buffett joined the ranks of the travelers as a result of their exile in 1834. Nobbs and Buffett traveled extensively thereafter for one reason or another. The journeys of James Russell McCoy, Chief Magistrate or President of Pitcairn for twenty-two of the thirty-seven years from 1870 to 1907, were so frequent and extensive as to foster occasional grumbling.

"Whereas from 1859 to 1893 only nine men and a woman had

ventured to visit the outer world, quite a few were now following
McCoy's example; in particular, many of the surplus Island women
were taken as mission helpers to Fiji, Samoa, Tonga and other Pacific
islands, and even as far afield as Australia and the United States.''
The "surplus" nature of the women derived from inequalities in the
number of girls and boys who returned from Norfolk to refound the
Pitcairn Colony.

When Mrs. Scoresby Routledge[10] visited Pitcairn in 1915,

> A large portion of the population asked for passages to Tahiti, but the
> hearts of most failed before the end, and we on our part drew the line at
> taking more than two men, who would work their passage. The two men,
> brothers Charles and Edwin Young, proved "intelligent . . . good work-
> ers" on the passage to England, where they were examined by Sir Arthur
> Keith and were "commanded to Buckingham Palace as representatives
> of England's smallest colony."

After being "impressed with the kindness and condescension of their
Majesties," the Young boys returned to Pitcairn by way of Tahiti.

The Young boys had been preceded to England in 1881 by two
Pitcairn youths, one of whom was

> . . . almost immediately on landing . . . secured as a highly prized
> specimen of the human species, to be exhibited in the Westminster
> Aquarium. Entirely ignorant of the intention of the parties who had
> obtained him, he consented to their proposal to accompany them, and
> were soon speeding away from Liverpool to London, where he was duly
> settled in his place in the aquarium and advertised. "Does he eat like
> other people?" was one of the many questions that amused him, as it
> was earnestly put by one of the spectators. A bluff old sea captain was
> very indignant that he had to pay for the privilege of seeing an old
> acquaintance whom he had twice visited in his faraway island home.[11]

Rescue was effected by the staunch friend of the Pitcairners,
Reverend A. W. Drew, and the two youths eventually returned to
Pitcairn.

FOREIGN RESIDENTS

The late nineteenth century initiated a new type of immigrant,
who could be distinguished from a visitor chiefly by the length of his
stay, frequently indeterminate. After the conversion of the Pitcairn
Colony to Seventh Day Adventism in 1886, missionaries and teachers

were sent them by their church at irregular intervals for varying periods. Other visitors came for protracted stays for one reason or another. Thus, when Dr. Shapiro visited Pitcairn in 1934, he found thirteen foreigners. Six were members of the family of a New Zealand dentist, Cooze, including himself, his wife, three children, and his father. The others were Aggie and Harriet Ross, retired spinsters from New Zealand; Dick Fairclough and his sister, Jessie Westall, from Birmingham, England; and Adella (Schmidt) Young, daughter of a Danish father and Chilean mother who had sent her to Pitcairn at an early age to go to school and learn English. She had, on maturing, married Arthur Young. Roy Clark was from California.

A notable addition was a young Mangarevan girl, Aunoa, (called Ruau Tahow by the Johnsons) who had been married to Sterling Warren (called Andy by Shapiro). Warren had arrived at Mangareva by way of Norman Hall's shipwrecked "Pro Patria." There he courted his bride-to-be, but could not be married to her for lack of a birth certificate, until he was rescued by the friendly Johnsons in their "Yankee" and carried back to Pitcairn with other stranded Islanders. Captain Johnson performed the marriage ceremony at sea in 1934.

Aunoa was the "only Polynesian addition since the original cross," and her name brought back to Pitcairn the nomenclature of mellifluous vowels for which the "Bounty" men had substituted easier "Marys" and "Susans," and which had not been represented in the names of the Pitcairn children.

EMIGRATION AFTER WORLD WAR II

But, as the twentieth century progressed, the dominant note became emigration rather than immigration; fear of overpopulation was replaced by the threat of depopulation. Dr. Shapiro estimated that in 1934, when the population was approximately two hundred, some twenty-five Pitcairners had emigrated. Curiously, if not unexpectedly, as economic conditions improved on Pitcairn by reason of development of curios and stamps, and refrigerators and radios became commonplace, the urge to try one's wings in the great world became stronger.

The immigration-emigration pattern on Pitcairn Island in the twentieth century presents a picture somewhat obscured by the return, temporary or permanent, of some of the emigrants, but the later trend is unmistakable. Only a small number of outsiders have been allowed to settle on the Island, despite yearly requests for permission, frequently made by Americans. Emigration has increased; in 1958 twenty-four migrated to New Zealand and three returned; in 1959 ten migrated and seventeen returned. The population figures indicate a dramatic downtrend, only intermittently halted. In 1965 there was a total of only eighty-eight.

Once again Pitcairn is faced with a population problem, only now it is a problem of underpopulation.

⚜ VISITORS ⚜

The strong desire of the mutineers to avoid visitors was one of the chief motives for the selection of isolated Pitcairn for their settlement in 1790. This situation, like many others, was to undergo a complete reversal, to the point where an Islander's eye-view of the history of Pitcairn might be written largely in terms of the visits of touching ships.

Before their discovery by Mayhew Folger in 1808, the mutineers had had several scares. In one incident a boat was sighted, but nothing came of it. In another, the Islanders concealed themselves in the bush when alarmed by the sight of two vessels standing in for shore. Evidence of an undetected landing came to light the following morning when one of the Quintals discovered a strange clasp-knife on a rock by the shore near a number of broken coconut shells.

The Pitcairners were still somewhat apprehensive when Folger stumbled on them, but they were reassured by his statement that he was an American from Boston, rather than an Englishman (they asked him whether America was in Ireland). The impact of Folger's visit can be discerned from the fact that generations later his given name, Mayhew, was affixed to Pitcairn children.

The next visit to Pitcairn, by Captains Staines and Pipon in 1814, representing as they did, His Majesty, sent a tremor of fear through the Colony. But the captains wisely forbore to take away from the Pitcairners their cherished patriarch, John Adams, last of the mutineers and potential yardarm bait. After this, the Islanders breathed more easily and welcomed subsequent ships eagerly.

With the advent of the whalers, visits by ships soon became more frequent. Because a visit to Pitcairn was a notable event, many captains published valuable reports of their stays, such as that of Captain King in 1819. Their reportorial prowess and accuracy were markedly uneven. The most extended stay by any of the early visitors—over two weeks—was that of Captain Beechey in 1825. It was a momentous visit because it resulted in the most complete account by far of the life of the Colony and the fate of the mutineers and their entourage (practically all of the many subsequent books draw heavily on Beechey) and because it ultimately resulted in the removal of the Pitcairners to Tahiti in 1831.

The arrival of Moerenhout in 1829 gave the Pitcairners their first "outside" employment; he took some of the men with him on a pearl-diving expedition to the Gambiers. His admiring account of the Pitcairners is also extremely valuable for a variety of reasons; unfortunately, it has never been translated into English and is rare and difficult to obtain even in the French editions.

Most welcomed of the sojourners who came to Pitcairn in increasing numbers in the 1830s were the British men-of-war. They represented the mighty Empire which the Pitcairners liked to imagine as standing behind them; they were of the race to which the Islanders preferred to be affined, probably because of the orientation provided by Adams and, later, by Buffett and Nobbs.

They brought with them, besides their impressive vessels, new faces, news of the great world, medical aid, and officers and gentlemen who adopted a correct, polite, and protective stance, but responded warmly to the Pitcairners' eager overtures of friendship. Moreover, they returned to England to sing the praises of the Colony, albeit their reports were sometimes tinged with reservations.

Another category of visitor might be classified as "accidental." In 1850, Walter Brodie and four fellow passengers, including the famous Baron de Thierry, were stranded on Pitcairn for sixteen days when they went ashore for a quick look and the vagaries of wind persuaded the captain of their ship to abandon them. The ship was headed for California with a list of passengers eager to join the gold rush; this accounted for considerable traffic at the time. Brodie incorporated his experience in a book which has become one of the "standards."

Other accidental visitors came from shipwrecks on nearby uninhabited islands, such as Ducie. Pitcairn was the nearest habitation for miles around and the natural destination of any survivors adrift in adjacent waters. Sometimes the number of these sailors and the enforced length of their stay taxed the Island resources, but the hospitality of the Pitcairners added luster to their reputation.

In addition to whalers, trading ships, men-of-war, and accidental guests, visitors came to Pitcairn in the interests of scientific investigation. Reference is not intended here to those who came primarily for other purposes, but seized advantage of the occasion to observe, sometimes to poke, to pry, to measure, and to assess, nor to government officials who came in pursuit of their colonial duties and performed like operations. The category refers to representatives of recognized disciplines and arts, licensed, so to speak, to examine, describe, and analyze.

The many traces of the pre-''Bounty'' Polynesian society brought archaeologists and anthropologists such as Mrs. Scoresby Routledge in 1915; a Franco-Belgian expedition in 1935[12] (which produced the most thorough report); and a 1955 Norwegian expedition headed by Thor Heyerdahl of Kon-Tiki fame. Dr. Shapiro in 1934 realized a dream frustrated in 1923 and produced the most comprehensive survey of the physical and cultural anthropology of Pitcairn.

The professional globetrotters, Captain and Mrs. Irving Johnson, visited Pitcairn six times during the 1930s, '40s, and '50s, and incorporated their engaging experiences and observations in well-illustrated magazine articles and books. Writer and skin-diver Luis Marden came to Pitcairn in 1956 to search for remnants of the ''Bounty'' in the bay named after it. Besides discovering copper fittings, a rudder pintle, an oarlock, and other objects, he returned with magnificent photographs incorporated in a fascinating account of his visit.

Already mentioned have been the passenger ships which stopped for periods of half an hour to two hours offshore to give their passengers fleeting contact with the legendary Islanders. The passengers sometimes seized the opportunity to quiz them on their sex life.* As an experience in human relationships it left something to be

---

* Dr. Shapiro acutely observes: ''I've never been able to determine exactly why quite decent people automatically become insufferable the moment they start traveling. Perhaps it is because subconsciously they metamorphose the new and strange into the inferior, and, as a corollary, a note of condescension creeps in.''

desired, but it did offer opportunities to get and send mail, pick up supplies, and sell fruit and souvenirs.

This far from complete list of visitors, omitting such notable events as the visits of Polar explorer Admiral Byrd in 1939 and Queen Salote of Samoa on her way to Queen Elizabeth's coronation, is sufficient to indicate that the famed isolation of Pitcairn, if at times of keenly-felt duration, at others provided a respite from company sometimes awkwardly bunched. At any rate, there is no record of any blemish on the Islanders' well-deserved reputation for hospitality.

❦ NOTES: PART FOUR ❦

1. Buffett.
2. Lady Belcher, pp. 233, 234.
3. Nobbs dominates large parts of the Pitcairn literature; the most valuable source is the work of his friend Murray, which quotes autobiographical material and many letters of Nobbs. For a report on Nobbs shortly after his arrival at Pitcairn, and of the Nobbs-Bunker-cutter tangle, see Moerenhout. Brodie and Belcher include Nobbs material not elsewhere available. An unusual view of Nobbs is provided by a seaman who visited Pitcairn in the mid-1840s (Extracts from the *Journal of John A. States,* Stonington, Connecticut; *On a Whaling Voyage, 1844–46: A Visit at Pitcairn's Island,* Publication of Marine Historical Association, Inc., Mystic, Connecticut, Vol. 1, No. 4, Nov. 20, 1931) :

    "Dominie Nobbs . . . was a sleepy looking little old man, dressed out in black pants with pumps, and white cotton stockings, a sack coat of drab and all surmounted with a belltopped beaver, the brim of which was about half an inch wide; he never took notice of any of our crew, but made himself acquainted with our officers, thinking I suppose, that a foremast hand was not worthy of notice. However, no love was lost, for he was not worthy of a decent man's notice, and with his gentility, served to make a laughing stock by the contrast between his dried form, and the healthy form of his parishioners. His wife was present with a child in her arms, but was dressed in the common dress of the Islanders. I shall not soon forget him, or his air of affected gentility, as he lifted his hat from his bald head and spoke compliments to our lady (the Captain's wife). . . ."
4. Buffett's own *Narrative* is the best single source for the career of Pitcairn's first immigrant.
5. The Tahiti migration is most thoroughly treated in Maude(2).
6. Hill's autobiographical statement has been quoted in much of the Pit-

cairn literature from Brodie to Shapiro. Because it is a classic of paranoia and illuminates the wishful interior life of the Pitcairn dictator, it will bear repeating, in part:

"I am aware that pedantry and egotism become no one, and myself perhaps less than any. (Prov. xxvii. 2.) But for certain reasons, the following credentials, as a memorandum, I hope will be pardoned on the present occasion—they are truths.

"I observe, *in limine,* that I have visited the four quarters of the globe, and it has ever been my desire to maintain, as far as lay in my power, the standing of an English gentleman. I have lived a considerable while in a palace, and had my dinner parties with a princess on my right, and a General's lady upon my left. I have had a French cook, a box at the opera. I have drove my dress carriage (thought the neatest then in Paris, where I spent five or six years; as well I have known Calcutta), and the handsomest lady (said), Madame R——, to grace my carriage. I have drove a curricle with my two outriders, and two saddle-horses, besides a travelling-carriage. A valet, coachman, footman, groom, and, upon extraordinary occasions, my *maître d'hôtel.* I have (at her request) visited Madame Bonaparte, at the Tuileries, St. Cloud, and Malmaison. I might thus mention many others of note abroad.

"I have frequently dined with that remarkable woman, Madame Carburas, afterwards the Princess de C——. I have had the honour of being in company; *i.e.* at the same parties, with both his late Majesty George IV. then Prince Regent, and his present Majesty William IV. then H.R.H. Duke of Clarence, as well with their royal brothers. I have ridden in a royal Duke's carriage, with four horses and three footmen, more than once, and have dined at his table, and drunk the old hock of his late father, George III. I have visited and dined with some of our first families, and have been visited by a Duke, and others of the first noblemen. I have known and dined with (abroad and in England), Madames Catalini, Grassini, Georges, etc. And I have given the arm to Lady Hamilton (of Naples renown), whom the hero of the Nile has given his (one) to more than once. . . ."

7. Moerenhout.
8. Young and Buffett.
9. Shapiro, *"Descendants of the Mutineers of the Bounty,"* Bishop Museum, Honolulu, 1929.
10. Mrs. Scoresby Routledge's visit is reported in her *The Mystery of Easter Island,* London, 1919.
11. Young.
12. The Franco-Belgian Expedition resulted in the most comprehensive report of Pitcairn archaeology, "Contribution À L'Étude de L'Archéologie de L'Ile de Pitcairn," *Bulletin de la Société des Américanistes de Belgique,* vol. 19, pp. 3–42.

For the writings of the other visitors mentioned, see the selective bibliography on pages 246 ff.

Part Five

THE SOCIETY OF PITCAIRN

ꙮ COLOR, CASTE, AND CLASS ꙮ

The Bounty-Pitcairn story is suffused with issues of class, caste, and color, but conscious discussion of these questions in the literature is meager.[1]

COLOR

One could fill a sizable volume with voyagers' descriptions of the color or complexion of the Polynesians. Such a venture would be of dubious profitability; confusion rather than enlightenment would be the likely result. The mutineers early eliminated any difficulties by crudely describing the Polynesians as "black," in contrast to themselves as "white," although it is likely that some of the sailors were darker than some of the "blacks."

"Black" was certainly simpler than the involved descriptions of color by the early travelers and their determined, if dubious, efforts to equate lightness of skin with superiority of class. One description has the Tahitian girls of "light copper colour, others darker, and some almost white. . . . The men's complexions were olive or tawny. . . . Their hair, which was neat and anointed with coconut oil, was usually black, but in some cases brown or red; while with young boys and girls it was often bleached."[2]

137

A leading authority, William Ellis, tells us that Tahitian babies were close in color to Europeans, but were tanned by the sun, and that the women were lighter than the males, such as the fishermen, exposed to the sun. That the Polynesians did not share the European attitude is indicated by his statement that, "A fair complexion was not an object of admiration or desire. They never considered the fairest European countenance . . . handsomer than their own."[3]

But, as is still true, the actual color was of less portent than the psychological effect of the difference and the ease with which it could be seized upon as a basis for divisiveness. This is evidenced by the exclusion of the Polynesian men from land ownership when the Englishmen divided Pitcairn amongst themselves and by the relegation of the "blacks" to the role of servants or retainers. The "failure in race relations" brought the community near to extinction. The implications of this experience need no elucidation.

When Pipon and Staines stumbled on Pitcairn in 1814 (the second to do so), it would seem that color prejudice was already well established among the first generation born on the Island, completely half-caste as it was. As Shillibeer tells the story, while young Thursday October Christian was breakfasting aboard the ship, "A West Indian Black, who was one of the servants," waited on the table. "Christian looked at him sternly, rose, asked for his hat, and said, 'I don't like that black fellow, I must go.' It required some little persuasion to stop him." Shillibeer concludes that "the hatred of these people to the blacks is strongly rooted."

While later increasing contacts with Europeans could and did foster European identification and prejudices, it is difficult to understand at this early date, unless it developed from stories of the "massacre" which identified the villains as "black." The Island natives escaped the evil effects of color prejudice themselves only by virtue of the fact that they were all half-castes and that they received especially considerate treatment from visitors, probably because of the "romance" which surrounded them and their reputation for piety and morality.

CASTE AND CLASS

Caste and class entered the Bounty-Pitcairn story with the Bligh controversy. A considerable portion of the criticism of Bligh emanated from, or was bulwarked by, the notion that he was "not a gentleman." His defenders asserted his right to this classification. Implicit in the discussion is the assumption that, once this delicate question were decided, any problem as to the propriety of Bligh's conduct must perforce be settled. Thus, Mackaness:

> It was the fashion for many critics of Bligh . . . to sneer at him because, they asserted, he had been a common sailor, and in his early days had been contaminated by association with the riff-raff who in those years inhabited the forecastle . . . it was his misfortune not to have been educated in the gunroom of a man-of-war, among young gentlemen—which is to the Navy what a public school is to those who are to move in civil society.

Mackaness demolishes this line of attack on Bligh. He quotes in support a most unlikely authority, George Borrow, who in the Appendix to *The Romany Rye* inveighs against the worship of class in the following manner: "The Lord help brave soldiers and sailors who are promoted; they have less to undergo from the high airs of their brother officers, and those are hard enough to endure, than from the insolence of the men."

An interesting observation comes from Danielsson,* to the effect that ". . . the mutiny on the 'Bounty' can also very well be interpreted as a class struggle; a revolt of the oppressed, neglected, poverty-stricken and homeless seamen against a privileged and overbearing gentlemen-class, the chief representative of which in their eyes was Captain Bligh." This convenient simplification overlooks the fact that the mutiny was led by a member of the elite with at least as much claim to belonging to the "gentlemen-class" as Bligh himself, but its suggestion that mutiny was an instrument of class warfare cannot be dismissed out of hand.† Leadership of the "Bounty" mutiny by an

---

* *What Happened on the Bounty*, New York, 1964.
† Another interesting theory of the mutiny, again based on reliance on an exclusive part of the facts, is that of Dr. Bernard Smith in his *European Vision and the South Pacific*, London, 1960. ". . . the mutiny provided a clear case of men born

officer was one of its distinguishing marks, and was regarded by more than one sea captain, as well as others, in the light of a betrayal of class.

Of more concern to the Pitcairn story is the nature of the arrangement under which the Polynesians, particularly the men, embarked on the last voyage of the "Bounty." The Tubuaians, Titahiti and Oher, were taken aboard under the banner of "taioship," a relationship which the sailors were disposed to take full advantage of at Tahiti and Tubuai, whatever their disinclination to honor it on Pitcairn. What of the other four Polynesian men? Adams' description of the Polynesians as "servants" is suspect. Assuming they were not kidnaped, why would these other four join up as "servants"? Is it not more likely that they, too, were "taios" of the "Bounty" men and that this accounted for their presence on the ship and a belief that they were engaged in a joint adventure?

Whatever notions of equality the Polynesian men may have entertained were dissipated shortly after settlement on Pitcairn by their pointed exclusion from the division of land. This immediately set up a class division of "white" against "black," European against Polynesian, landowner against landless, master against servant. "The white men began life in Pitcairn with a feeling of their solidarity of interest as a dominant caste; they assumed a right to govern the coloured people, to exploit their labor, and to enjoy their women."*

The problem of class warfare achieved a "final solution" on Pitcairn; the "lower" class was eliminated. Thenceforth all were

---

and reared in a civilized society deliberately choosing to live permanently among native people. There had been earlier cases but none that drew such public interest. That interest was due not only to the exciting story but also to the fact that the mutineers chose to accomplish in real life an ideal that lay close to the romantic view of life—the desire to live in intimate and continuous contact with nature. The mutiny was a sharper criticism of civilization than any of the clever remarks voiced by literary noble savages."

* Prof. W. K. Hancock, "Politics in Pitcairn," *Nineteenth Century*, May 1931, vol. 109, pp. 575 to 587. The following remarks from this article, made after pointing out that white solidarity lapsed after achievement of victory over the Polynesians, are also of interest: "The mutineers had lapsed into a state of nature. They had divided their world into nine parts; each mutineer took his own part, and became his own law, each established himself as a sovereign, supreme and unchallenged within his territory, combining with his neighbors only for the joint exploitation of coloured labor, or to ensure his own security in face of a rival combination. The world of Pitcairn was divided into rival alliances; the tiny island became Christendom in miniature."

landed and, in the next generation, all were identically half-European and half-Polynesian, the "black" men having left no progeny.

There were, of course, class differences among the whites before the landing on Pitcairn. Christian and Young were officers and of the gentry; the others were "people" from socially inferior classes. The weight of the evidence indicates that only traces of any distinction survived the landing. Distinction was ignored in the division of the land and there is no indication that Christian was accorded special benefits either by reason of his lineage or previous leadership of the mutiny and of the Pitcairn expedition. The other mutineers were hell-bent on equality—for themselves at least. In this connection it is amusing to note Barrow's reaction, at a remove of thirteen thousand miles, to the information that Adams, in speaking of Christian, "never omits to say 'Mr. Christian.'" The British viewpoint is epitomized by Barrow's statement: "Why indeed should he? Christian was a gentleman by birth, and an officer in his Majesty's service, and was of course always so addressed." We may indulge in presumption that, had Barrow been on the Pitcairn scene, he would have found highly irregular the proceedings and attitudes of the "Bounty" men, including their persistent cry of, "We are our own men."

With the liquidation of the Polynesian males, and the death of all but one of the whites, social equality obtained, subject until his death to the commanding position of Adams. There were other limitations, one created by the fact that land descended equally to all the children of an owner, so that after one or two generations, variance in fertility created like variance in the amount of land each child could claim. Nonetheless, class distinctions were reduced to a minimum in the subsequent history of the Island, although a special attitude governed relations with "strangers" (those not born on the Island) who settled on Pitcairn, such as Nobbs and Hill. This attitude commingled suspicion and awe of the outlanders' experience in the great world over the horizon. To the rest of the world, their strange history made Pitcairners unique; for themselves it was a leveling force.

The half-caste character of the Pitcairners subjected them to no penalties on the Island, and was further transcended by their growing identification with the Western World. In the first half of the nineteenth century, contact was largely with American whalers and British men-of-war, plus a few Western trading and passenger vessels.

The three permanent immigrants were Englishmen. It is to this identification with the West that Maude(4) attributes in considerable part the failure of the Tahiti migration. ". . . the Pitcairn people, for reasons implicit in their history, were strongly race-conscious. For them miscegenation obviously meant assimilation, and the only race they were prepared to be assimilated into was the European, to which they felt they rightfully belonged."

Infusions of new blood in the last half of the nineteenth century were largely from the United States. Pitcairn became part of the British Empire in 1838, at least as the Islanders viewed the matter. When emigration, largely to New Zealand, swelled after the Second World War, the Pitcairners apparently suffered little difficulty in marrying into the society of their adopted countries. There is no indication that any distinctions developed on the Island on the basis of varying amounts of Western blood, although one parent indicated distaste for the pure Polynesian ancestry of his son's bride.

Differences in the amount of land owned by individual families have been accentuated with the passing of time, and have caused some difficulties.* The growth of the curio industry into the mainstay of the Island economy has probably increased the gap between the most and least efficient producers. Nonetheless, Pitcairn society was and is notably egalitarian. But it is inadequate to describe the Pitcairners as egalitarian. Pitcairners formed a *sui generis* class, simultaneously incorporating the traits of peasants, landed proprietors, seamen, traders, and manufacturers.

Before leaving the subject of class, it is pertinent to recognize the class of reporters of, and commentators on, the Pitcairn scene. Almost invariably these gentlemen, ships' captains and officers, government officials, missionaries, and scientific observers, were representatives of the European, Australian, and American middle class. Some were imaginative enough to assess the Pitcairn society with an unslanted eye, recognizing its special circumstances, but others did not hesitate to apply to it yardsticks derived from their own milieu. Thus, Pitcairn housing and housekeeping were measured against European ideals, Pitcairn alternate bursts of heavy labor and deep relaxation against time-clock employment, and Pitcairn morals against a standard perhaps more theoretical than actual even in the West. This tendency

---

* See pp. 226–228.

accounts in part for some of the less sympathetic reports of Pitcairn life which intersperse the record and counterbalance the sometimes overlavish praise heaped on the Islanders.

☙ RELIGION ☙

Nothing so excited the first visitors to Pitcairn as the evidence of piety and religious observance. Whether the captains' surprise at this revelation was sharpened by their own devoutness or lack thereof is a matter of speculation. It can be accounted for simply by the sheer improbability of finding the usages of the Church of England—whatever sea change they may have suffered—being followed on this remote Pacific rock by such an unlikely congregation, all the members of which, except John Adams, were either full or half-blooded Polynesians.

The early accounts glowingly reported the Islanders' practice of saying grace before and after every meal. Lt. Shillibeer gave this aspect of Island life its most dramatic rendering:

> I must here confess I blushed when I saw nature in its most simple state, offer that tribute of respect to the Omnipotent Creator, which from an education I did not perform, nor from society had been taught its necessity. 'Ere they began to eat; on their knees, and with hands uplifted did they implore permission to partake in peace what was set before them, and when they had eaten heartily, resuming their former attitude, offered a fervent prayer of thanksgiving for the indulgence they had just experienced. Our omission of this ceremony did not escape their notice, for Christian [Thursday October] asked me whether it was not customary with us also. Here nature was triumphant, for I should do myself an irreparable injustice, did I not with candour acknowledge, I was both embarrassed and wholly at a loss for a sound reply, and evaded this poor fellow's question by drawing his attention to the cow, which was then looking down the hatchway, and as he had never seen any of the species before, it was a source of mirth and gratification to him.

By the time Beechey arrived in 1825, and Moerenhout in 1829, religious services had developed to the extent that the visitors wavered between boredom at their length and repetitiousness, and awe of what they were witnessing. How did this unlikely dispensation come to

143

pass? Especially as the adults were all, save John Adams, Polynesians in a strategic position to foster the tenets of their own faith, both because they were in the majority and because they were the mothers of the community?

Clearly suggested as the answer is the commanding stature of Adams on Pitcairn. His version, as related by Beechey, follows:

> Adams and Young were now the sole survivors out of the fifteen males that landed upon the island. They were both, and more particularly Young, of a serious turn of mind; and it would have been wonderful, after the many dreadful scenes at which they had assisted, if the solitude and tranquillity that ensued had not disposed them to repentance. During Christian's lifetime they had only once read the church service [Jenny(3) has it that Christian observed Sunday and divine service was read], but since his decease this had been regularly done on every Sunday. They now, however, resolved to have morning and evening family prayers, to add afternoon service to the duty of the Sabbath, and to train up their own children and those of their late unfortunate companions, in piety and virtue.
>
> In the execution of this resolution Young's education enabled him to be of the greatest assistance. . . . The loss of his last companion [Young] was a great affliction to him [Adams], and was for some time severely felt. It was a catastrophe, however, that more than ever disposed him to repentance, and determined him to execute the pious resolution he had made, in the hope of expiating his offences.

There is added a story that two vivid dreams of Adams, involving his past transgressions and the dire punishments that awaited him in hell, were motivating factors in his repentance and conversion.

The cause of Adams' conversion offered no difficulties to one school of thought: "But there can be only one simple and straightforward explanation of what took place, that it was the handiwork of the Almighty, whereby a sailor seasoned to crime came to himself in a far country and learnt and taught others to follow Christ."[4]

A variant suggestion has it that, "It is possible Adams began his exercises in the Scriptures as a mere refuge from the unaccustomed tedium of peace. Yet in the end they mastered him and overruled him. . . . They dominated him—overwhelmed him in a conviction of sin and a revelation of the way of salvation."[5]

Turning from the particular to the general, two observations may be relevant. The first comes from William James: "Were we writing the story of the mind from the purely natural history point of view . . .

we should still have to write down man's liability to sudden and complete conversion as one of his most curious peculiarities.''[6]

The second comes from a sailor who visited Pitcairn in the same year as Beechey, 1825: ''There are mysteries in Heaven, in the Earth, and in the Ocean, which move the Sage to meditate, the Poet to think, and the Fool to laugh; but they are alike, inscrutable to all.''[7]

Two very important pillars, representing the physical manifestation of the religion, supported the triumph of Christianity on Pitcairn. Both were drawn from the ship's library, that potent collection which was also responsible for the choice of Pitcairn as the home of the mutineers and their followers. One was a King James version of the Bible and the other a copy of the Book of Common Prayer. The Bible, after some vicissitudes, is now on Pitcairn, a cherished relic.

Adams, according to Rev. Murray,

> . . . observed the rules of the Church of England, always had morning and evening prayers, and taught the children the Collects, the Catechism, and other portions of the Prayer-book. He was very particular in hearing them say the Lord's Prayer and the Apostles' Creed. The youthful pupils took such delight in Adams' instructions, that on one occasion, on his offering to two of the lads, Arthur Quintal and Robert Young, some compensation for their labor in preparing ground for planting yams, they proposed, that, instead of his giving the present held out to them, consisting of a small quantity of gunpowder, he should teach them some extra lessons out of the Bible,—a request with which he joyfully complied.

The religious background of Adams must be guessed at from his workhouse upbringing, which undoubtedly exposed him to some of the rites and usages of the Church of England.* He had occasion to dredge arduously for these childhood memories. It is not surprising that his recollection or understanding faltered at times, or that he was inclined to extremes of biblical exegesis. Thus, the injunction to fast on Ash Wednesday and Good Friday became transmuted into the ordination of weekly Wednesday and Friday fasts, to the discomfort of his parishioners. It was only after the advent of Buffett in 1823

---

* Some instruction on this point is derived from the experience of Adams' fellow alumnus, Oliver Twist. Describing a meal at the poorhouse, Dickens says: ''The gruel was served out; a long grace was said over the short commons.'' Quite likely this was the source of Pitcairn emphasis on saying grace. Dickens describes other instances of religious instruction at Oliver Twist's ''home'' in a similarly kindly vein.

that he was "set straight" on this point, and even afterwards he continued his Friday fasts. One decision of the patriarch indicated a misconstruction of the prohibited degrees in marriage. Levitical laws, such as those requiring the abstention from unclean birds, were observed.

The devout attitudes and observances of the Pitcairners, admiringly reported to the outside world, invoked a wave of approval so forceful that it swept all the way back to the Island and intensified the piety or religiosity (depending on the particular commentator) of its inhabitants. What was reported from Pitcairn served as a dramatic argument in support of some of the most cherished tenets of both organized religious institutions and believing individuals. The Pitcairn Island story was the biblical tale of the fall and the redemption. Bad men (the mutineers) and bad women (the Polynesians) ate of the apple (unlicensed sex) and fell into discord and bestiality too horrendous to be more than hinted at.

When all seemed lost, the word of God appeared through the media of the ship's Bible and Prayer Book, relayed by a regenerated John Adams (the Island Moses), lone survivor of the bad men. This brought the little Pitcairn remnant to salvation. Thereupon it became transmuted into an idyllic community, where Christian precepts prevailed, sex was subdued into sanctioned channels, and harmony reigned. Here was living, flourishing proof of the efficacy of the Christian ethic and the salvation which lay in the Gospel and in religious attitudes and observances.

Small wonder that the Pitcairners should be led to increase the emphasis on piety by the heart-warming chorus of praise which reverberated from the mightiest nations of the world. The apogee was reached in an incident described by Captain Waldegrave. He arrived at Pitcairn in 1830 aboard a ship freighted with supplies, brought in somewhat tardy response to a plea by Captain Beechey. When Captain Waldegrave and his ship's chaplain were brought ashore, they were met by the Pitcairn women.

"I have brought you a clergyman," says the captain.

"God bless you," issued from every mouth, "but is he come to stay with us?"

"No."

"You bad man, why not?"

"I cannot spare him, he is the chaplain of my ship; but I have brought you clothes and other articles, which King George has sent you."

"But," says Kitty Quintal, "we want food for our souls."

At this point, even some of the admirers of Pitcairn piety began to draw the line, Barrow among them. On the side of the line furthest from admiration we find Montgomerie, over a century later, describing early Pitcairn religion as "a peculiarly nauseating brand of pietism . . . which would have seemed to Joseph Surface overdone and to Tartuffe inartistic." Montgomerie's interest in the question derived from his desire to rehabilitate the reputation of Captain Bligh, which he felt had suffered by reason of the adulation heaped upon the Pitcairners.

Of the possible impression "that a strong taint of sanctimony flavored all this hyperreligiosity," Shapiro says that it "seems justified by the actions and words of a few of the later islanders. . . . But at this period (1825), the islanders were still fresh in their contact with the world, and their devotions must be regarded as sincere and free from cant." Shapiro attributes any excesses to the "hyperbole showered upon them by their visitors for their simple and sincere faith. Pride in worship and eagerness to inspire a repetition of praise are an insidious pair of human traits."

The applause of the outside world was not confined to expressions of admiration. As early as 1819, the Society for Promoting Christian Knowledge, in response to a suggestion of Captain Staines, sent the Islanders a "small stock of religious books" by Captain Henderson of the "Hercules." The gift was accompanied by a letter which voiced a frequently expressed notion for utilizing the devout bent of the Islanders: "At some future time, perhaps not very far distant, you may find opportunities of imparting the knowledge which you acquire, to the natives of other islands, in which the name of Jesus Christ is not known; and may become blessed instruments in the hand of God for extending the kingdom of his Son our Lord." This hope was not to bear any fruit for some time.

In the middle of the nineteenth century the Pitcairners were to serve religious education far from home, if only by way of example. Says Dr. Shapiro: "At this time Sunday schools throughout the United States were glutted with tracts in which the lesson of Pitcairn was neatly pointed."

Religion on Pitcairn derived from Adams. Despite a very sketchy

147

background, he was sole authority and functionary until the arrival in 1823 of John Buffett, Pitcairn's first immigrant. Buffett was already conducting religious services at the time of Beechey's visit in 1825, apparently with Adams' full approval and collaboration. Nobbs, who was to become spiritual leader of the community until and after the exodus to Norfolk in 1856, arrived in November of 1828, and Adams died the following April.

Trader Moerenhout arrived at Pitcairn in early 1829 at a time when all three were still alive. Moerenhout, too, was strongly impressed with Adams, "depuis longtemps si justement célèbre en Europe," and recommended his name to "la dernière postérité." But he was strongly suspicious of Nobbs, even though he found him possessed of talent and a gentle nature. Where he had no question of Adams' sincerity, Nobbs struck him as affected and pharisaical, and he expressed the hope that the Pitcairners' evident faith in Nobbs was well-founded. He noted that rivalry between Nobbs and Buffett had resulted in separate services in different houses.

Moerenhout's faith in the sincerity of Pitcairn piety was clinched by an episode which took place when he was put to bed in the same room with some of the Islanders. After they thought him asleep, the elders woke everybody and said their prayers on their knees. "Quel peuple! J'étais vraiment dans un autre monde!"

The rivalry between Buffett and Nobbs culminated in the complete victory of the latter, most probably because of Nobbs' superior resources and forcefulness. He became a triple functionary in the roles of pastor, schoolteacher, and doctor, as well as taking over the Island Register. Whatever bitterness may have survived the contest with Buffett was diluted by the coming of the dictatorial Hill in 1832 and by Hill's successful efforts to exile all three previous immigrants, Buffett, Evans, and Nobbs. This pretender held sway over every aspect of Pitcairn life, including the religious, for several years. Despite his ability to effect revolutionary changes, he could not move his congregation in the direction of his own Wesleyan inclinations.

On the return of the exiles, Nobbs again took up his triple duties. His position as spiritual leader was sanctified when, through the good offices of Pitcairn's leading patron, Admiral Fairfax Moresby, he voyaged to England in 1852. In a little over a month Nobbs qualified for ordination as a deacon and priest by the Bishop of London, being described in the Letters of Order as "Chaplain of Pitcairn Island."

After being entertained by many notables, he was received by Queen Victoria herself, on presentation by Prince Albert. Loaded down with portraits of the royal family and a per annum of fifty pounds from the Society for the Propagation of the Gospel, Nobbs returned in triumph to Pitcairn in 1853. His position was now unshakably firm, though not immune to occasional sniping, at home and abroad, and survived the total removal of the Pitcairn Community to Norfolk. Nobbs died there in 1884.

The first emigrants to Norfolk who returned to Pitcairn in 1859, although only sixteen in number, continued religious observances, according to the 1860 report of Captain Montresor of H.M.S. "Calypso." "Mr. Arthy [Chaplain of the "Calypso"] questioned both the men and women as to their observance of religious duties, and ascertained that the children had been baptized when born, and that they had church service morning and evening on Sundays, besides daily morning and evening family prayers."[8]

In 1869, by which time twenty-seven more had returned, we find John Buffett, on a visit to Pitcairn from Norfolk, writing Admiral Moresby that, "Mr. Simon Young is school-master and pastor, and attends well to those duties." Simon Young, a "man of superior parts and with a high sense of social responsibility," fathered Rosalind Amelia, who authored *Mutiny of the Bounty and Story of Pitcairn Island, 1790–1894.*"

New seed which was to grow into a change in the theological allegiance of the Islanders arrived in 1876 in the form of a box of literature sent by elders of the Seventh Day Adventists.

The Islanders, who had developed a taste for religious tracts, nibbled at this theological fare suspiciously, their resistance weakened by the wealth of biblical citations offered to support the tenets of this new sect. But habit prevailed and nothing might have come of this overture had there not arrived on the scene, after a more than suitable interval of ten years, an emissary in the form of John I. Tay, Adventist communicant and seaman.

This gentleman, whose urge to reach Pitcairn is reminiscent of Nobbs, after many obstructions and working a passage to Tahiti as a carpenter, wangled a passage to Pitcairn on the British man-of-war "Pelican" in 1886, and was unanimously voted permission by the Islanders to stay until the next boat arrived. In the space of six weeks of instruction he won over a majority to his beliefs;[9] the minority averted a threat of schism by agreeing to join the new faith. A rearguard opposition which flared up after the departure of Tay was snuffed out at a meeting in March of 1887. The church recorder, Mary McCoy, noted: "The forms and prayer book of the Church of England laid aside. During the past week, meetings were held to organize our church services on Sabbath." (Sabbath meaning Saturday.)*

Pitcairn conversion to the Adventist sect caused varying reactions abroad. It was the genesis of the widespread Pacific Missions initiated by the Adventists. Excited by their conquest, they conceived the idea of a missionary ship. An "unseaworthy" boat, "Phoebe Chapman," purchased by Elder A. J. Cudney at Honolulu, with the intention of going to Pitcairn, was never heard of again after it sailed to pick up Tay at Honolulu. But Adventist Sabbath schools contributed pennies and chose the name "Pitcairn" for a vessel approximately the size of the "Bounty," built at Benicia, California, and launched in 1890. The "Pitcairn" arrived at its namesake island late in the year with six missionaries. Amidst religious and social celebrations, Pitcairn communicants were baptized in a rock-bound pool.

But, as the Pitcairners feared, the shift in religious allegiance did not escape criticism in the "mother" country. Adherents of the Church of England naturally regarded it as a matter for regret, and some of the more bitter were not above suggesting that advantage had been taken of the Islanders' lack of sophistication. Otherwise, how could they have been persuaded to trade their respected traditional faith for an upstart sectarianism without cachet?

Pitcairn survived this, as well as previous and subsequent criticism, and has remained generally faithful to the Adventist creed. In adopting Adventism, the Islanders took on, besides tenets which included belief in the imminent second coming of Christ and the concurrent beginning of the millenium, a Hebraic emphasis on Sabbatarian observance on Saturday and dietary prohibitions against pork and scaleless fish. The new creed further involved acceptance of the Bible as the only rule of faith and practice, the doctrines of

---

* Maude(4) points out the interesting circumstance that the Sabbath was celebrated on Saturday until 1814 by virtue of the fact that the "Bounty" proceeded by the Eastern route. The error was pointed out to John Adams by Staines in 1814. "Thus the only wholly Adventist society in the world was also the first to observe the Sabbath, if unwittingly."

salvation by faith, baptism by immersion, footwashing before communion, and tithing.

The "Pitcairn" returned in 1892 with Elder Gates, first of a number of Adventist emissaries to assume spiritual leadership of the community. That gentleman and his wife initiated a variety of activities, including a literary society, and a monthly handwritten newspaper.

Elder Gates departed in 1893, but there arrived in his place a young United States college graduate, Hattie Andre, who came to teach school. She started classes for adults and soon won the affection of the community. Her efforts were supplemented by those of Rosalind Amelia Young, native daughter of literary ambitions. Shapiro calls her "the best example of a type common in the Colony: a deeply religious nature schooled to a gentle and deprecating tolerance for the weaknesses of the less rigorously faithful members of the community."

The taking over of the Pitcairn school proved, in later years, during some of which the Adventists did not retain their pristine interest in Pitcairn, a source of some friction with British Government officials, who were sometimes critical of the standards of instruction. After the new school was built with stamp money in the 1940's, as part of the effected reorganization, it was agreed that the British Government assume responsibility for providing outlanders as teachers.

In 1954 the Islanders asked to allow control of the Church to be reinstated. Consent was conditioned on the provision of "a qualified teacher who would meet the needs of the local government," but nothing came of this, despite the eagerness of the Adventists to have a teacher who "cares . . . for those issues that mean so much to us."

Some notion of the Pitcairn Sabbatarian services as of 1934 is provided for us by Shapiro, who ran the complete gamut. The bell for Sabbath school rang at 7:30 A.M.

> There are two assembly rooms in the church, one on the ground floor and another identical in size and similar in decoration on the floor above. The Sabbath school service began as a general meeting held downstairs. . . . Practically every able-bodied man, woman, and child attended. The service commenced with hymns. A prayer was offered by Fred Christian, assistant elder. Fred is a Titan, with a voice which seems to well up from the bottom of his entire six feet six inches. In vibrant 'cello tones he uttered his prayer in the ever-moving and hypnotic words of the Old Testament. Then followed a reading by Fred from some

Seventh Day Adventist missionary literature. . . . This being the thirteenth Sabbath since the last missionary drive, he collected the sum of 8 pounds, 10 shillings. . . . I was astounded that a congregation of only about 178 poor islanders was able to roll up such a figure. . . . While the collection was being taken, the congregation sang a tune with the *andante* words "dropping, dropping, hear the pennies dropping," and ending with "every one for Jesus". . . .

After the collection had been taken, the congregation divided itself into five classes, each of which retired to its own accustomed place. Several gathered in opposite corners of the upstairs meeting room. One went outdoors for its lessons. . . . Eleven o'clock services . . . were in the upstairs room and were principally attended by adults, though there was a good sprinkling of children. As before, the meeting began with hymns, then a passage was read from the Scriptures. After Roy had finished his reading, he called on five of us, among them myself, to rise and read designated verses. . . .

Roy, being the elected elder, now proceeded to deliver his text and his sermon, based on the significance of the communion which was about to be taken. The lack of professionalism lent an air of sincerity and devotion to the preacher who acquitted himself acceptably. After the services two young men went forward to receive trays of biscuits which were passed around, then a native wine poured into tiny glasses was distributed. . . ."

Following was the foot-washing ceremony,

. . . the symbol of humility. It was done in utmost seriousness. It was deeply impressive. . . . Then back again to another prayer, more hymns, and dismissal. . . . At 3:30 in the afternoon there was another service— the young people's—which was a repetition of the earlier ones. . . . Family prayers followed [supper] . . . the bell rang again—7:30 and time to attend the church business meeting. . . . As usual the session opened with the singing of a hymn. No gathering of Pitcairners is decent without the chanting of a hymn."

Then followed a reading of reports, votes, and a discussion of changing the Sabbath school hour and other matters. As can be seen from this description, despite the adoption of a new creed, Sabbath services had not diminished notably on Pitcairn since they had astonished Beechey more than a century before.

Seventh Day Adventism, whatever the reaction of outlanders, proved particularly congenial to the Pitcairn Community, according to the testimony of more than one observer. James Norman Hall, who complained after his brief withdrawn visit in 1933 of "the atmosphere of primitive evangelicism," was in the distinct minority. Thus, the outgoing Johnsons, who visited Pitcairn for extended periods over a term of twenty-one years, reported:

> Pitcairn seems only to have benefited from their [the missionaries'] influence. The straightforward simplicity and the definite discriminations between right and wrong of this faith fit very readily into a primitive, unworldly community. . . . But though we had to smile at some of these customs [religious and other practices], the general advantages of Seventh Day Adventism as practiced on Pitcairn are very great. Their faith and their consequent attitude of kindness, temperance and peacefulness can only be admired. The people are absolutely sincere and conscientious.

And Ferdon acutely observes that, "If there is a focal point that brings and holds the Islanders together, it is their religion."

A judicious appraisal is that of Mr. Maude(4), entitled to especial weight both because of his incomparable knowledge of Pitcairn history and his lengthy personal contact with life on the Island:

> On balance Adventism has probably proved a benefit to the Islanders by providing new motivations and interests, increasing community cohesion and adding a much-needed feeling of consequence. The exacting demands made by the new faith have, however, resulted in constant backsliding on the part of individuals and, as a result, in the growth of double standards of profession and conduct. The effect of the change on personal character and morals has, therefore, been marked only in the case of the few.*

Evidence of the sincerity of the modern Pitcairners' faith is both abundant and impressive. Their close observance of its tenets involves not merely the practice of rituals; it requires many material sacrifices. Dietary restrictions eliminated the most important source of meat— pork—as well as many forms of seafood previously enjoyed. The Sabbatarian restrictions on labor frequently proved galling, as when, on one of their all-important trips to gather miro wood in the Johnsons' "Yankee," unfavorable winds landed them at Henderson Island on the Sabbath. The Pitcairners chose to return without the coveted wood rather than cut and load it on the Sabbath. When the arrival of a ship, a red-letter event in Island life, falls on a Saturday, the Pitcairners forego the keenly-anticipated opportunity to trade, although they go out to the vessel and give some fruit away. This unfortunate coincidence occurred fourteen times in 1956.

---

* The same objection, of course, might be raised to some extent to most religions which are not permissive.

Pitcairn Island

There can be few societies where religion has played a more central and important role than on Pitcairn. Religion provided a community shattered by lawlessness with a standard of conduct conducive to survival in place of threatened annihilation. It created a strong unifying force and replaced savagery and the rule of force with order and a standard of value. It gave the Islanders, after their existence was discovered, a fruitful bond with the outside world. And it became the basis and focus of the social life of the community.

If believers have found in the Pitcairn experience compelling evidence of the power of God and the efficacy of His word and message, who can gainsay their right to so read its testimony? What could be more natural for them than to hear in the story the echo of biblical parable?

⚜ MORALS ⚜

CHASTITY

Next to the flourishing of religion, the aspect of Pitcairn life which particularly captured the first visitors and the outside world was the high morality of these descendants of "pirates, mutineers, and murderers" and, it might be added, of loose-living Polynesian women. Morality, in this context, is to be equated largely with sexual chastity.

As early as 1814, we find Adams boasting well, if not wisely, to Captain Pipon that

> . . . not one instance of debauchery or immoral conduct had occurred among these young people, since their settlement on the island; nor did he ever hear, or believe, that any one instance had occurred of a young woman having suffered indecent liberties to be taken with her. Their native modesty, assisted by the precepts of religion and morality, instilled into their young minds by John Adams, had hitherto preserved these interesting people from every kind of debauchery.*

This represented a startling contrast to the first decade of the community, when promiscuity was perhaps closer to the norm.

Failing any Island Kinsey (a lack partially remedied by Dr.

* The same claim had been made to Folger in 1808, according to Delano.

154

Shapiro in 1934), we are left to speculation on the veracity of Adams' boast. Skepticism may draw support from explorations made, for example, in the field of the vaunted strict morality of the Puritans and Victorians. But the early visitors to Pitcairn had no difficulty in accepting the claim of sexual immaculacy, reporting that the young women's "manners and demeanour exhibited a degree of modesty and bashfulness, that would have done honour to the most virtuous and enlightened people on earth."

Whatever the situation before 1814, the record thereafter indicates that perfect chastity was not to be a permanent condition. Ironically, the first transgression reported (by Captain Henry King of the "Elizabeth," who visited Pitcairn early in 1819) involved Adams' own daughter, Diana, who had already borne a son to Edward Quintal without benefit of matrimony. Adams had forbidden them to marry, but was persuaded by Captain King, "after a great deal of conversation upon the subject," to permit the union to be sanctified.

John Buffett, Pitcairn's first immigrant in 1823, despite his marriage, his religious bent, and his position as school teacher, managed to father two children out of wedlock.

Another recorded instance of seduction in the 1820s involves Jane Quintal, who succumbed to the blandishments of an English ship captain and left Pitcairn in 1826, never to return. As Moerenhout tells the story, she followed her lover to Tahiti, where she clung to him despite his obvious desire to abandon her. The awful result was that he brutally forced her ashore at Rurutu, "alone and pregnant." But the story did not follow the usual Victorian scenario. Jane married a native of Rurutu because the missionaries were "so very particular.
. . . I could not talk to any male creature when single, so I got married."[10] She had no desire to return to Pitcairn, which she claimed to have left because it was too small and had too few eligible males. Apparently she was not too unhappy with life on Rurutu.

Nobbs, who arrived at Pitcairn in 1828, either found a snake in the Pitcairn Eden or introduced it by fiat. Roared Barrow, all the way from England,

> . . . this man [Nobbs] has already thrust upon them what he calls a code of laws, in which he enumerates crimes, such as murder and adultery, unknown and unheard of among these simple people since the time that Adams was sole legislator and patriarch. The punishment of adultery, to give a specimen of Nobb's legislation, is whipping for the

first offence to both parties, and marriage within three months; for the second, if the parties refuse to marry, the penalties are, forfeiture of lands, property, and banishment from the island. . . . It is quite clear this silly person does not understand what is meant by adultery.

The short-lived Tahitian exodus in 1831 revealed that the vaunted virtue of the Pitcairners, like some delicate wine, did not travel well. Most of the chroniclers throw a kindly veil over the Tahitian episode, suggesting that it was revulsion to, rather than participation in, the unashamedly flaunted Polynesian fleshpots that was the source of the Islanders' disenchantment with "the land of the Golden Haze." But reports based on visits made after return of the Pitcairners indicated a noticeable deterioration of morality, continuing as late as 1834.

Whaling surgeon Bennett, who arrived at Pitcairn in March of 1834, at the height of the dissension created by Hill's thrust to dictatorship, though he noted some restoration from the injurious effects of the stay at Tahiti, found Pitcairn morals at a low ebb, evidenced by the "restless and dissatisfied state of many amongst them, as well as in a licentiousness of discourse . . . vices of a very deep dye were hinted at in their mutual recriminations." Matters seem to have improved after the banishment of Hill. Had they not, the increasing traffic with whalers would have put an end to the Pitcairn tradition of chastity.

The whalers with their hard-bitten and sex-starved crews presented a real threat to the chastity of Pitcairn women. It would not be difficult to envisage Pitcairn being turned into a brothel, as were other Pacific islands, unless there was a considerable restoration of shattered Island morals. This disaster was avoided, most probably by the combination of Pitcairn's reputation and the surprising delicacy of the whaling captains, most of them New Englanders. The latter frequently admonished their crews against any transgressions with the "innocent" Islanders.*

---

* An interesting, if somewhat enigmatic, sidelight on this problem derives from Whaler Captain King's visit in 1819, long before the Tahitian migration. "In the evening, after supper, they entertained us with an Otaheitian dance, which consisted of various writhings and distortions of the body, by no means obscene, yet in no respect pleasant. While some were dancing, the rest sat down to look on, in company with six sailors belonging to the ship, when suddenly one of the young women jumped up and ran to her brother, saying, 'she would not sit any longer near that naughty man (pointing to one of my sailors), for he wanted her to commit fornication.' I asked the man why he behaved so rude to people that had treated him so well. He told me that it was by mere accident he put his foot against hers, and that he had never spoken to her.''

That the Islanders did not escape wholly unscathed is indicated by an incident which involved part of "the ruffian crew of a whale ship on shore for a fortnight, during which time they offered every insult to the inhabitants, and threatened to violate any woman whose protectors they could overcome by force." Fortunately, this episode was not typical.

After the return of part of the Pitcairn Colony from Norfolk in the 1850s, the record offers few indications of the trend of Pitcairn morals until the report of Captain Doughty, H.M.S. "Constance," in 1884, that he had "no reason for believing they have departed from the laws of that adhesion to propriety with which they have ever been accredited." But by 1898 Judicial Commissioner Hamilton Hunter was describing the Pitcairners as "lax in morals" and relaying the plaint of McCoy, president of the governing body, "that things were not as they used to be," a complaint buttressed by reference to "the large number of illegitimate births on the Island." Be it noted, in passing, that this complaint that morals were not "as they used to be" reechoed through the decades which followed Adams' prideful boast of immaculacy in Pitcairn's "golden age." It need hardly be added that this dolorous cry from the remote rock was part of a chorus that encircled the globe, in many instances dating back hundreds and thousands of years before the Pitcairn Colony was founded.

These lamentations reached their apogee around the turn of the century (roughly 1893 to 1913) in official reports and correspondence which, besides indicating a general deterioration of moral and intellectual fiber and increasing criminality, made frequent reference to sexual immorality in general, unsupported by statistical data or analysis, but bulwarked by reference to specific offenses such as a case of sodomy, an illegal operation on a girl of fifteen, and increasing bastardy.[11]

Assessment of these reports presents almost insuperable difficulties. Taken at face value, some of them would indicate that, not only had the snake entered the garden, it was threatening to swallow it. Many factors support skepticism in evaluating these reports. They were in part colored by the prevalent folk belief in degeneration as a necessary consequence of inbreeding; they were not infrequently based on very hurried visits and on hearsay; they were at times interspersed with countervailing notes; and they applied standards more theoretical than realized even in the European middle class experience used as a yardstick.

Nevertheless, it is impossible to escape the conclusion that sexual morality on Pitcairn, however it might compare with that of the West, if valid statistics were available, had reached a very low point. From this nadir, the record suggests some very gradual rise, but Pitcairn was never again to even approach its pristine image of chastity. The critical might say it had "reverted" to a Polynesian level, the sympathetic that it had joined the mainstream of Western sexual mores.

In 1934 Dr. Shapiro combed the Island records and supplemented these efforts with oral revelations from the Islanders to arrive at some notion of the extent of illegitimacy. (Illegitimacy does not, of course, equate with the level of unlicensed sexual activity, but admits of some connection.) After indicating acceptance in large part of the claims of innocence in the early days of the Colony, Professor Shapiro remarks that

> A noticeable change has affected the sex morality of the community. The days when the virtue and chastity of Pitcairn women were recognized as inviolable by the hard-boiled crews of whaling ships have disappeared. Illegitimacy in the early part of the nineteenth century was unknown except in a couple of instances. All this has changed in the last fifty years. Practically 25 per cent of births at present are illegitimate and a considerable number of the permanent unions are not legitimatized, even though they may have produced large broods of children. . . . It is to some extent a distortion to consider some of these births illegitimate even when the parents have not been legally married. Extra-legal unions, as permanent as the legal variety, have been contracted, and are regarded as just as binding in the eyes of the community. Such marriages might well be considered as an expression of a community change in procedure and not as evidence of an alteration in attitude toward sex. But besides these respectably "illegal" matings there are many examples of a roving taste in sex relationships. The older members of the community are well aware of the change occurring among the younger people, and they lament the breakdown of the older *mores* in terms that seem very familiar. Not even Pitcairn has escaped the problem of the "younger generation."

A report based on hearsay, acquired on a visit a decade later than Shapiro's, indicates that at that time Pitcairn had thirty unmarried men as against only four eligible girls.* "What we call 'immorality'"

---

* This is a reversal of the situation earlier in the century, when part of the blame for alleged immorality was laid at the door of an excess of unmarried women. Figures for 1966 have the eligible women outnumbering the male prospects.

is definitely on the increase . . . there are so many more men than women that some of the former are beginning to encroach upon the domestic preserves of the others.''[12] Three illegitimate children had arrived within a two-year period. But this very report quotes a "missionary minister" as saying, ''Yet on the whole the moral standard of Pitcairn, like the physical and mental, is probably as high as in any other community anything like ours.''

The claims for Pitcairn chastity have altered (possibly more radically than the actual sexual habits). Now the assertion is that Pitcairn is no worse than other societies. Whether the alleged deterioration of morals is attributable to any particular cause or may be regarded as an inevitable return to a more "normal" level of unsanctioned sexual practices is a question unlikely to be answered conclusively.

MARRIAGE

In describing the original Pitcairn ménage, the literature frequently refers to the women as "wives" of the mutineers. No wedding ceremonies are mentioned and none can be postulated. We can only guess at how these representatives of two diverse civilizations regarded their pairing.

Whatever their original notion, the birth of children and the looming question of land inheritance must have inclined the mutineers to equate their matings with Western concepts of marriage.[13] From unpropertied sailors on the prowl, they had been transformed into landed proprietors and, in some cases, into patresfamilias. Other times, other manners.

The pattern of monogamy (polyandry in the case of two of the three women allotted to the six Polynesian men) was shattered with the extermination of eleven of the original fifteen males. The surviving four, McCoy, Quintal, Young, and Adams, divided the ten remaining women among them. There is reason to suspect that they were not always scrupulous about observing the lines of this division.

When Adams became the lone adult male and leader of the community in 1800, his "regeneration" insured the predominance of the Western view of the marriage institution. The question remained academic for the short interval until the first Island-born generation reached puberty. Adams then opposed early marriage on the ground that motherhood removed the bride from productive labor in the fields. The age requirements were eighteen for the women and twenty for the men, and biblical prohibitions of incest were to be observed. Nonetheless, there were several "under age" marriages even in the first generation, and it would have been impossible to avoid for long an increasing amount of inbreeding without the importation of considerable outlander blood.

Adams carried his prejudices to the extent of refusing his own daughter Diana permission to marry for some eighteen months after she had produced a child, when he was persuaded to sanction the union by visiting Captain King in 1819. He also separated a married couple on the ground that their relationship was within the prohibited degrees, although it is not clear how he arrived at this seemingly insupportable conclusion. (See p. 172.)

The weddings to which Adams agreed were marked by a ceremony derived from the liturgy of the Anglican Church and a gold ring was used which had belonged to Edward Young. Adams evinced his faith in the virtue of the nuptial rite in 1825 by having Captain Beechey wed him to his now aged spouse of many years, Teio (Mary). Beechey also cut a Gordian knot by releasing Polly Young from an oath, since regretted, that she would *never* marry George Adams. With the wisdom of a Solomon he judged the vow null and void because it had been made before Polly's judgment was mature.

The abnormal age structure created by the peculiar early history of Pitcairn produced some unusual marriages. Thus, Thursday October Christian, first-born of the Colony, married Teraura (Susannah), widow of Edward Young, who was his senior by fifteen or more years and possibly twice his age at the time of marriage. His only full brother, Charles, married Sarah, the daughter of Teio, who had been brought to Pitcairn as an infant, but here the discrepancy in age was not so dramatic.

An amusing story comes from Rosalind Young concerning the courtship of John Evans, who jumped ship at Pitcairn in 1823 at the tender age of eighteen or nineteen. When he applied for the hand of John Adams' daughter Rachel, a maiden in her thirties, that patriarch offered the obvious objection. "However, the matter was referred to the daughter for decision. Her answer came, quick, short, and decided, 'Try it, daddy.' He at length consented. . . ."

160

The imbalance of men and women of eligible age was to plague Pitcairn at intervals long after the early days. The composition of the parties which returned from Norfolk in 1859 and 1864 to resettle Pitcairn provided a notable example. Of the total of forty-three who began a third Pitcairn community, there were six married couples, two widowed grandmothers, and twenty-nine children of assorted ages—preponderantly girls. The consequence, according to Maude(4), was that in the latter part of the nineteenth century "many of the surplus Island women were taken as mission helpers to Fiji, Samoa, Tonga and other Pacific Islands, and even as far afield as Australia and the United States." A reverse situation marked the 1940s when a scarcity of eligible women led to charges of "poaching" and proved a cause for concern.

Legal prohibition of marriage to outlanders followed an attempt by a shipwrecked sailor from the "Acadia" in 1881 to "cut out" a suitor betrothed to an Island girl. Later the law was changed to permit marriage with "strangers" whose admission was deemed beneficial. Islanders who married while abroad were permitted to bring their spouses back to Pitcairn. Curiously, no legal provision was made for divorce, and incompatible couples were forced to their own stratagems to effect separation, until recent years, when divorce became possible by resort to the Supreme Court of Fiji.

The failure of ceremonized marriage to become the universal practice has been discussed in the preceding chapter. Pitcairn, like the western world, developed the patterns of "common law marriage" and of totally unsanctioned matings, and the consequent problem of "illegitimacy." The Pitcairn experience with the venerable institution of marriage offers little in the way of novelty or instruction to the western world.

CRIME

The leading element in the original Pitcairn settlement, the mutineers, might themselves be considered criminals or outlaws. They adopted no criminal code. The definition and punishment of "crime" was largely on a catch-as-catch-can basis. The first reported "crimes" were the carrying off of a pig by Manarii and some yams by Teiuma, for which they received sound beatings. These "thefts" may reflect as much on the harshness and parsimony of the mutineers as on the Polynesian aptitude for appropriating what was needful.

The carnage which marked the first decade of the Colony would probably have occurred in the teeth of the most elaborate criminal code that could be devised. The reprisals and counter-reprisals were unsanctioned by law and no legal punishment was ever applied, nor was law operative in the ''war between the sexes'' which ended in a truce.

From this era of near anarchy, survivor Adams emerged as the law on Pitcairn Island. With him, too, the law was largely an *ad hoc* proposition. In an era when the major portion of the population consisted of young children, all regarding Adams as father, there would have been little need for a criminal code. As the children grew older and sex became a factor, new problems arose. Thus, confronted by the fact that his daughter Diana ''had committed an offence against the laws of God'' (produced a bastard), Adams was prevented from imposing the death penalty only by public dissent, if his own account to Captain King is to be trusted. (See p. 172.)

Seduction of an Island girl by Buffett went unpunished until the advent of Hill some five or six years later. A similar offense by a visiting sea captain, involving Jane Quintal, was likewise unpunished. He was beyond the reach of Island justice, even had there been any inclination to impose punishment. But crime remained an insignificant feature of the Pitcairn landscape—at least until the arrival of Nobbs in 1828.

As he consolidated his status, Nobbs added the role of lawgiver to his many other functions. Before long he drew up a list of punishments for theft, murder, removing a landmark, and fornication (which he miscalled ''adultery''). Provision was made for a trial of offenders before a bench of three elders.[14]

Even this revolutionary change was to appear as nothing when Hill became czar of Pitcairn. He concocted an elaborate governmental structure, artfully designed to enable him to buy and keep allies by appointing them to numerous offices with imposing titles, such as Chief Elder, Elder, Sub-Elder, Cadet, and Privy Counsel, reserving for himself the title of President.

Under pretense of legality, he imposed and had executed *ad hoc* punishments for whatever displeased him, whether it was unfavorable gossip relayed to him or the indiscretion of Buffett which antedated

162

Hill's arrival. Punishment took the form of publicly-administered floggings, exile, and the calling down of the wrath of God during devotions.

Hill's earnestness was underlined by the building of Pitcairn's first jail, so that sentences of imprisonment could be enforced. Hill's fixation on punishment caused him to come a cropper when an attempt to penalize Arthur Quintal's daughter for stealing yams was met with stout physical resistance by her father. This shattered Hill's authority.

The code of laws drawn up by Captain Elliott, at the instigation of the Islanders, in 1838, a year after Hill's removal, placed little emphasis on common criminal offenses. The code which Brodie found in existence in 1850 provided fines for such offenses as a dog chasing a goat, killing a cat, procurement of liquor from a vessel, and losing the public anvil, but ignored most of the felonies and misdemeanors recognized by Anglo-Saxon law. One provision of special interest prohibited "bringing up things that are past to criminate others, with a view to prevent justice with the case before the Magistrate." In short, the plea of "You're another" was interdicted.

Omissions were rectified by provisions added to meet contingencies not provided for in the code, sometimes with amusing ineptitude. Thus, one law provided that "no two persons of different sex are permitted to lie in bed or have any such unlawful connection." The tailored-to-measure nature of some of these supplements to the catalogue of crime indicates the actual, rather than merely potential, existence of the offenses defined therein. As reported by Captain F. P. Doughty after a visit in 1884, these offenses included bastardy, uttering of profane and obscene language, assault, slander, manufacturing false reports, and insulting the Magistrate and questioning court decisions.

Further indications that Pitcairn had rediscovered sin comes from the criminal code revised during the reorganization of Pitcairn government, which followed a conference with Captain Rookes of H.M.S. "Champion" in 1893. This code provided punishment for adultery, fornication, wife beating, conduct prejudicial to morals, cruelty, contempt of court, threatening another's life, carrying concealed weapons, misuse of drugs, and peeping at bathing women.

Later reports reinforce the suggestions of increasing criminality. A climax was reached in 1897 when a man brutally murdered his wife

163

and child to make possible his marriage to another woman. Prompt punishment was administered with the assistance of a Judicial Commissioner sent from Fiji. But the subsequent report in 1908 of the Government Secretary indicated little improvement in the first decade of the twentieth century. "Crime is of frequent occurrence; of Law there is almost none, every man does practically as he sees fit—while the idea of restraint in any form, is abhorrent to them."

Improvement of the situation is indicated by official reports of 1921 and 1937. During Dr. Shapiro's ten-day visit in 1934, he noted that the prison built by the community remained untenanted most of the time, although it had one occupant during his stay, held on a charge of wife-beating, "a prisoner only in the loosest sense of the term." Imprisonment was onerous for the community; parole was a frequent substitute.

Little evidence of major criminal activity emerges from the record of the second quarter of the twentieth century, although such matters as bastardy continued to be troublesome. Even were statistics of crime available,* we should be faced with the usual difficulties in equating them with criminal activity. But the record indicates that problems in the administration of law, criminal and civil, were compounded by lack of professional competence in the Island court, by the fact that parties were likely to consider themselves "as good as" the court, and by the fact that enforcement was frequently awkward.

ALCOHOL

The "Bounty" was well supplied with rum and other spirits when she set out from England, as might be expected, even if the record did not make it clear. In addition to the rum required for that Navy indispensable, the daily grog ration, there were the private stocks of Captain Bligh and Surgeon Huggan. The latter's store must have been prodigious to outlive his thirst, which expired with the surgeon at Tahiti.

How much of this treasure survived the demands of the seventeen months preceding the mutiny, the hard drinking which followed the

---

* Some statistics are available for the period 1956 to 1962. In that time, the Island Court tried eighteen cases and convicted twelve offenders, of whom three were imprisoned. Principal offenses were abusive language, assault, and trespass.

mutiny, the Tahiti split-up, and the subsequent wanderings of the vessel, to be salvaged for the Pitcairn landing, is uncertain. There was probably some, but not nearly enough to meet the demands of daily consumption, rationed or unrationed, for very long. The involuntary ''climb on the wagon'' which followed exhaustion of the remaining spirits must have been one of the more trying aspects of their exile for habitual drinkers like the mutineers.

Some were unwilling to surrender to this dreadful drought without stubborn resistance. McCoy, combining his distillery experience, the seemingly innocent ti root (which developed a similar history in Hawaii), and Quintal's kettle, demonstrated anew that necessity is the mother of invention. He arrived at a distillation of awesome potency which was to play a leading part in the reign of terror and brutality that marked the first decade of the settlement. The date assigned this historic event is April 20, 1798.*

Apparently the sailors, accustomed to limited daily grog rations and a very occasional spree on shore, were unable to introduce discipline and limits into their consumption of this formidable concoction. The result was that they were frequently reduced to subhuman levels by its staggering effects, and committed acts of senseless violence and cruelty with the tragic results already noted. Indeed, McCoy himself, the author of this notable contribution to the arsenal of spirits,† was so heedless of the fearsome nature of his own product that he succumbed to delirium tremens and threw himself over a cliff, achieving a destiny beyond temptation.

McCoy's ''melancholy fate . . . created so forcible an impression on the remaining few, that they resolved never again to touch spirits.'' This noble resolution, like many efforts in the outside world to control the problem of alcohol, was to thread early Pitcairn history like a cross-stitch, that is to say, go in and out. Unlike the outside world, it was to achieve notable success in later days.

Beechey was convinced that Adams kept the pledge to the day of his death, but the record contains many contrary suggestions. Captain King reported that after he secured Adams' permission in 1819 for the

---

* Jenny(1) indicates that Young had taught the art long before this date, and this indication is corroborated by her statement that Manarii was ''inflamed with drinking the raw new spirit they distilled'' when he shot Temua in 1793.

† Maude(4): ''No doubt 'the Real McCoy' was a particularly villainous beverage; correctly speaking, it was a brandy, though it has been called both whisky and rum.''

marriage of Adams' daughter Diana to Edward Quintal, father of her child, "I now gave him some porter, wine, and spirits to regale themselves with at the wedding." The generous captain records no protest.

If the Pitcairners had even temporarily bested the Demon Rum, they became reacquainted with this malevolent fellow during their short-lived exodus to Tahiti in 1831. Captain Freemantle, reporting the condition of the Colony after its repatriation, found it "much altered for the worse, having, since their return, indulged in intemperance to a great degree, distilling a spirit from the tee root, which grows in great quantities on the island."

The problem of alcohol was very much alive at the time of Captain Freemantle's visit in 1833. As Hill told the story to the captain, when Hill arrived some four or five months previously on a Sunday, he had found most of the Islanders intoxicated, and Nobbs so drunk he could not perform his pastoral duties. Hill immediately formed a temperance society as part of his campaign against Nobbs, Buffett, and Evans for domination of the Island. It was because of Hill's fight against John Barleycorn, Hill "having broken up their stills," that Captain Freemantle "gave him all the assistance in my power to support him in his mission."

Hill told Freemantle that Nobbs was habitually drunk, a charge which the captain apparently accepted, despite a seeming distrust of Hill.

Nobbs' version, significantly, contains no categorical denial of indulgence. It is interesting for several reasons, including its strong suggestion that the distillation and consumption of spirits had never ceased on Pitcairn.

Said Nobbs, in a petition protesting his treatment by Hill:

> A short time after our return to Pitcairn's Island, some of the natives [Edward Quintal, William Young, and Fletcher Christian], determined to recommence distilling rum—*a practice they had been accustomed to in John Adams's time.* [Italics supplied.] Your petitioner remonstrated with them on the impropriety of their conduct, but to no purpose; the answer they gave to your petitioner's advice was, "We are our own masters; we shall do as we like; no one shall control us." Many times your petitioner talked with them, and begged them to desist from distilling spirits; but your petitioner always received abuse in return, and twice narrowly escaped a beating from Edward Quintal. . . . Capt. Freemantle informed [the Pitcairners] that he . . . came on shore with

the intention of removing Mr. Hill from the island; but, on hearing that your petitioner had partaken of the spirits distilled by the natives, he, [Capt. F.] informed your petitioner that he could not reinstate him in the situation of which Mr. Hill had deprived him.

Whether as a result of Hill's campaign or because the Islanders had witnessed so many instances of the murderous potential of alcohol in their situation, prejudices against its use on Pitcairn survived Hill's banishment. The necessity for control was accentuated by the growing intercourse with whalers in the second quarter of the nineteenth century. Legislation forbade the bringing of spirits on land, save for medicinal purposes, and the sale of spirits on shore. The law was later modified to permit "Other residents and foreigners . . . to . . . import sufficient for their personal use with the written sanction of the Chief Magistrate."

Island intolerance to alcohol was reinforced by religious sanction when the Colony was converted in 1886 to the tenets of Seventh Day Adventism.

Dr. Shapiro's report, on the basis of his 1934 visit, indicates that this prejudice was extended beyond alcohol. "Even to this day the islanders abhor intoxicants. None were to be seen, and no one privately dropped a word that a wee drop might be good for the health. As a matter of fact, the islanders are as abstemious in respect to drink as to food. The standard bearers of the community disapprove of coffee and tea, confining themselves instead to pure water or 'tea' steeped from bran husks." This observation has been confirmed by later visitors.

The Pitcairn experience indicates that, at least under special circumstances, it is possible for a community to eliminate the hazard which our most highly-developed societies have been unable to hurdle.

CHARITY

The Pitcairners won a greater reputation as recipients of charity than as givers, but their material contributions, internal and external, to benevolent purposes were notable, especially when considered in the light of their limited resources.

An early effort to mitigate the vagaries of fortune among the Islanders is indicated by Beechey. "There was also a mutual accommodation amongst them in regard to provisions, of which a regular account was taken. If one person was successful in hunting, he lent the others as much meat as they required, to be repaid at leisure; and the same occurred with yams, taros, etc., so that they lived in a very domestic and tranquil state.''

We are given no indication of what resulted when repayment was not forthcoming, but it seems plausible that many transactions initiated in the guise of business transactions wound up as charitable contributions.

The scarcity of money on Pitcairn (Island produce was generally traded with touching ships for other commodities rather than money) in the first century of Island history precluded cash contributions to charity. But the Pitcairners not infrequently shared what they had with outlanders without prospect or actuality of reward, in some instances at heavy expense to themselves. Nobbs and his sick companion, Bunker, were taken in and fed (the latter was nursed as well) despite grave suspicions of both. Brodie and his four fellow passengers, stranded on Pitcairn for more than two weeks, were treated in a manner that evoked high tribute: ''Thrown thus upon the hospitality of the islanders, avowedly destitute . . . we were not only received with the most cordial welcome, but treated with a prevenance of attention (the offspring of natural politeness) which could not have been exceeded in the most polished European society. . . .''

More taxing yet were the occasions when Pitcairners were invaded by shipwrecked sailors in burdensome numbers. One notable incident of 1875 involved a 51-day invasion by shipwrecked mariners of the ''Khandeish.'' External charity was exhibited also in incidents when Pitcairners came to the aid of vessels in distress, in one case working long and arduously for a ''thank you.'' (See page 199.)

The conversion of the Pitcairners in 1886 to Seventh Day Adventism and the increasing availability of money expanded the role of charity in the Community. Their new Church placed emphasis on tithing, and tithes became as much a feature of Island life as taxes in other communities.

Elder Gates,[15] the first missionary of the Seventh Day Adventist Church to serve on Pitcairn, in 1892, introduced tithing and the tithe barn, with the injunction to ''see if the Lord will not devise a plan for marketing your tithe products.'' Every tenth coconut tree was marked ''L.X.'' to represent the Lord's Tenth. The tithe barn

suffered as a fund-raising device from the erratic nature of ships'
visits, resulting not infrequently in the rotting of produce placed
therein, but the growth of the curio trade made it possible for the
Pitcairners to increase their charitable contributions. Elder Gates
was able, years later, to note with pride that cash and produce provided $740.83 in tithe offerings in 1920, and $1,014.18 in 1921.

In addition, the Pitcairn Church made the following offerings
during the year 1921:

> To the China Famine Relief—8 pounds.
> To Queen Mary's Limbless Hospital—4 pounds, 10 shillings.
> To India School Building Fund—2 pounds.
> To England "Save the Children" Fund—11 pounds.
> For the Naked Poor of Europe—13 pounds, 10 shillings.

By 1937 we find Mr. Neill complaining that the Islanders were

> . . . neglecting the education of their own children and paying more
> than they can afford for work in the mission field. The position is diffi-
> cult, as the payment of tithe and free-will offering, apart from being
> a matter of faith, appeals to the Pitcairners. [It is] traditional for the
> Pitcairners to expect things to be done for them while at the same time
> they make contributions . . . for the advancement in other parts of the
> Pacific of the work of the mission to which they adhere.[16]

The official reports and correspondence for the last decade of the
nineteenth and first two decades of the twentieth century are marked
by frequent criticism of Island reliance on the charity of passing ships
and outlanders, and its deteriorating effect.

A kindlier attitude is voiced by Sir Cecil Rodwell in his official
report of a 1921 visit:

> Equally unjust is the term "beggars of the Pacific," which I have more
> than once heard applied to the people of Pitcairn. Where charity is
> concerned they are self-respecting and even sensitive. Their chief am-
> bition is to find opportunities of earning a little money with which to
> buy essential commodities. And, considering their limited means and
> the scarcity of cash on the island, they are generous contributors to
> charity themselves: in recent months they have sent several small con-
> tributions to various objects, including the Chinese Famine Fund, and
> I have with me a sum of 11 pounds for the "Save the Children" Fund,
> which they asked me to convey.[17]

A passenger on a touching steamer of this era noted with awe and
admiration a contribution of 20 pounds for the Missionary Society
entrusted by the Pitcairners to the captain of his ship. ''This from the

people with such scanty store, the people almost forgotten by the world, who might well have been excused had they the world forgot."[18]

In the next decade, Shapiro was "rather hot," but "astounded that a congregation of only about 178 poor islanders were able to roll up" the sum of 8 pounds, 10 shillings as a "Sabbath offering" in response to a plea for funds to help build a boat for missionaries laboring in Melanesia.

In the field of charity, the Pitcairners may be said to have enjoyed the worst of two possible worlds; they were criticized both for receiving too much and for giving too much. They managed to survive both criticisms.

HARMONY[19]

Pitcairn's strongest claim to the Arcadian state arose from the superlative harmony repeatedly reported as prevailing. The bloody history of the first decade indicates that, contrary to what might be anticipated, harmony was not indispensable to survival, even on this tiny "rock." Despite wholesale slaughter of the original males, by the time Folger discovered the settlement eighteen years after it was initiated, the population had increased from twenty-eight to thirty-five. This accords with world experience, marked thus far by the astonishing ability of the human race to outlive, or to coexist with, its own follies.

Special factors worked toward the establishment of harmony when John Adams, about ten years after the settlement, became the lone adult male survivor. One was the deference accorded Adams, whether by reason of his age, sex, ingenuity or personality. This respect was reinforced by the religious instruction given the children by Adams without hindrance from schismatics or dissenters. On many questions, Adams constituted a majority of one. All the children regarded him as "father," with Polynesian indifference to physical parenthood, and he was the object of devotion as well as respect. Said the youngsters, " 'We mind what Mr. Adams tells us, because he knows best'; in truth they live together in the greatest amity and brotherly love."[20]

Concord on Pitcairn owed much to ameliorative and conciliatory attitudes and institutions derived from the Polynesian culture. The

Polynesian concept of "family" was broader than the Western idea of those "immediately" related. "Within very wide limits, no matter how incompetent or sluggish he might be, a Polynesian never lacked minimum food and shelter so long as a relative of his, and that theoretically included the whole community, had a piece of taro and a roof. This was not communism, as early observers thought, but a wide application of the principle of mutual back-scratching among blood relatives."[21]

The principle was bolstered on Pitcairn, not only by the smallness of the population and the Island, but by the fact that, as Brodie witnessed it in 1850, the inhabitants "are as one large family bred up together; they are, in point of fact, all more or less related to each other, and look upon each other more as brothers and sisters than anything else. The children appear to be more nursed by their relations than by their mothers, which makes it often difficult to distinguish the married from the unmarried." Among Polynesians, childhood was a privileged estate, physical parenthood an incident.

Beechey, noting a "mutual accommodation amongst them in regard to provisions," implies that it was a matter of borrow when you need, pay back when you can.

Another visitor of the same year, 1825, Seaman Bechervaise, describes the economics of Pitcairn, as explained to him by Adams, as even closer to the socialistic ideal: "When each of the families have gathered the produce of their ground, it does not belong to them individually, but is put into the general store, from whence it is withdrawn to supply the wants of all without regard to the quantity each has put in." Further, no "purchase" from touching ships is "private . . . all tend to the general comfort, and to the general stock." The Pitcairn "shareout," frequently noted by twentieth century visitors, obviously derives from this time.

The picture of concord on Pitcairn was early epitomized by Pipon's statement that no serious quarrels ever occurred, though a few hasty words might now and then be spoken, but were only "quarrels of the mouth," and that the Islanders were "strictly honest, lending and exchanging live-stock and produce in the most friendly manner, and submitting to the settlement of any little dispute by Adams without rancor."

This generalization was frequently reinforced by later observers, but, like most generalizations, was subject to exception.

171

In the report of a visit in 1819 by Captain Henry King of the whaler "Elizabeth," we find indications of stress, as well as of limitations on Adams' authority, wisdom, and benevolence.

We were all sitting down in conversation, when a little child ran down to go into the surf. I ran to prevent the child, and so did the wife of Charles Christian, saying at the same time to Diana, the eldest daughter of John Adams, "Diana, your child will be drowned." Adams having told me, prior to this, that his daughters were not married, I expressed my surprise to the wife of Christian. Old Adams, hearing this, took me aside, and gave me the following account: Notwithstanding his paternal care of his daughters, Edward Quintral [sic] and Diana had committed an offence against the laws of God, for which he supposed them worthy of death, and accordingly gave orders that they should be shot; but as no person seemed willing to execute his orders, he made the necessary preparations for executing them himself, when he was strongly opposed by Auther [sic] Quintral, who said that though the offence was certainly a great one, and the more so, as a similar one had not been committed since the death of Christian; yet he did not conceive it to be a crime worthy of death. The rest being of the same opinion, Adams changed his mind also, but forbade them to marry. Adams, upon this occasion, probably changed his mind through interest, for he will not suffer his daughters to marry for fear of losing their labor in cultivating his plantation.

A further source of friction is described by Captain King:

While Adams was on board the ship, he gave me a brief account of the different occurrences that had taken place upon the island; and, among others, he mentioned his divorcing Christian and his wife, in consequence of having read in the Old Testament that marriages should not be allowed among those who were at all related to each other, and they had lived separate a long time.

In true story book fashion, Captain King brought an end to the enforced separation of the two pairs of lovers.

After a great deal of conversation upon the subject, I persuaded him [Adams] to allow Diana, his daughter, to be married to Edward Quintral, and Christian to live with his wife, both of which he promised to do; and calling Edward to him, he took him by the hand, saying, "Come here, my son, you shall have my daughter Diana, and to-morrow we shall keep the wedding."

The picture presented by Buffett, who lived on Pitcairn with Adams for six years before Adams' death in 1829, adds a somewhat puzzling note to the symphony of harmony played by the earlier reporters:

> Mr. Adams had no concern with their secular affairs, that is, no control over them. Sometimes little disputes would arise between them when trafficing for fowls, but if Mr. Adams had a dispute with any he would follow the precept, "Let not the sun go down on thy wrath," and before night would make friends.

This may indicate a development peculiar to Adams' later years, when many of the children had come of age and were no longer amenable to parental rule. The fact that Adams' authority was not absolute is likewise indicated by marriages consummated by youngsters under the age limits fixed by Adams.

Suggestions in the record that Pitcairners were mortal, though they may substantiate Buffett's conclusion that "human nature is the same throughout the world," do not destroy the picture of accord painted by visitor after visitor during Adams' reign. Harmony is a comparative matter and claims of near perfection prima facie suspect. The picture may have been exaggerated also by the natural tendency of the Islanders to conceal "family" differences and present a happy front to guests, although a contrary disposition was exhibited after Adams' death on more than one occasion. Considering the many potential sources of friction indigenous to Pitcairn, the amount of harmony achieved must be considered remarkable.

The rivalry for pupils and religious leadership which developed with the arrival of Nobbs in 1828 was settled without excessive rancor on the part of the loser, Buffett. A real tempest developed with the arrival in 1832 of the imperious, if not imperial, Hill. His thrust to dictatorship brought the Islanders as near to civil war as they had been since the days of the mutineers. Some bitterness survived his expulsion, but the indications are that it was short-lived.

Potentially divisive issues, such as the proposed (and accomplished) emigrations to Tahiti in 1831 and to Norfolk in 1856 (the latter proposal was long simmering) created no lasting animosity. They apparently were regarded as the single problem of a single family; the minority might drag its heels, but would not accept options to follow a course different from that of the majority.

The return to Pitcairn in 1859 and 1864 of about one-fourth of the emigrants to Norfolk, in the face of strong admonitions and criticism, was accomplished with the use of funds of the community.

Unsuccessful attempts to get the repatriated Pitcairners back to Norfolk continued until 1872, when inducements held out included an offer to pay for the charter of a transport, if all would return. The strong desire of the community to remain intact and to avoid geographical division is forcefully argued by this offer.

Its sequel, as related by Rosalind Young, one of the children on Pitcairn at the time of the offer, evidences a case where the majority accepted a minority decision: ". . . most of the younger members of the community were eager to return, and some among the older ones were not unwilling. But a few of the families were determined to remain where they were, and there the matter ended."

It should be noted that the proposal of the Norfolk community came at a time when Pitcairn was suffering from a drought, poor yam crops, and a blight damaging to the potatoes.

Perhaps the likeliest source of trouble on Pitcairn was the constantly growing variance in the amounts of land owned, which developed from the varying fertility of the mutineers and their offspring. The means by which this threat was circumvented is discussed on page 227.

Another opportunity for schism arrived with the proposal in 1886 to convert the community from its long loyalty to the Church of England to the doctrines of the Seventh Day Adventists. (Adams had previously averted divisiveness by persuading the Tahitian women to adopt his beliefs.) Again opposition yielded to the desire for unanimity, and the Pitcairners went over in a body to the new sect. A second thought rearguard action was scotched. Homogeneity of religion, whether that of the earlier or later allegiance, has proved a unifying thread in Pitcairn history ever since John Adams "saw the light" and brought it to his fellow Islanders.

Summary accounts must of necessity overlook scores of Island disputes indicated by the record* (as well as unreported differences),

---

* The Pitcairn Island Register for May 2, 1840 records that, "A serious altercation took place between Edward Quintall sen. and John Evans sen.; the latter receiving several bruises on the head, back and throat and several scratches on the breast." Young (p. 92) tells us that Quintal, "being a powerful man, brought it to a termination by lifting Evans, who was small, as easily as he would a child, and throwing him violently into a pigsty, thereby causing him serious injury." Her comment that, "This wicked act was recorded in the register of those times, for it was customary to enter therein every occurrence, however trivial," is not supported by the Register itself, which was largely a bare-bones record and contains only the one quoted incident of this type. It would not be safe to assume that it was because no others occurred.

including recurrent suggestions of a running feud between the Christian and Young families. (It is not clear how the one could be distinguished from the other after three or four generations.)

Toward the end of the nineteenth century and for several following decades, the official reports and Island archives suggest a high level of acrimony, reminiscent of the period of "mutual recriminations" in the time of Hill. Among leading sources of trouble were the unmannerly habits of goats, pigs, and chickens, whose depredations had caused trouble on unfenced Tubuai. Frequent complaints of damage to crops by animals were brought to the Island court and voiced in public meetings. Life might have been simpler on Pitcairn without fauna; rats and wild cats created other problems. There were also accusations of theft of animals, as well as of fruit and vegetables.

Public work was a continuous source of controversy, and the Island records indicate that straggling and other resistance to this exaction was common. Quarrels between husband and wife or parent and child not infrequently were dumped into the lap of the local authorities, with results as unsatisfactory as those in most societies. Sexual trespasses occupied the Island court. The problem of illegitimacy was aggravated by lack of any institutional response. Defamation was an Island irritant.

Trading with passing ships involved disputes about who was authorized to engage therein and about the tendency to indulge in "private trading" before "public trading" was disposed of. Islanders accused of derelictions were not above exhuming past offenses of their accusers, and did not always readily accept decisions of the Island court.

Colonial officials bemoaned the lack of strong leadership, but the frequent terms of Chief Magistrate James Russell McCoy, a man of notable forcefulness, do not evince much superiority in maintaining order and subduing friction. Like Nobbs and Hill, he drew criticism, as well as support, from the anti-authoritarian Islanders.

That the Community was able to survive the frictions it engendered argues that cohesive factors were also at work. As the twentieth century advanced, visitors remarked on the cooperative and harmonious aspects of Island life. This is not to suggest that discord had been eliminated; it had merely been overcome. Which is perhaps the nub of the matter.

If Arcadia is a frictionless society, Pitcairn never achieved it. The Pitcairn experience suggests that, even in a closely confined community, it is not the absence of friction which is essential to survival, but the presence of assuasive agents which reduce the abrasive effects of inevitable differences of interest, viewpoint, and personality. Pitcairn concord, beset by indigenous booby traps and diminished by the difficulties common to mortal flesh, survived to an extent sufficient to insure continuance of the community. Much of the credit belongs to the ameliorative attitudes and practices derived from Polynesia.

❦ LAW AND GOVERNMENT ❦

Of the Pitcairn community, it could be said that never have so few been governed by so much law, if government be equated with legislation and the machinery of administration.[22] In the first days of the settlement, government was arrived at by consensus of the mutineers, with little attention given to the views or rights of the Polynesians. Civil war and near anarchy developed when the mutineers, following exclusion of the "Blacks" from land ownership, supported Williams' demand for the wife of one of the Polynesians. Order was not restored until the end of the first decade, after the eleventh murder, when Adams and Young, invoking a "right" to anticipatory self-defense, axed the ungovernable Quintal to death, leaving themselves the sole male adults.

When Young died in 1800, Adams became the law and the government on Pitcairn Island, as well as its theocratic head. Fortunately for the badly maimed community, he only occasionally abused his powers and was capable of yielding when he had placed himself in an untenable position. As the young Pitcairners told the first officer of the "Sultan" in 1817, "We have no king, nor lord, to obey here, and every one is his own master; but . . . we mind what Mr. Adams tells us, because he knows best."[23]

Adams achieved both respect and affection from the younger generation, and was regarded as universal father. The picture of Pitcairn society which won the ecstatic paeans of the early visitors was that of a closely-knit and harmonious family, wisely guided by a kindly patriarch. The obvious argument for the superiority of a benevolent despotism met its equally obvious rebuttal when Adams died in 1829.

Before his death, however, Adams had effected a rapport with the

British Government by his discussions with Beechey in 1825 of the problem of potential overpopulation. There had been suggestions, too, that a missionary be sent to Pitcairn, which evoked anguished howls from such outlanders as Barrow and Delano, who shared the characteristic antagonism of seamen to these evangels.* Indeed, the attitude of such men and of the early explorers, such as Captain Cook and Bougainville, offers a curious instance of Western ambivalence. In the very act of putting down footholds in the Pacific, some of these prescient sea captains foresaw the deteriorating effect which contact with the West must impose on Polynesian ways in which they found much to admire. Their surprising self-denigration, in which the noble savage showed to advantage against the corrupt Westerners, proved largely rhetorical; it was never to be matched by actions indicating relinquishment of the fixed notion of the superiority of Europeans over Polynesians.

Beechey's transmission to the British Government of Adams' and his own concern for the Pitcairners eventuated in the short-lived emigration of Tahiti in 1831. On their return, the vacuum of power created by Adams' death in 1829 was filled by immigrant George Hunn Nobbs, who had arrived in 1828. Nobbs never achieved totally unqualified acceptance, but his multiple roles of teacher, pastor, doctor, registrar, and minister plenipotentiary reinforced his leadership of the community, nominally in the hands of elected officials after 1838. Nobbs even tried his unpracticed hand at legislation.

Nobbs' power was dramatically usurped in 1832 by the megalomaniac Hill, who became a non-benevolent dictator of the Pitcairn community for a period of several years. Before describing his reign, note should be taken of the unwritten law of land tenure which had developed before his advent and was not questioned until Hill sought to bypass it for his own purposes.

---

* Thundered Captain Delano: "To send missionaries among them, according to the proposal of some good people, would be an unfortunate experiment upon their peace and virtue, unless the individuals selected should be much more enlightened and liberal than any of that class of persons with whom I have been fortunate enough to be acquainted . . . Let it be our fervent prayer that neither canting and hypocritical emissaries from schools of artificial theology on the one hand, nor sensual and licentious crews on the other, may ever enter the charming village of Pitcairn to give disease to the mind or bodies of the unsuspecting inhabitants." And Barrow invoked Providence to "throw round the shores of your enviable little Eden 'cherubim and a flaming sword' to guard its approaches from those who would endanger your peace; and above all, shield you from those, who would perplex and confuse your unsophisticated minds, by mysterious doctrines which they do not themselves comprehend!"

LAND TENURE

When the nine mutineers divided Pitcairn into nine parcels, shortly after settling the Island, they apparently assumed that title to the land would be inherited by their children. There is no evidence that the matter was discussed. Fragmentary as their acquaintance with the English law must have been, it is difficult to believe that they were unaware of the rule of primogeniture under which the first-born male inherited *all* of his father's land.

The harsh effect of this rule on younger sons was mitigated in England by the possibility of placing them in the church, navy, law, medicine, and the colonies. Pitcairn offered no such alternatives and, perhaps for this reason, the rule of primogeniture was never invoked. Instead, inheritance of land was equally shared by all the owner's children, whether male or female. This practice developed as a matter of custom rather than as a result of legislation.

The equity of this mode of inheritance is unarguable; unfortunately, it resulted in the very fragmentation of land ownership which the rule of primogeniture was designed to avoid. By 1849, Captain Wood noted that differences in fecundity had already resulted in a situation wherein one Islander had title to as much land as twenty-two members of another family.

Shapiro found in 1934 that the Pitcairners were very free with personal possessions, but that the "very rocks on the shore" were titled. Some twenty years later, Marden found "some people owned only four feet of ground. Others are completely landless." Individual trees had owners, and while it was permissible to pick a coconut or orange from another's tree, if one ate it at the site, carrying it away was unsanctioned.

THE REIGN OF HILL

Hill challenged the land ownership of the previous three Pitcairn immigrants, with the desire of getting at the "lousy foreigners," whom he considered obstacles to his complete domination of the Island. Nobbs, Evans, and Buffett had become landowners by virtue of marrying Pitcairn women. As Buffett described it, Hill "persuaded the natives to sign a petition to Government to deprive us Englishmen and our children of their lands; I am ordered, with my wife and five children to leave the island. . . . He has been the means of depriving one of my children of the land left her by her grandfather, and he proposes to deprive the others also, and as they grow up to send them to sea as cabin boys, etc."[24] The Pitcairn system of land tenure, however, survived Hill's eviction from the Island in 1837.

But a law voiding the immigrants' rights to land was only a small part of the legislation enacted by Hill during his brief regime. His passion for legislation and "legality" cannot, from this vantage point of time, fail to bring to mind the frantic efforts of the Nazis. The willingness of both Hill and Hitler to ignore or override any law that stood in their way was almost equaled by their passion for stamping their trespasses as lawful by the simple device of new decrees.

Thus Hill "framed laws" elaborate enough to provide against "high treason," built a prison, appointed "privy councilors," the while he had dissenters flogged, seized their muskets, evicted them from their houses, and forbade them access to visiting ships. After driving the "foreigners" into exile, he indulged his zest for the paraphernalia of power by appointing elders, subelders, and "cadets." The government of Pitcairn never regained such pomp and circumstance after Hill's departure.

PITCAIRN JOINS THE EMPIRE

The Hill imbroglio and the growing trade with the whalers brought home the vulnerable position of Pitcairn. Sans army, navy, or a big brother, it was "up for grabs" to anyone who could overcome its very limited manpower. This lent force to the Islanders' plea in 1838 to Captain Elliott, H.M.S. "Fly," that they were subject to contumely and the threat of being overcome by reason of lack of national allegiance, and that it was essential that the British Government take them in, so to speak, their loyalty having been demonstrated.

Captain Elliott did not allow lack of authority to add this dubious jewel to Her Majesty's crown to prevent him from indicating assent. The effect of his action was never put to the test. Pitcairn became a British settlement later under the British Settlements Act of

1887. It was brought within the jurisdiction of the High Commissioner for the Western Pacific in 1898, and in 1952 the Pitcairn Island Order in Council transferred administration to the Governor of Fiji, after separation of the offices of Governor and High Commissioner.

With that gift for improvisation demanded of Royal Navy captains, Elliott whipped up an instant Constitution, guided the Islanders in enacting a set of ten laws, and oversaw the election of Edward Quintal as Pitcairn's first "Chief Magistrate." Most notable were provisions for female suffrage and compulsory school attendance for children—both features far in advance of their incorporation into more "advanced" societies.

The new laws required the annual election of a Chief Magistrate (who must be native born) on the first day of the year by all natives over 18 years of age and residents of five years' duration, regardless of sex. The Magistrate was to be chief authority and arbiter of disputes, assisted by one elected councilman and one appointed by the Magistrate. These officials were answerable to the commanding officers of visiting British men-of-war, for whom knotty questions were saved, and took an oath of accountability to "Her Majesty the Queen of Great Britain."

LAWS AT MIDCENTURY

By 1850 the laws of Pitcairn had expanded considerably, although the increase in volume was not attended by a marked improvement in draftsmanship. These laws are of more than legal interest because of the light they throw on the community problems they were designed to meet and on community attitudes.

It is interesting to note, for example, that in the section describing the duties of the Magistrate (hearing complaints, committing to a jury, levying fines, and directing the execution of public works) it is stated: "He is not to assume any power or authority on his own responsibility, or without the consent of the majority of the people." This is an excellent example of the Pitcairn penchant for curbing authority; what they delegated with one hand they reached for with the other.

The laws provided for the payment of one shilling per month, or its equivalent in produce or labor, according to a prescribed schedule, for each child of school age, regardless of whether the child actually attended school.

Other provisions penalized the owner of a dog who chased goats, the killing of cats (valued as an antidote for rats), and the rooting of pigs, and allowed rewards for informers.

The stringently limited resources of Pitcairn fathered a number of miscellaneous provisions. Notice of intention to cultivate land was required. Wood remaining after completion of a house must be turned over to the next aspirant. Permission to cut timber, even on one's own property, was required. Slaughter of "white birds" was punishable by fine of one dollar unless the bird were killed to pamper a sick person. The dwindling miro and purau trees could be cut only for buildings, and must be used within a specified period on pain of confiscation. Carving on trees was forbidden. Fishing for squid or fish from certain rocks was forbidden to all but the owner of the rock. The magistrate must inspect landmarks once a year and replace those destroyed.

The increasing intercourse with whalers is reflected in prohibitions against the sale of spirits ashore and against women visiting ships without the Magistrate's permission. The Magistrate was required to watch over the women himself or appoint four men to accompany and protect them.

The Pitcairn Code, like that of mightier communities, contained a good many "dead letter" provisions, no sooner enacted than forgotten. The perennial wish, "there ought to be a law," was easier to realize on tiny Pitcairn than in more complex societies, and the latter did not lack for silly legislation. Perhaps the percentage of inert enactments was higher on Pitcairn; it is unlikely that so small a group could administer the considerable body of law enacted at one time or another, especially in the absence of lawyers. Even lawyers would have had their troubles with some of the free-hand legislation.

The notion that much Pitcairn legislation was more honored in the breach than by observance is borne out by repeated references to "laxity" and "lawlessness" and the failure of law enforcement, particularly in official reports around the turn of the century.

Custom and consensus, as in larger communities, were generally more effective than the attempt to mold conduct by prescribing it in writing. It is difficult to assess how much of the written law was operative, but the record suggests that *ad hoc* considerations, rather

181

than juridical principles, frequently controlled controversial questions.

The legal system which Captain F. P. Doughty, H.M.S. "Constance," found in force on a visit in 1884 made no reference to the Code of 1838. The probability is that, aside from alterations, it was considered operative in the same sense as the English considered the common law to govern those situations in which it was applicable. The difficulties of law enforcement on Pitcairn were indicated by a provision punishing insults to the Magistrate and attempts to "call in question" decisions of the Court. Fines or punishments were not specified, but apparently left to the discretion of the Chief Magistrate.

A notable enactment was: "No one is allowed to call the Magistrate without a good evidence or satisfactory proof against an opposing party or parties without laying himself open to whatever fine the Magistrate or jury might lay upon him for lost time." Maude(3) reports that this law, intended to prevent frivolous charges, was interpreted in the years preceding 1940 to make an accuser almost automatically subject to fine if the charge were not substantiated by the verdict. Like many laws, its purpose was laudable, but the result was that the Islanders usually preferred "to suffer wrongs in silence rather than risk a fine by making a complaint." This law was eliminated in the 1940 Code.

MODIFICATIONS OF LAW AND GOVERNMENT (1893)

The system of government was altered in 1893 as a result of a conference between the "principal men" of Pitcairn and Captain Rooke of H.M.S. "Champion" in October of 1892. Provision was made for a parliament of seven "to legislate, to plan for the public good, to execute all decisions of the court, and to see that all public demands are attended to without unnecessary delay." The executive powers were entrusted to a president, vice-president, and secretary, and litigation was to be decided by a separate judiciary consisting of two judges, whose decisions could be appealed to parliament. The doctrine of separation of powers had reached Pitcairn.

This revision of the government was accompanied by the enactment of "Laws and Regulations." Among the new contributions to

182

law and order on Pitcairn were provisions prohibiting the shooting of goats in specified areas, the bringing of coconuts from " 'TOtherside" except on specified conditions, and imposing fines for any action "contrary to the decency, peace and good order of the Island," whether or not otherwise specified.

REVISION IN 1904

The "Laws as revised in 1904," described as "Administration as laid down by His Majesty's Deputy Commissioner R. T. Simons," reinstalled the office of chief magistrate, "who must not be a church officer." This latter provision possibly resulted from Mr. Simons' "opinion that Mr. McCoy has become somewhat inflated in consequence of his status among the Adventists of America, and the deference shown to him as President of Pitcairn Island in his travels abroad."

The 1904 revision made the Chief Magistrate the "chief official authority," and provided for assistance from a council composed of two assessors and the chairmen of the committees for dealing with the Internal and External Affairs of the Island. The Chief Magistrate was also made "chief judicial authority." A new note was provided by exclusion of adultery and rape from local jurisdiction; "such matters must be referred to the High Commissioner's Court for the Western Pacific." Abortion was added to the catalogue of crimes. "To prevent the misuse of imported drugs, the Chief Magistrate will, alone, authorize a competent person to import ordinary and simple medicines for the use of the Islanders." The revised code regulated the residence of foreigners, the importation of alcoholic liquors, and public work.

New provisions appear on an important subject—boats. "Constant disputes having arisen as to the control of the boats, in the future the boats are to be under the control of the committee for Internal [External] affairs who will not only require the men for manning them, but will requisition men for keeping them in order, a certain number of hours each week."

Pitcairn's first and only money taxation, other than school fees, was legislated in the form of a fee of six pence a year for a firearms license, neither onerous nor productive of much revenue.

Quarantine was provided for by forbidding Islanders to board passing ships until definite ascertainment that no sickness of any kind existed on board.

A 1909 addendum provided for the payment of fines in arrowroot or fungers at the discretion of the Chief Magistrate and for prison rules and routine. A 1913 extract from the promulgations of the Deputy Commissioner, copied in the Book of Records in 1915, also is of interest: "It is suggested that before any outside person should be allowed to come and reside on Pitcairn Island that he should have the permission of the Deputy Commissioner [and] deposit with the Deputy Commissioner a sum of money, the money to be forfeited should he have an illegitimate child while resident in Pitcairn. If he should marry the money to be returned to him."

Regulations of the Internal Committee concerned public work, littering, clothes suitable for bathing in the sea, a hunting season, damage by livestock, and, in much detail, the proper conduct of goats, goat owners, and goat killers. (See p. 237.) These samples of Pitcairn laws indicate that, if the Island lacked for anything, it was not for legislation.

PUBLIC PROPERTY AND PUBLIC WORK

The concept of public property entered the Pitcairn scene almost simultaneously with the mutineers. "A suitable spot of ground for a village was fixed upon, with the exception of which the island was divided into equal portions. . . ." Quite probably Brown's Well was treated as public property from the very beginning. As the assets of the community grew, public ownership, with obvious sense, was extended to the roads, the church, the courthouse, and the schoolhouse.

The advent of the longboat or whaleboat necessitated the more novel inclusion of this indispensable of Pitcairn commerce into the framework of public property. When not received as gifts or trades to the community, these large boats could not be built without community effort. They required large crews to handle them and keep them in repair. (Small boats remained subject to private ownership.) The sugar house and sugar boiling trench were other unusual additions to the list of public property.

In a society without money taxes or slavery, public property could be maintained only by public work, that is, by the exaction of labor from every able-bodied male of reasonable age. Little of specific nature appears from the record about how public work operated in the early days. The Pitcairn Code contains scattered references to public work, including the statement, "All persons liable for public work shall assemble at the Courthouse within fifteen minutes after the ringing of the bell."

Apparently the extent of this unwelcome labor varied with necessity. Dr. Shapiro in 1934 found seven days of labor required of each male over eighteen and under sixty, devoted to such tasks as road-making, repair of public buildings, and work on the boats. The Code provided for payment of fines and school tuition by public work, and placed its direction under the jurisdiction of the Committee for Internal Affairs.

Public work, taking men from their individual pursuits or leisure, achieved equal popularity with money taxes in other communities, even though its necessity was likewise recognized. With the growth of money-producing commerce and increasing aid from the British Government, it has not gained in appeal.

As reported in *A Guide to Pitcairn,* the situation is:

> . . . in recent years that part which is not traditional has been reduced as far as finance reasonably permits. . . . a government school . . . government-provided radio communications . . . public buildings which house a free dispensing service for the sick, a post office, a library and a combined Court House and community hall . . . are all services which fall outside the old tradition, and public work on them is kept to a minimum.
>
> Perhaps the most essential of the public duties that are still recognized as being traditional are concerned with Bounty Bay and the maintenance of the public boats. . . . Installations in the Bay, however, are provided mainly from general revenue and grants from Britain and, since they are vital to the life of the people and the outcome of older custom, there exists a degree of give and take in their maintenance. Public trading, the landing of cargo, the 'share out,' and the maintenance of roads and paths are also part of accepted community service as, in very much the same category, is the voluntary work undertaken for the Church. . . . It is all too evident that a small community, so dependent on co-operative action, could not change over entirely to a system of paid labour, so the grumbles and compromises are likely to go on as they have always done.

THE CURRENT PICTURE

Government on Pitcairn was reorganized by the Pitcairn Island Government Regulations of 1940, resulting from the labors of Mr. Maude. By Ordinance No. 2 of 1952 these Regulations, providing for local government by an elected Council and limited jurisdiction for an Island Court, were given the force of law under the new Order in Council. The Pitcairn Island Council consists of the Chief Magistrate, two Assessors, the Chairman of the Internal Committee, the Island Secretary, and the Education Officer in the role of Adviser.

The Council, charged with the management of internal affairs, meets in the first week of each month. It is chaired by the Chief Magistrate, possessed of executive and judicial powers. The Council is empowered to enact rules of the nature of bylaws which must be notified to the Governor of Fiji, who may revoke or alter them. The Internal Committee arranges for and supervises public work.

Candidates for the offices of Chief Magistrate and Assessors must have twenty-one years' residence; voters must be eighteen with three years' residence. The Chief Magistrate is now elected for three years, but other offices are filled at the annual election on Christmas Day. The Governor of Fiji, with the advice of the Council, appoints the Island Secretary, the Postmaster, Radio Operator, and Chief Constable. The Education Officer is Government Adviser and local Auditor ex officio, but cannot vote in the Council.

The Island Court consists of the Chief Magistrate and the two Assessors. Its jurisdiction is confined to criminal cases involving maximum punishment of ten pounds fine or imprisonment for three months, and civil cases where the disputed amount does not exceed ten pounds. Appeal to the Supreme Court of Fiji is provided for, and the law of England is applied in instances where there is no local law.*

---

* Recent changes in Pitcairn government are embodied in Ordinance No. 1 of 1964, ''Relating to the Local Government,'' and Ordinance No. 1 of 1966, ''Relating to the Administration of Justice,'' enacted by the Governor of the Islands of Pitcairn, Henderson, Ducie and Oeno. Notable features of the latter Ordinance include punishment for disrespect to the Island Court, for persons who ''live together as man and wife unless they are legally married,'' for failure to vote ''in any poll for the election of an island officer,'' and for failure or refusal to keep children of five to fifteen in regular attendance at the Pitcairn public school.

DETAILS OF PITCAIRN'S FINANCES

REVENUE

	1957 £	1958–59* £	1959–60 £	1960–61 £	1961–62 £	1962–63 £	1963–64 £	1964–65 £
Stamp sales	20,349†	9,087	2,614	2,852	10,424	3,886	16,391	29,063
Interest	1,583	2,837	2,155	2,111	2,098	2,082	1,964	2,063
Miscellaneous	23	190	44	36	69	111	260	339
Development Grants	—	—	2,159	1,525	1,704	7,219	3,620	6,789
	21,955	12,114	6,972	6,524	14,295	13,298	22,235	38,254

EXPENDITURE

	1957	1958–59*	1959–60	1960–61	1961–62	1962–63	1963–64	1964–65
‡Administration	2,340	5,108	2,526	2,518	3,136	3,771	4,444	4,023
Education	1,640	2,230	2,944	1,971	2,659	2,069	2,972	2,645
Health	351	358	543	334	557	833	2,564	1,400
Postal	1,493	2,624	672	248	2,127	549	3,105	15,658
Works	1,123	1,096	1,110	538	1,700	2,303	4,207	1,877
Development Grants	—	—	2,567	1,496	2,060	7,270	3,611	6,854
	6,947	11,416	10,362	7,105	12,239	16,795	20,903	32,457

ASSETS AND LIABILITIES

	1957	1958–59*	1959–60	1960–61	1961–62	1962–63	1963–64	1964–65
Assets								
Cash	3,312	1,512	2,314	1,322	918	1,391	1,385	2,307
Investments	49,775	57,085	52,563	51,353	54,504	53,734	54,989	60,013
Sundries	698	204	164	343	298	156	406	419
	53,785	58,810	55,041	53,018	55,720	55,281	56,780	62,739
Liabilities								
Loans	—	1,000	—	—	—	—	—	—
Sundries	605	1,622	1,315	1,272	1,623	1,450	978	2,116
General Revenue Balance	53,180	56,188	53,126	51,746	54,097	53,831	55,802	60,623
	53,785	58,810	55,041	53,018	55,720	55,281	56,780	62,739

† New stamp issue.   * 15-month period.

‡ Includes normal administration services, radio communications, agriculture and miscellaneous expenditure on Pitcairn and in Suva.

Pitcairn was never a prize of empire. Its administration has always required efforts disproportionate to the number of people involved, and the paternal and sporadically generous attitude of the Crown has not precluded complaints that it was not doing enough for these distant cousins of the Empire. By reorganizing Pitcairn government and laws, by providing a fertile source of public revenues in the issuance of stamps, by sanctioning a development plan for improvement of landing facilities in Bounty Bay, and by providing a new radio installation, agricultural surveys and technical training overseas, supported by grants, the British Government has gone a long way to silence critics of its Pitcairn policy, although grumbling has not entirely ceased.

The economic importance of stamps in financing Pitcairn government and education, and some notion of public finances, can be derived from the table on the preceding page from *A Guide to Pitcairn*.

The Pitcairn experience suggests that the need for law and government is not necessarily proportionate to the size of a community or the complexity of its economy. It brings out with unusual clarity the adaptation of law to terrain (what other Code devotes such attention to goats?), the human inclination to legislate and adjudicate *ad hoc*, and the tendency of many enactments to fall into desuetude.

❧ EDUCATION ❧

The beginnings of education on Pitcairn recall the familiar rhetorical picture of James Garfield on one end of a log and Mark Hopkins on the other. John Adams was as far from Mark Hopkins as one could get short of complete illiteracy, but in the kingdom of the blind the one-eyed man is sovereign. The exact degree of Adams' literacy is beyond definition, but it might fairly be described as marginal.* The most

---

* See p. 36. The author, examining a copy of the rare "Pitcairn Island Register Book" in the Congressional Library, encountered a comment in the introduction by Sir Charles Lucas on a supposition by the author of Adams' biography in the *Dictionary of National Biography*, that Adams must have had an exceptional education: ". . . this supposition is inconsistent not only with other accounts but also with Adams' handwriting which, as the facsimile (reproduced in the book) shows, was that of an uneducated man." Opposite Sir Charles' statement, in which the word "uneducated" is underlined, appears, bristling with indignation, the penciled notation, "It is not!"

plausible source for such formal education as Adams had was the poorhouse in which he was reared.

Shortly before his death in 1800, Young had begun instruction of the children in reading and writing. Adams carried on in defiance of his own limitations, apparently learning as he taught, so that in later years he was able to write. That he achieved creditable results is indicated by Delano's statement that in 1808 "the girls and boys were made to read and write before Capt. F, to show him the degree of their improvement. They did themselves great credit in both, particularly the girls."

Suggestive of the physical difficulties involved, as well as of eagerness for learning, is the report of Officer Newell of the "Sultan," which touched on Pitcairn in 1817: ". . . they were very anxious to obtain a spelling book, that they might learn to read, for, said they, all that we now know, is what Mr. Adams has told us, and if we can get a spelling book we can read all the good things ourselves; but unfortunately we had not one on board."

When Buffett arrived in 1823 as Pitcairn's first immigrant, he found that "all but two or three of the first generation could read. . . . It is generally thought that Mr. Adams brought them up in this manner from childhood, but it was many years after the Massacre [1793] before he taught any to read, and McCoy's son has told me, that they could not believe for some time that Adams understood what he read, but they thought (to use his own words) 'he spoke out of his own head.' " Buffett notes also that some of those instructed by Adams taught others to read.

The advent of Buffett brought the Pitcairn children a teacher with a more extensive, if limited, educational background. The arrival of Nobbs in 1828 resulted in a rivalry for students, as well as for religious leadership. The contest was an unequal one; Nobbs was better qualified, more forceful and aggressive. Whether by formal schooling or considerable reading, he had acquired an effective education, apparent in his many letters and Register entries, which evidence definite literary talent. Buffett eventually accepted the new dispensation.

Education now took on increasing organization and formality.[25] A schoolhouse was erected after Nobbs' advent. Attendance was made compulsory; here Pitcairn was in advance of most other communities. Parents were required to pay one shilling per month per child or its equivalent in a prescribed schedule in yams, sweet potatoes, Irish potatoes, plantains, or labor. The charge could not be escaped by failing to send a child to school, although Island tradition has it that some parents achieved exemption by naming Nobbs godfather to their children.

It was inevitable that religious matters were emphasized in the school. John Adams' texts had been the Bible and the Prayer Book, and Nobbs was a man inclined to stress rather than subdue piety. Thus we find Captain Waldegrave expressing in 1830 "gratification" at hearing William Quintal "say part of the Catechism, and answer several questions as to his knowledge of the redemption in Christ, and of the different habits of the Jews, their sects and diseases, perfectly, clearly, and distinctly—showing that he understood their meaning."[26]

But the secular also had a place, as attested by the observation of Captain Freemantle in 1833 that: "The present generation of children is the finest I ever saw; and out of the whole number, seventy-nine, there are fifty-three under twenty years of age, who appear to have been well instructed, many of them capable of reading, and nearly on a par with children of the same age in England."[27]

It may be of passing interest to note that during the reign of terror of Hill, although he apparently preempted for himself sovereignty in every facet of Pitcairn life, he signed one 1833 communication, "Joshua Hill, Teacher, etc." and referred to himself in another (1834) as "an humble teacher upon Pitcairn's Isle for the time being." Classes may have had an added luster under this self-admitted man of affairs; it is to be regretted that no account of them can be found. When Nobbs returned from exile, he resumed his teaching duties.

Some concrete evidence of the level to which education, now conducted in "a substantial building, about 56 feet long by 20 wide, conveniently supplied with forms, desks, slates, books, and maps," had attained by the middle of the nineteenth century is available in a letter from some of the "elder pupils" to Captain Hope, in August 1847:

> We attend school five days in the week, five hours each day. Our routine of school duties is as follows:—namely, commence with prayer and praise; conclude with the same. Monday, recital of weekly tasks, reading the Holy Scriptures, writing, arithmetic, and class spelling. Tuesday, the same as on Monday. Wednesday, reading in history and geography, transcribing select portions of Scripture, &c. Thursday, similar to Monday and Tuesday. And on Friday, which is the busiest day of the week, transcribing words with their definitions from Walker's Dictionary; read hymns, or rather devotional and moral poetry; re-

The Society of Pitcairn

peat Watt's and the Church Catechism; arithmetic tables, &c, &c.; and emulative spelling concludes the whole: we are generally an hour longer at school on this day than any other. On Wednesday afternoon the elder scholars attend the Bible class, with their parents. On the Sabbath, Divine service is performed twice, and all who can possibly attend do so.

If the request is not improper, will you, honoured Sir, procure for us some copy-slips, or models for writing, and a few of Walkinghame's *Arithmetic*, with a Key to the same? We often hear our teacher say, if he had these helps, the work would be much easier.[28]

The commendable degree of literacy apparent from this letter is also evident in other communications of the Islanders. Without resort to odious comparisons, it is clear that schooling in the time of Nobbs was more than could have been expected in so disadvantaged a locale.

After the return to Pitcairn of some of the emigrants to Norfolk, a new teacher was required, Nobbs having remained with the Norfolk colony. Good fortune again shone on the Islanders. Simon Young, "a man of superior parts and with a high sense of social responsibility," took over as both schoolmaster and pastor.* Some indication of the quality of his instruction can be found in the accomplishments of his star pupil, his daughter Rosalind Amelia. She it was who authored *Mutiny of the Bounty and Story of Pitcairn Island, 1790–1894* (Oakland, California, 1894).

After the conversion of Pitcairn to Seventh Day Adventism in 1886, the church sent missionaries and, in 1893, a teacher fresh from college in the United States, Hattie Andre, who won the respect and affection of the community. In this same era, Rosalind Young assisted with the instruction of the children.

In the first forty years of the twentieth century, turnover of teachers became more rapid than in the days of Nobbs. The educational fortunes of the Pitcairners varied, as did the interest of the Adventists and the British Government, to the accompaniment of drumbeats of internal and external criticism, not unfamiliar to Western ears. Much of the criticism centered on the quality of the instruction, but sometimes the interest or teachability of the Pitcairn youth was called into question.

Dr. Shapiro in 1934 observed school being conducted by Roy Clark, son of an American immigrant to Pitcairn, in a commodious

---

* One of his successors, Roy Clark, gave him this accolade, many years later: "Even to this day the name of Simon Young calls up respect and reverence for one that was more than a man of God."

191

building housing forty-five children. For his services, Clark received three pounds quarterly, and three Pitcairn-educated assistants had a quarterly stipend of from one pound, ten shillings to two pounds. The church paid the running expenses of the school.

> According to Clark . . . the curriculum reaches the level of the fourth grade in New Zealand. Reading, writing, and arithmetic are the principal studies, and history, geography and kindred subjects are taught to the older pupils.
>
> All children between six and sixteen years of age are required to attend school. On the whole, in the opinion of the master, the children are neither very eager nor apt pupils. But this opinion is based on a limited teaching experience. Evidence on the other side cites one of the island boys, Richard Christian. Eager to pursue his education, he left Pitcairn for New Zealand where he entered college, and, according to a report received by his parents, was doing satisfactory work.

A teacher's-eye view comes from this same Roy Clark in magazine articles[29] in which he notes two peculiarities of Pitcairn education: the dismissal of school when ships arrive and the seeming immunity of Pitcairn children to the academic competition elsewhere so keen. Having noted that "none of the school children are ever required to pass an examination," Clark decided to introduce that American institution known as the "report card." The result was laugh-provoking and, perhaps, thought-provoking. "The children simply looked at the report cards and threw them aside, and I do not believe that one was carried home to parents."

THE MODERN PICTURE

The age of affluence which followed World War II brought Pitcairn many educational improvements financed by the "phenomenal" sale of stamps to acquisitive philatelists. Stamp proceeds paid for a school and teacher's residence of timber and iron construction completed in 1950. Equipment includes a 240-volt lighting plant, a film projector, apparatus for technical training, and a school library.

Between 1917 and 1938, when the Seventh Day Adventist Church again appointed a resident pastor, non-religious academic training had been left to the Islanders. In 1948 the British Government assumed responsibility, separating Church and State (not without some indecisive objection by the Church), and providing for the appointment of an Education Officer (teacher) by the Governor of Fiji in consultation with the New Zealand Department of Education, which furnishes a professional teacher for a two-year tour of duty.

School attendance has increased from an average of twenty in the fifties to thirty-six in 1962. The New Zealand syllabus is used as a basis and practical training is given in "home studies, farming, commercial practice and typewriting. Correspondence courses in post-primary education were introduced in 1957. . . ."[30]

Pitcairn schooling is now in the mainstream of Western educational practice and goals. It has lost its unique Island flavor, but is better adapted to the outward-looking stance of modern Pitcairn youth. Those guiding its course are now confronted with a novel dilemma: How to satisfy Island needs for skills in nursing, midwifery, mechanics, building, radio, government, and teaching without stimulating emigration of the initiated and without developing a class of semi-professionals and technicians which will prove top heavy in the small, simple, and egalitarian structure of Pitcairn society. The time is past when one man can be preacher, teacher, doctor, and general factotum—but how many "specialists" can a limited population develop, retain, and support?

⚜ BOATS AND BOAT-HANDLING ⚜

BOATS

Boats play an important part in most island communities. In the case of harborless Pitcairn, their role was a commanding one throughout its history. As Admiral Moresby well put it, "the boat is to them of the first consequence."

The complement of the "Bounty" included a 23-foot launch, a 20-foot six-oared cutter, and a jolly boat or small cutter. At the time of the mutiny, after much bickering and unsuccessful attempts to use the jolly boat and the cutter, both much too small, the mutineers put over the launch in which Captain Bligh and his crowded eighteen "loyalists" made their epic forty-one-day journey to Timor.

The ship presumably arrived at Pitcairn with the two smaller boats. The jolly boat had been so worm-eaten at the time of the mutiny that it began to sink rapidly after being put overboard. Possibly it was repaired; its existence within a year or two of the arrival at Pitcairn is suggested by the report of Williams' threat "to leave the island in *one of the boats of the 'Bounty'* (italics supplied), unless he had another wife" to replace the one he had lost. (Hindsight indicates that giving up the boat, prized as it doubtless was, would have been the better bargain.)

This deduction would seem to outweigh the tradition recorded by Buffett that, "They destroyed their remaining boat, that none of the party might escape from the island or be the means of making known their retreat, should a vessel approach in the vicinity." But the short-livedness of the boats is indicated by the incident recorded in Young's journal for 1794, when the dissatisfaction of the women reached such a pitch that, "since the massacre it has been the desire of the greater part of them to get some conveyance, to enable them to leave the island."

In puzzling acquiescence to this desire, "the men began to build them a boat; but wanting planks and nails, Jenny . . . tore up the boards of her house, and endeavoured, though without success, to persuade some others to follow her example." We are given no description of the nature of the vessel, but it upset on launching, which Beechey termed "most fortunate," although the women presumably had a contrary reaction.

Young's diary further states that, "On the 4th of May, 1795, two canoes were begun, and in two days completed." (It is difficult to understand why the mutineers would have waited this long to build canoes if the "Bounty" boats were unavailable from the time of the landing five years previously.) Judging from Folger's description of what he found on discovery of the Pitcairn settlement in 1808, the canoes were of a portable dugout type. Although without outriggers, they could be joined like a Polynesian double canoe. They were used for fishing.

With the advent of the whalers in the 1810s, the Pitcairners must have cast a covetous eye on the whale boats, much better adapted than canoes to the booming Pitcairn surf and capable of carrying larger loads to and from the harborless Island when a ship appeared offshore. Their dream was realized in 1819 when Captain King, captivated by the Islanders and their hospitality, "gave" them a whale boat and other items "in return for their refreshments," which included water, poultry, hogs, goats, plantains, and "everything the island produced." In the same year a subscription of 3500 rupees raised by the *Calcutta Journal* brought the Pitcairners, via Captain Henderson and the "Hercules," a 22-foot cutter as one of a number of generous gifts. Their later history is dotted with gifts and purchases and building of whale boats.

The whale or long boat, now 37 feet long and rowed by fourteen oars, capable of carrying large numbers, has become a Pitcairn trademark. Sometimes sails are hoisted in the open sea, and, in more recent times, diesel engines have been added to several of the boats. These boats, which the Islanders attempt to keep at a level of four, are their life line to the outer world; touching ships are wisely reluctant to use their own boats to negotiate the treacherous Pitcairn surf and the bull's-eye landing practically impossible to any but the Island breed. The importance of the whale boat in the Pitcairn economy is illustrated by the fact that concern over the diminishing population is centered on the fact that there will not be enough males of the proper age to man the boats.

Around the turn of the twentieth century, Pitcairn began dreaming of maritime ventures more grandiose than whale boats. After the Seventh Day Adventist vessel, named in honor of the Island, was sold in 1899, British Consul Simons, stationed at Tahiti, yielded to the request of President McCoy of Pitcairn and purchased a cutter, also named "Pitcairn," with a view both to developing trade with the Gambier Islands, Pitcairn's nearest populated neighbor at a distance of some three hundred miles, and to thwarting any French designs on Oeno, Ducie, and Henderson.

The vessel, entirely manned by Pitcairners, was employed in carrying produce to Mangareva, where it was traded for money which the Gambierians earned in the pearl fisheries. Three Pitcairners were stationed at Mangareva to look after the business. When the "Pitcairn" foundered in 1904, the British Government did not insist on repayment of the 218 pounds loaned to buy it.

A second project proved even more immediately abortive. A collection of 124 pounds to replace the "Pitcairn" was supplemented by 150 pounds from the British Government, and a cutter named "John Adams" was purchased. When it arrived, it proved unseaworthy and was eventually sold for 60 pounds.

A third and last attempt to join the maritime powers almost proved the most costly of all for the Pitcairners. This involved the "Messenger," a 25-ton schooner built on Pitcairn itself circa 1919. After several voyages to Tahiti, the ill-fated vessel was caught in a hurricane on returning to Pitcairn from Mangareva.

> Gallantly the little vessel tried to weather the storm, but it was too much for her, and her masts were whipped out like sticks. Wallowing in the trough of the sea, her position was desperate. Every moment the big curlers threatened to swamp her. Her crew had, in fact, given up hope except in God, and their trust was rewarded, for an American steamer, the "Sassenach," arrived upon the scene in the nick of time, and rescued them as their vessel foundered.[31]

If the Pitcairners forsook dreams of maritime glory, the dwindling supply of Pitcairn timber and the necessity of acquiring it to build and repair boats and for the ever-growing curio trade pushed them into nautical expeditions at least equally as dangerous as their larger-scaled ventures. The nearest place to acquire the treasured miro wood was uninhabited Henderson Island (Elizabeth), some one hundred five miles east-north-east from Pitcairn and now one of the "Pitcairn Islands." The first reported trip by Pitcairners to Henderson, on the ship "Sharon," is recorded in the Register entry for November 11, 1851. "Eight human skeletons were also found upon the island, lying in caves. They were doubtless the remains of some unfortunate ship-wrecked seamen, as several pieces of wreck were found upon the shore."

But in the 1930s and 1940s the Pitcairners attempted the dangerous passage to Henderson's in their whale boats in pursuit of wood. The first voyage was successful, but on the second they were becalmed for fourteen days, and on the third encountered a storm that nearly foundered the longboats. On several occasions the Pitcairners were carried to Henderson by the friendly Johnsons in their brigantine "Yankee."

In more recent years, annual expeditions have been made possible by the courtesy of the Shaw Savill liner "Corinthic," which takes two longboats and a complement of Islanders to Henderson. Three or four days are spent in cutting the precious miro wood and in fishing, and the return journey is made under sail in eighteen to twenty-four hours.

Pitcairn's closest neighbor, if an uninhabited atoll can be so designated, is Oeno Island, some seventy-five miles northwest. It is sometimes visited (for nine days in 1961) by the Pitcairners on an expedition which is part picnic and part camping trip, part sport and part business. The sport is fishing; dried and salted fish are taken back home. The business is hunting for coral shells and pandanus leaves used in manufacturing island curios.

Recent developments, such as diesel engines for two of the long-boats, have aided the Islanders in the commerce with offshore boats. These include a power hoist for transporting goods from Bounty Bay to the village above it, power winches for the slipways, and a sea wall and jetty to improve landing facilities.

While these improvements have lightened the arduous task of handling cargo and wrestling it up the "Hill of Difficulty," they have not lessened the perennial dependence on boats nor the central role they play in Pitcairn life.

This role requires making contact with the passenger liners which began touching on Pitcairn, after the opening of the Panama Canal in 1914, to break the monotony of the long 7500-mile passage from New Zealand to Panama.

> Once the liners of Shaw Savill and Albion and New Zealand Shipping companies made Pitcairn a regular mid-Pacific call the old days of iso-lation became merely a memory of the past. Since then, if we except the war years, the number of ships stopping at Pitcairn has averaged over one a week; yet even today few are prepared to believe the prosaic fact that of all of the many ports of the South Seas, not excluding Noumea, Apia or Papeete, only Suva has a larger visiting tonnage.[32]

The number of calls has drifted downward in recent years, one factor being withdrawal of the passenger services of the New Zealand Shipping Company. Only vessels of the Shaw Savill Company now make regular calls. Where 1956 registered sixty-five calls; 1957, fifty-five; 1958, fifty-eight; 1959, fifty-three; 1960, forty-seven; and 1961, fifty; only thirty-nine calls were made in 1962. But 1963 saw forty-eight calls, 1964 and 1965 each included forty-one. The fall in number of passenger vessels touching the Island has increased the emphasis on selling Island curios by mail order and retail outlets. But touching ships still provide a substantial portion of the curio market, and the long boat is still essential to capitalize on it.

197

BOAT-HANDLING

From the time in 1814 when Captains Pipon and Staines made the journey to Bounty Bay "attended with some degree of danger," suffering "only a good wetting," this brief voyage in Island boats through turbulent rollers to a slapdash landing which threads huge boulders has become a minor classic of navigation. Few visitors have not been excited to graphic comment. Made necessary by lack of harbor and varying with the distance from shore at which touching ships hove to, this journey was no millpond voyage in the best of weather. In rough seas it took on an epic stature.

There is nothing so consummately Pitcairn as the verbal and photographic pictures of the Islanders straining at their oars in heavy surf to guide their longboats into the rock-strewn "bay" overhung with dramatic cliffs. It is their "moment of truth."[33]

From an embarrassment of riches, it is difficult to choose a description, but the account of Dr. Shapiro's experience in making a landing in "exceptionally calm" weather will serve very well.

> . . . even though we were now close in shore, the men seemed almost phlegmatic, even disorganized, to my apprehensive frame of mind. Ahead of us were rocks and more rocks, then the narrow shingle at the base of a steep cliff. This so-called Bounty Bay was no bay to me. It was not even a cove. Nothing protected it from the swelling pulsations of the Pacific, as they rhythmically threw masses of surf and spray against the rocks. At last, as I had finally decided that these were not superskilled boatmen but foolhardy idiots, the rowing ceased without a spoken command. We paused. Wave after wave came up, lifted our boat high on its crest, passed on again as we dropped down into the trough. Once or twice a voice cried, "Now." But apparently the men recognized it as premature, or else they waited for the command of a more trusted voice, for suddenly someone yelled, "Now," and eagerly the word was taken up. "Now, now," "pull, pull," came from all parts of the boat. In response to the exhortations, oars were dug into the sea, and the boat gathered a momentum to match the oncoming swell. With a turn and a skilful pointing of the boat we had rounded the huge boulders into a narrow channel hardly visible to an inexperienced eye, and carried by the force of the awaited swell we were thrown straight and true down the short, narrow channel and hard onto the pebbly shingle.

The Pitcairners courted disaster not only on the inbound trip, but in launching their boats, particularly when there was a bit of weather.

An occasional breaker afflicted with gigantism might dash a cherished boat against keel-breaking rocks. The Pitcairners earned their reputation (confirmed by winning races with the Australian Navy) as topnotch surf boatmen the hard and necessitous way.

Pitcairn seamanship was put to dramatic use on more than one occasion by distressed ships. The incident recorded by the Register entry of November 4, 1853* evokes the "Bounty" mutiny:

> . . . an American whale-ship, which left us the day before, made her appearance again . . . the captain landed with the melancholy information that his ship was in a sinking state, occasioned by two of his crew having, the night before, with an inch-and-a-quarter auger, bored eight holes through the bottom, hoping to sink her off the Island!
> . . . one half our men went immediately on board . . . After fourteen hours of hard labour, they, with the assistance of the crew, succeeded in pumping out all the water, and in stopping the holes. After endeavouring in vain to be allowed to leave the mutinous characters on the Island, he again left us . . . It is a most providential thing for us, that she did not sink. For having been within eighty miles of this Island, whoever were saved would naturally have come, expecting hospitality from us; and as there were twenty-seven persons on board, it would be a heavy draw upon our at all times circumscribed means . . . Besides which, it is impossible to imagine how much mischief might be occasioned by having among us so many individuals, who, by all we have learnt of them, are by no means the best of characters.

To which account may be added Admiral Moresby's comment: "They asked no reward, nor did they get any, beyond the Captain's thanks, that I know of; for all they mentioned to me was, 'The Captain thanked us very much.' "

Another incident provided the basis for Jack London's wellknown short story, "The Seed of McCoy." In 1901, Captain Bryce of the barque "Pyrenee," confronted with a burning cargo which days of fire fighting by an exhausted crew had failed to extinguish, proposed beaching her on Pitcairn. McCoy, then President of Pitcairn, objected that the ship would be lost if beached and offered to pilot her to Mangareva. The trip was made in the burning ship in twenty-eight hours, the "Pyrenee" was beached under Mount Duff, the fire was extinguished, and the vessel salvaged.

The importance of boat-handling in the Pitcairn community was underscored by the Island's nearest approach to a trade school. At

---

* The quotation is as given by Murray, page 279, but the *Pitcairn Island Register Book,* curiously, has only a much abbreviated version.

fourteen the already water-wise boys are put into the boats to train. At fifteen they join the crews and pull oars.

Lack of a harbor increased the appeal of Pitcairn for Christian and his party. For their descendants it meant that they must either become superb boatmen or resign themselves to isolation.

❧ RECREATION AND CULTURE ❧

Pitcairn accomplishments in the realm of fun and games, as viewed by Beechey in 1825, were not impressive. His account of an entertainment which he instigated indicates that, in addition to the inhibitions of natural shyness, the Islanders were already conscious of their international reputation for piety and nonfrivolity and were disinclined to step "out of character." Their tepid and unenthusiastic dancing would have drawn no huzzas in Tahiti, giving Beechey the notion that dancing was rarely enjoyed. But Rosalind Young's description of a celebration of the Queen's birthday some twenty-five years later indicates the survival of the Tahitian "ihari." The lone remaining original settler, Susannah, entering her last year, flashed through the "uri" in a farewell gesture to life and her unforgotten Polynesian youth.

Music for the dance witnessed by Beechey was provided by gourds beaten with hands or sticks, a piece of musical wood, "porou," worked with the toes, and the "Bounty" copper fish kettle. When the Pitcairners failed to respond to a performance on the violin by one of the officers of the "Blossom," Beechey felt justified in consigning them to the musical limbo. This judgment was rendered suspect by the 1850 experience of marooned sojourner Carleton, who in short order was able to evoke choral singing from the Islanders that prompted a later visitor to compare it with that "at Cathedrals" and repeatedly won lavish praise. The impressive singing of hymns by the Pitcairners as they rowed back to Bounty Bay after bidding visitors farewell became a Pitcairn signature.

Sports activities of the youngsters naturally centered on the water. They learned to swim and thread the difficult passes of the rocks at an early age. Swimming around the Island was a common achievement. Surfing with a canoe-shaped board gained an added thrill by the danger of being dashed on the rocks by heavy incoming waves. Kites, tops, balls, and swings provided other diversions. Among the older children and adults, fishing was the "number one love." Shooting of sea birds, pigs, and goats provided a relished sport at times.

The high point of Pitcairn fun was visitors, particularly British men-of-war, even though they entailed a lot of hard work. In young Moresby's glowing account of an 1852 visit (quoted in part on page 209), references to entertainment involving the young women spoke of "uninterrupted fun and laughter," of a "country dance" aboard ship at the request of the officers, of singing, blind man's buff (several times), in addition to dining, churchgoing, and intellectual discussions. Moresby was "quite astonished" at the intelligence of the Pitcairn belles, "and the answers they gave, making use of many expressions that I should have thought them quite ignorant of, particularly Susan; she is very clever, and can repeat a great deal of Milton."[34]

READING

Milton in all probability was not a Pitcairn favorite, although literary interest may have been at peak level at the time of Moresby's visit. Another visitor of this time noted the presence of a few works of fiction by Scott, Cooper, Marryat, and Dickens, besides many other popular books.[35]

Early Pitcairn reading was largely confined to the King James Bible and the Prayer Book, on which beginning readers cut their teeth. The Society for Promoting Christian Knowledge supplemented this basic library with other religious books, and Adams was reported to be fond of reading one of the Society's publications, "The Knowledge and Practice of Christianity; an Instruction for the Indians," product of the pen of the Right Reverend Dr. Wilson, Bishop of Sodor and Man. Interest in religious books and tracts remained a constant on Pitcairn, while the stock of other types of literature fluctuated.

The Pitcairners early evidenced a thirst for literary knowledge. They were anxious to obtain a spelling book from a ship touching in 1817. Two years later, "nothing pleased them so well as the books" which Captain King gave them, "as they wished much to read and write." In later years the Islanders evidenced an appetite for newspapers and magazines, undulled by the fact that they were generally stale when received. Later reports indicate that Victorian novelists, to say nothing of Milton, are no longer popular fare; ". . . few read anything more than magazines or children's stories."

LATER DEVELOPMENTS

This may result in part from the advent of radio, phonograph, and even movies on Pitcairn. Many homes have "old-fashioned organs which are played with acceptable skill." Music has become secularized, and the traditional-minded can now complain of "hill-billy and jazz" music, and "the present tendency is towards these more primitive and degenerate forms." But the Islanders are still able to switch from jazz to hymns with amazing speed.

Movies fascinate the Islanders; natural favorites, such as "Mutiny on the Bounty," are screened repeatedly. "A comic short meant to illustrate a point in national economics became a great favourite because of its catchy musical accompaniment and was screened regularly once each week for upwards of a year, even though the theme of the film was never understood."

In the field of sports, cricket has become popular with male and female. From a vivid description of traditional matches "played in a pre-Hambledon spirit," one gains the impression that whatever they may lack in formality is more than balanced by spirited action, culminating in "some eight hundred runs . . . agreed and recorded by the rival scorers." Naturally, the famed trenchermen of Pitcairn seize on the occasion for a public feast.

Partying is prompted by the slightest excuse (birthdays are sure-fire) and reaches its peak on departure of a visitor, when "food is laid on in great abundance." Christmas is celebrated with gifts placed in baskets hung outside the house by the children and hung on Christmas trees in "The Square."

Noteworthy sporting events on Pitcairn include annual boat races on New Year's Day and a tug-of-war between men and women, with the women perennial winners. Fishing maintains its strong appeal when weather permits.

Beginning with Elder Gates in 1892, outsiders have sought to organize recreational and cultural clubs with impermanent results. They tend to dissolve shortly after the organizer departs. Recent organizations include a Women's Club, a League of Mothers, a Red Cross society, and a church-sponsored equivalent of the Boy Scouts and Girl Guides. Pitcairn's third attempt at a journal, the monthly *Pitcairn Miscellany,* was commenced in 1959 and has proved longer-lived than its predecessors.

Social life on tiny Pitcairn is more difficult to isolate than in more compartmented societies. In such communal activities as government, boating, wooding expeditions, and trading with touching ships, there is a "social" element not present in complex and fragmented communities. Back and forth visiting takes on a remarkably casual cast. The visitor, unworried by lack of invitation, drops in, perhaps joining a conversation in progress, perhaps picking up a magazine to leaf through it silently. He departs when the mood strikes him, having made no claim to being entertained, although both host and guest may find enjoyment in the visit.

Pitcairn fun and games are distinguished by the relaxed and informal manner in which they are pursued, and by the fact that they involve a large part of the community. Even an "exclusive" birthday party, confined to the "closest relatives," is likely to include a third of the Island population.

☙ LANGUAGE ❧

THE TRIUMPH OF ENGLISH

Among the enigmas of Pitcairn history, the language "mystery" is not the least.

Recall the circumstances: After a stay in Tahiti of some five or six months, mutiny, and two failed attempts to settle in Tubuai, nine English seamen sail from Tahiti with a ménage of six Polynesian men, twelve Polynesian women, and an infant girl. After four months of roaming the South Seas they find an uninhabited island on which to settle. Within ten years, accident, disease, and internal warfare have reduced the original settlers to a single Englishman, ten Polynesian women, and the girl. There are also twenty-three hybrid offspring of the mutineers ranging in age from infancy to ten years. There is a complete absence of contact with the outside world for another eight years, when the settlement is discovered by a Yankee sealing captain.

Query: What language is spoken on the Island?

Answer: English for one, and perhaps predominantly.

How was it possible for the youth to grow up speaking the language originally exclusive to the lone male survivor with an excellence that astonished Captains Folger, Staines, and Pipon, and many others, when all their mothers had Tahitian or cognate tongues as their native speech? As Dr. Shapiro points out, "Not only do we usually think of mothers as teaching their offspring the rudiments of language, but where the women so outnumbered the one surviving man who had no English companion to exercise and to keep agile his mother tongue, we might logically expect the natural influence of the maternal language would have predominated."

The evidence indicates that the early Pitcairners were bilingual. Pipon noted that in 1814, "The old women who are from Otaheite, retain the mother tongue . . . they have pick'd up many English words & understand the English language tolerably," but that English was "the general language among them [the descendants]." Pipon's conclusion was probably correct, but the Pitcairners would naturally use a common language in conversing with the visitors, who expressed amazement that they spoke English "uncommonly well," regardless of the speech current among themselves. Moerenhout, who visited Pitcairn in 1829, noted the bilingual abilities of the Islanders and drew therefrom the suggestion that they would make good missionaries. And Hon. Captain Waldegrave, reporting observations made in 1830, said: "One of the remarkable circumstances is the correctness of their language and pronunciation. The general language is English; their divine service, also, is in English; but they frequently converse in Otaheitan, the language of the mothers."

The survival and, indeed, triumph of English could hardly be predicted in the circumstances. It is difficult to explain after the fact. Dr. Shapiro, one of the few to devote much attention to this interesting question, suggests that the British are "proverbially bad linguists, and have, according to the French, forced the world to speak their language by their inability to use another." This suggestion draws some support from the statement of Jenny(1) that, "The first settlers discouraged the Tahitean language, and promoted the speaking English.'' Her interviewer says of Jenny that she ''can speak neither English nor Tahitean, but a jumble of both.'' On the basis of an interview five years later, von Kotzebue said that Jenny ''spoke English well enough to carry on a conversation.''

If the survival of English on Pitcairn cannot be fully accounted for, some factors favoring it may be mentioned. The fact that Young, shortly before he died in 1800, and Adams thenceforward, undertook the instruction of the Pitcairn children with the aid of the ''Bounty'' Bible and Prayer Book was undoubtedly significant. It meant that the only literary education offered was conducted in English and involved understanding of English books and prayers. The prestige added to English by corporeal existence, as contrasted with the unwritten and bodiless Tahitian, did not work to the disfavor of the language of the mutineers.

Add that English was the language of the sole surviving adult male, leader of the community, and the person with widest experience of the world. The coming of the ships, with their English-speaking officers and their exciting importance in the Pitcairn cosmogony, enhanced the prestige of English, reinforced by the ties which developed with the great Empire and the English-speaking Yankee whalers. The first immigrants, notably Buffett and Nobbs, who took over the education of the children, conducted classes in their native English tongue. By this time, before 1830, the die was cast. English had been staked out as the basic language of Pitcairn.*

THE FATE OF TAHITIAN

Tahitian, as did English, survived for a considerable time after the settlement. As we have seen, it became a supplementary or alternate language. The last of the Polynesian settlers, Susannah, did not die until 1850; the decline of Tahitian probably began before this date, although it is difficult to chart its course with any accuracy. It is equally difficult to trace the emergence of a third language, which may

---

* The first draft of this chapter was completed before the availability of the very interesting study, *The Pitcairnese Language* by Alan S. C. Ross and others, Oxford University Press, New York, 1964. This invaluable book, of which more later in the chapter, adds little that is helpful in solving the question of how English, with the numerical odds so heavily against it, emerged as the language of Pitcairn.

have been a parallel development, consisting of an amalgam of English and Tahitian into what came to be known as the Pitcairnese language. An 1850 visitor reported that, "The language of conversation among themselves is fast degenerating into a dialect," although "They can speak English, when they take the trouble, with remarkable purity, but with a formality of expression which shows it to have been acquired from books."[36]

There are indications that the ability to speak Tahitian, if failing of pristine fluency, continued after 1850 for an indeterminable period, although the 1878 report of Admiral deHorsey states flatly, "English is the only language spoken or known."

THE PITCAIRNESE LANGUAGE

Tahitian as a separate language expired slowly, but not without leaving a notable mark on Pitcairn speech. This was its contribution to Pitcairnese, described variously as "dialect," "patois," and "language," a mixture of English and Tahitian. The first reference to this "third language" found in the literature is the one above quoted from an 1850 visitor, although Pitcairnese could hardly have been an overnight development.

The early accounts suggest that the Pitcairners spoke a "plain" English readily comprehensible from Tipperary to Tacoma. The few direct quotations of Pitcairn speech in these reports support this view, although it is conceivable that the Islanders stifled their local dialect for the occasion, just as a schoolboy might suppress in the classroom taboo words and syntax natural on the playground, without even thinking about it. Indeed, subsequent visitors, particularly in the twentieth century, repeatedly reported a swift transition from Pitcairnese, in talking to one another, to English for the accommodation of outlanders. But 1825 callers, such as Beechey and Bechervaise, whose visits were on the order of three weeks, were likely to have noted this phenomenon if it had developed by that time. Pitcairnese was probably slow in development; the best inferential guess would have it emerging in the 1830s and 1840s. Survival of some Pitcairnese in the Norfolk colony indicates that it had caught on before the 1856 exodus.

But Pitcairnese reached its greatest development on the Island of its origin, where isolation was more complete than on Norfolk. Dr. Shapiro found in 1934 that "Pitcairnese still flourishes, the children hardly speaking any other form than this to which they are bred, and the adults frequently lapse into it when they are not on their company manners." He describes Pitcairnese as consisting of "mispronounced English and Tahitian words with a spattering of coined words, the whole employed in a degenerate English syntax." To extract a few plums from his "word list": "illi-illi" is used to describe a rough sea, deriving from "hilly" plus the characteristic Polynesian repetition for purpose of emphasis. "I'sa dona school" indicates the speaker has finished school, "cah fetch" that it can't be done. The elision of the letter "r" is typical, as are a drawl and rhythm that "transmute the caricatured words into a cadence."

Writing of the same period, Hall notes that Pitcairn English "still has something of the biblical flavor* first acquired by their forefathers at John Adams' knee; but when talking among themselves they speak a jargon in which scarcely a word is, at first, understood by a stranger. They change from this to English with the greatest ease."

The speech of Pitcairn-born Mayhew December Christian, interviewed by Frederick O'Brien at Tahiti circa 1920, was described as a peculiar patois, English, Tahitian, and American—middle western—with admixture of Tahitian words.[37]

Despite the opposition of the Pitcairn school to Pitcairnese, and frequent predictions of its demise, it continued to develop and flourish. Thus schoolmaster Roy Clark in the 1930s noted that "common Island vernacular . . . as spoken today is not nearly so corrupt and difficult to understand as it was two generations back." But visitors in the 1950s almost invariably reported its current use and cited examples of Pitcairnese to demonstrate it.[38]

---

* Col. Edouard R. L. Doty, who was born in Tahiti in 1901, son of the U. S. Consul there, had a Pitcairn-born nursemaid, Mary McCoy, and other contacts with Pitcairners "who frequently came to Tahiti for a few months, for they all seemed to rotate around the Consulate." In correspondence with the author, his recollections of Pitcairn speech are of much interest, and bear out Hall's observation of three decades later. "They spoke slowly, never in a hurry, and this was an extreme contrast to . . . the Tahitians, who, because of their French assimilation rambled along like any Frenchman. The Islanders were always calm, much as a mid-west farmer is portrayed to be. But of particular interest was their 'biblical' construction of all sentences. They spoke 'Bible English' using 'thee,' 'thou,' and 'ye' with often reference to the deity, such as . . . 'We shall go to Faaa, if our Good Lord be willing.' And when Mary greeted Christian or Young in the morning, it was usually, 'And the Lord has been kind to thee?' and the reply . . . 'Yea, he has been merciful.' "

PITCAIRN PLACE NAMES

Pitcairnese is further imbedded in such place names as "Illy Illy Ridge," "Popoi Stool," and "Johnny's Tuny-nut." Pitcairn place names, only some of which employ Pitcairnese, are prodigious in number and color when the two-square-mile extent of the Island is considered. Several hundred are listed in *The Pitcairnese Language.** Many of them embody the history of former ownership, such as "Big George Coco-nut" (a coconut grove originally belonging to George Young, son of the mutineer), "Isaac's Stone" (an offshore rock which was claimed by mutineer Isaac Martin), and "John Mills' Harbour" (an inlet which was the mutineer's fishing place).

Other Pitcairn place names constitute a catalogue of disaster, commemorating the scenes of accidents, some trivial, but many tragic. "Down-under-Johnny-fall" marks the place where John Mills, son of the mutineer, plunged to his death in 1814 while gathering seabirds' eggs on a cliff. "Where-Minnie-off" refers to the place where Minnie Christian was washed from the rocks by a big wave; she was rescued. "Bane's Edge" fixes the spot where a Tahitian fell into the sea and was drowned in 1852.

Pitcairn place names derive from a variety of sources. Some are simply descriptive of physical features, such as "The Edge," a small ledge at the top of the path from Bounty Bay, or "Flattie," a flat rock at the landing place. Others commemorate the scene of events in Island history, such as "Timiti's Crack," where one of the Polynesian settlers was murdered. Places associated with particular birds, fish, trees, or plants are distinguished by names descriptive of that fact, such as "Itei," "Out-the-small," "Under-the-Coffee," and "Ginger Valley." As Mr. Ross points out, whereas the origin of most place names is lost, Pitcairn is a mine of "pristine" place names; that is, names "of whose act of creation we are cognizant."

If Tahitian as a separate tongue is apparently defunct on Pit-

---

* *The Pitcairnese Language*, by Alan S. C. Ross and others, published by the Oxford University Press at New York in 1964, is a scholarly work which has assured the immortality of Pitcairnese. It removes the Pitcairn contribution to the dialects of the world from the realm of visitors' casual observations and fragmentary word-lists to the more rarefied atmosphere of professional philology, and is highly recommended to those with a more than cursory interest in Pitcairnese.

cairn, it still survives in the words, phrases, place names, and syntax which have been welded into Pitcairnese in recognizable, if frequently altered, form. This is less surprising than if it had disappeared completely and English had survived without suffering a sea change on its long journey across the oceans under the strange circumstances which landed it on Pitcairn. But the survival of English after the Colony was reduced to a single man who had it for native tongue is in the nature of a miracle, comparable to that whereby the same unlettered Adams was able to lead his exotic flock into the Church of England.

⚜ HOSPITALITY ⚜

If there be one aspect of Pitcairn on which there is complete agreement, it is the hospitality of the Islanders, lauded in a hundred reports. Pitcairners have frequently received the accolade of "the most hospitable people in the world." Their very first visitor, Captain Mayhew Folger, called them a "very humane and hospitable people."

It was not always thus. The original settlers were averse to guests dropping in, as can readily be understood. Even when Folger arrived in 1808, and only Adams remained of the original mutineers, apprehension had not disappeared. But as the fear of Adams' removal vanished and friendly relations and commerce developed with visitors, fear was replaced by eagerness for guests. Accounts of the visitors are replete with descriptions of hearty welcomes, especially demonstrative in the case of Royal Navy vessels, inquiries after previous visitors, and correspondence by the Pitcairners with departed guests.

Some notion of the reception given these visitors is derived from the unreserved account of Mr. Fortescue Moresby, inspired by the 1852 landmark visit of H.M.S. "Portland," commanded by his father, Rear Admiral Fairfax Moresby. Reported young Moresby:

> Never were seen so many happy smiling faces, all eager to look at the first admiral that ever came to their happy island, but not one tried to push his way or make any attempt to get before another: if we said a kind word to any of them they looked happy and pleased, and we did not neglect to do so . . . I was forthwith introduced to all the girls. . . . It was now church-time, so away we all went to church. Mr. Nobbs officiated, and read the prayers earnestly and impressively; the most

solemn attention was paid by all. . . . Every family has a regular turn to entertain the captain of any ship that arrives. . . . The officers are all billeted off to different families, because it makes the cooking and attendance easier, and they say the officers talk more, consequently they obtain more information. The most implicit confidence is placed in English officers; no restraint is thought necessary, and the girls walk about with them by day or night, alone or together. I was generally accompanied by one or two with their arms around me; almost as often by three or four. . . . All the time the stream of fun and laughter was uninterrupted, but their demeanor is so virtuous, modest, and natural, while they show so much affection, that I could not help feeling quite a love towards them all; and I feel convinced that the most hard-hearted villain and the greatest reprobate must loathe himself and detest his own sins in contemplating the high moral standard to which these simple islanders have attained.

. . . We made them dance a country dance; but the band was their great treat, for it was the first ever seen . . . we then went to the singing-school . . . We then proposed blind-man's-buff, and it was fun . . . The parting with the men was worse almost than with the girls; to see big stout fellows crying, and hardly able to look up, was too much. All the officers were deeply affected, and I saw some of the men nearest me, old hardy seamen and big marines, not only wipe away a tear but regularly crying.[39]

Buffett, Pitcairn's first immigrant, was accepted into the community in 1823 on the basis of Adams' approval. His shipmate, Evans, apparently had no permission, jumped ship, and was nonetheless accepted into the community. Nobbs and Bunker arrived in 1828 under circumstances which inevitably aroused the Islanders' suspicions. Nevertheless they were given refuge on the plea of Bunker's illness, and Nobbs remained to become the spiritual leader of the community after the death of Bunker.

Pitcairn hospitality was no mere formalized ritual, devised to cope with guests regardless of whether they were welcome. On Pitcairn, the desire for visitors could be assumed; it was necessary to evolve rules for rotating them among eager hosts so that all could share. The genuine warmth of the Pitcairn greeting, combined with the simplicity, naïveté, and unpretentiousness of the Islanders, won visitors over and brought out in them their kindliest manners.[40]

This observation covers even the hairy-chested whaling crews. Captain King of the whaler "Elizabeth" capsuled the matter in his statement that in 1819, "Even the sailors belonging to the ship behaved with a modesty in the presence of these naked (meaning above the waist) females, that would have surprised a Joseph Andrews.'' The relationship with the whalers, while not infused with as much sentiment as attended calls of Royal Navy ships, resulted in some warm friendships, especially when an occasional prolonged stay was involved. This occurred when the captain of a whaler left his wife on Pitcairn for a badly-needed shore leave or with the intention of making available to her the services of the Island women in a forthcoming childbirth.

Not infrequently, hospitality involved more than an exchange of good fellowship, or of bed and board for thank-you gifts. There was more than one instance in which the Pitcairners provided refuge for shipwrecked sailors in numbers that taxed severely the limited resources of the Island and for periods longer than was convenient. The Pitcairners passed even this test of hospitality on four occasions in the 1870s and 1880s, when shipwrecked sailors sought succor on the Island. The wreck of the ''Cornwallis'' on Pitcairn and of the ''Khandeish'' on Oeno both occurred in 1875. The ''Acadia'' was wrecked on Ducie in 1881 and the ''Oregon'' on Oeno in 1883.

The most taxing demand was that imposed by the 51-day stay of the ''Khandeish'' crew in the year following the punishing drought of 1874. Some notion of how well the Pitcairners acquitted themselves in the awkward role of involuntary and poorly-heeled (with worldly goods) hosts can be gleaned from the sequel. As a result of interest aroused by the returned sailors' lavish praise of their treatment, the citizens of San Francisco sent the Pitcairners a stream of gifts, including utensils, clothing, cloth, and even a ''beautifully-toned organ, of the Mason & Hamlin Organ Company.''

🙟 NOTES: PART FIVE 🙟

1. See "Politics in Pitcairn" by W. K. Hancock, *Nineteenth Century* (1931), Vol. 109, p. 575.
2. Rowe, Newton, *Voyage to the Amorous Isles,* London, 1955. This book is based on Wallis's expedition, during which he discovered Tahiti in 1766.
3. Ellis, William, *Polynesian Researches,* London, 1831.
4. Lucas, Sir Charles, in introduction to *The Pitcairn Island Register Book.*

5. Hancock.
6. *The Varieties of Religious Experience.*
7. Bechervaise.
8. The standard sources all treat of religion on Pitcairn Island. Rev. Thomas Murray is most valuable for the early days.
9. For the story of the conversion to Seventh Day Adventism and the role of that Church on Pitcairn, *see* Gates, H. E.: *In Coral Isles,* Washington, D.C., 1923; Christensen, Alta Hilliard: *Heirs of Exile,* Washington, D.C., 1955; and Young.
10. Bennett.
11. Many of the voyagers' and official reports include comments on Pitcairn sexual morality which run the gamut from awed admiration to unrestrained horror. The "standards" include some material; most valuable is Shapiro, which contains the nearest equivalent of a "survey" and the most judicious comments.

    It is obvious that, by reason of the subject, the data are as unsatisfactory for Pitcairn as for other communities and conclusions are equally suspect.
12. Greene, Marc T. "Lonely Isle," *Asia,* December 1945, vol. 45, p. 588.
13. Shapiro is the most valuable authority on Pitcairn marriage in general; the other "standards" and Beechey on the early days are helpful. Young is of particular interest on the shipwrecked sailors who married into Pitcairn society and the general picture in the latter part of the nineteenth century.

    There are only scattered references in the record to the rearing of children. These suggest that the attitude was permissive, after the Polynesian fashion, and that Pitcairn boys and girls were early imbued with freedom and independence.
14. Brodie and Shapiro are valuable generally, and in addition, they include the text of criminal legislation. The official reports listed in the bibliography are the basis of much of the material in the latter part of the chapter. Maude (3) gives the most comprehensive and coordinated picture. See *A Guide to Pitcairn.*
15. Gates, *In Coral Isles,* Washington, D.C., 1923. This is the best account of Pitcairn indoctrination into tithing and missionary giving.
16, 17. See offical reports in Bibliography for quoted and other reports.
18. Fullerton, W. Y. *The Romance of Pitcairn Island,* London, 1923, page 17.
19. For idyllic pictures of Pitcairn harmony in the "golden age" of Adams, see almost any of the early voyagers' reports, but particularly Beechey and Bechervaise. Brodie gives a similar picture of Pitcairn in 1850. For Pitcairn at a high point of discord, the reign of Hill, see Bennett. For the period around the turn of the twentieth century, see the official reports. Murray is a good source for many of the reports of the Navy captains and other visitors in the period from Adams' death in 1829 to the Norfolk emigration.
20. Newell.
21. Furnas, J. C., *Anatomy of Paradise,* New York, 1948.

22. For the actual texts of Pitcairn law, see Brodie, containing the contents of the Code existent in 1850, and Shapiro, Appendix A, which contains the *Laws and Regulations of the Pitcairn Islanders* from the Book of Records of Pitcairn Island. Maude(3) gives the most comprehensive history to 1941 of Pitcairn laws and government. *A Guide to Pitcairn* is the best source for updating of the laws and governmental changes. Much of the Pitcairn literature touches on aspects of law and government, and they are dealt with particularly in the official reports.
23. Newell.
24. Buffett's petition is quoted, among other places, in Shapiro, p. 84, which also includes some of the other documents related to the Hill episode.
25. All the "standards," notably Brodie, Murray, and Shapiro, contain valuable material. Murray quotes many letters from the Islanders and their educational mentor, Nobbs, indicative of the talents of the teacher and the achievements of the pupils. Miss Young's book demonstrates the quality of literary expression attainable by a girl educated on Pitcairn, and at a period when there were no European-educated teachers. Official reports cited herein contain comments on the educational scene, generally marked by comparisons rather than objective descriptions. Reading habits and culture are treated on pp. 200 ff. of this book.
26. Quoted by Murray, p. 141.
27. Quoted by Shapiro, p. 77.
28. Quoted by Murray, p. 200.
29. "The Schoolmaster of Pitcairn," *Atlantic Monthly*, Vol. 157, pp. 576–579, May 1936; "School on Pitcairn," *Atlantic Monthly*, Vol. 159, pp. 482–484, April 1937.
30. *A Guide to Pitcairn.*
31. Fullerton, W. Y., *The Romance of Pitcairn Island*, London, 1923.
32. Maude(4).
33. Pitcairn boats and boat-handling are described in a large part of the literature. For Pitcairn experience with larger vessels, see Maude(3) and Fullerton, supra. For excellent descriptions and photographs of Pitcairn boat-handling, see the Luis Marden article and the articles and books by the Johnsons.
34. Mr. Moresby's account is reproduced in Belcher, p. 220 ff.
35. Shipley, C., *Sketches in the Pacific, the South Sea Islands* (1851), p. 6.
    Other quotations are from the chapter by E. Schubert on "Pitcairn Island Today" in *The Pitcairnese Language* and from *A Guide to Pitcairn*.
    Some pertinent material will be found in much of the literature, but Beechey, Brodie, Murray, Young, and Shapiro are particularly valuable, and, for the last decade, Marden, Schubert, and *The Guide*. The latter contains an excellent account of cricket à la Pitcairn.
36. Metoixos (Hugh Carleton), "Pitcairn's Island," *The Shipping Gazette and Sydney General Trade List*, vii, 272–3.
37. O'Brien, F. *Atolls of the Sun*, London, 1922.
38. Marden contains many colorful direct quotations of Pitcairn speech and Pitcairnese, as well as Islanders' explanations of such place names as

"Oh Dear" and "Headache." A.G.H., writing in *Blackwood's* for July 1959, vol. 286, p. 1 ff., describes the Pitcairners as having "a funny trick of speech . . . the splitting of all the long vowel sounds into two; things on Pitcairn are never all right, they're always ri-aht." Ferdon also provides interesting linguistic data in his article in the *Geographical Review,* January 1958.

Besides these and the authorities cited in the text, a large number of references to Pitcairn speech is scattered throughout the literature, many of them collected in *The Pitcairnese Language.*

39. Moresby's account is much more fully quoted in Belcher.

40. The hospitality of the Pitcairners is eulogized in most of the numerous accounts. Perhaps those of most value in recording this aspect of Pitcairn life in the nineteenth century are Brodie, Belcher, Murray, and Young. A more recent report appears in the articles and books of the Johnsons.

Part Six

EUGENICS LABORATORY —
THE PITCAIRN BREED

⚜ CROSS-BREEDING ⚜

All the children born of the original adult settlers of Pitcairn were sired by six of the Englishmen (Adams, Christian, McCoy, Mills, Quintal, and Young) out of Polynesian women. The result was the production of a hybrid race of marked interest to geneticists and eugenists, especially as the community received little new blood for generations.

The effect of this cross-breeding was one of the major interests of Dr. Shapiro on his finally-realized arrival on Pitcairn in 1934. Noting that experiments, plant and animal, indicated that the production of hybrids "often leads to an increase in size and vigor," he measured the Pitcairners to find the men slightly taller, on average, than either ancestral stock (173.0 cm.), but with the difference diminished as compared with that (177.8 cm.) indicated by measurements recorded in 1825 of the first born Pitcairn generation. He found, too, that the English width of face was dominant, that the minimum frontal diameter was narrower than that of either parent stock, that the width of the nose was roughly intermediate between the broad Polynesian and the narrow English nose, and that mixed eye colors showed a dominance in the women of the Polynesian brown over the English blue, but in the men there appeared to be "an additional factor operating to modify the expected dominance of brown pigment." Further, that the range of variability otherwise to be expected was reduced by intense inbreeding.

217

After indicating that each Pitcairner was "a varying mixture" of both English and Polynesian stocks, Dr. Shapiro makes the "subjective rating" that "not one [Pitcairner] was sufficiently Tahitian in appearance to be able to pass as such, whereas a number of the Islanders might readily escape detection in an English community. Of course, this preponderance of the English type is natural, for all the new additions to the colony have been of English stock."

The verdict on this point was not unanimous, but rather reminiscent of a colloquy between maternal and paternal grandparents as to whether the baby looks more like one side than the other.

Thus naturalist Michael John Nicoll, after his visit to Pitcairn in 1903, found the children fair and the older people dark, and came to the conclusion that the Pitcairners "resemble their ancestors, the 'Bounty' mutineers, every alternate generation."[1]

Mrs. Scoresby Routledge, after her 1915 inspection, adjudged the Pitcairn men "definitely European in appearance and manner; they were mostly of a sallow white complexion, though a few had a darker tinge."[2] Mrs. Scoresby Routledge brought to England two Young brothers, examined by Dr. Arthur Keith, F.R.S., and he came to the conclusion that the boys were "decidedly more Tahitian than European."[3]

A government official in the late 1920s dismissed the physical appearance of the Pitcairners as typical of Polynesian half-castes.

Examination of many photographs of Pitcairners in books and magazine articles indicates the difficulties involved. In the field of the subjective, grandma and grandpa yield to no man. What the photographs do suggest, however, is a homogeneity of visage in the Pitcairners clearer than their resemblance to either parent race. It may be arguable whether they look more English or Polynesian; it is less questionable that they look more like one another than like either root stock.[4]

❦ INBREEDING ❦

Accidents of history and geography made Pitcairn perhaps the closest available approach to a laboratory of human inbreeding. As all the children in the first generation born on the Island were descended from six of the mutineers, and immigration was minimal until recent times, it was not very long before relationships were, as Mark Twain put it, "wonderfully, even astoundingly, mixed up and complicated." The humorist found this situation an irresistible target.

A stranger, for instance, says to an islander,—
"You speak of that young woman as your cousin; a while ago you called her your aunt."
"Well, she *is* my aunt, and my cousin too. And also my step-sister, my niece, my fourth cousin, my thirty-third cousin, my forty-second cousin, my great-aunt, my grandmother, my widowed sister-in-law—and next week she will be my wife."[5]

Anthropologist Shapiro, avoiding the difficulty of describing the intricate relationships evolved after five or six generations, resorted to a "simple index" of the degree of inbreeding, arrived at by dividing the total number of ancestors theoretically possible, dating from the generation of the mutineers, into the actual number. The average for adults in the 1910–1916 period was 51.53 per cent. "One subject had an index of 25.56. In his family tree Fletcher Christian appeared seven times, Edward Young six times, John Mills three times, William McCoy three times, Matthew Quintal three times, John Adams once, and John Buffett once." It may surprise some that, according to Professor Shapiro, "This inbred young man is a healthy islander and shows no obvious stigmata of his restricted ancestry."

Prevalent taboos against marriage within prohibited degrees and a host of folk beliefs caused some visitors to scrutinize the inbred Pitcairners for tell-tale signs of degeneration as the mother of an exposed child might examine it for measle spots. In more than one case, finding no stigmata, they invented them or attributed whatever common human failings they discerned to the "inevitable" degeneration which must result from inbreeding.

Thus, the official report of the High Commissioner for the Western Pacific (1898) found the Islanders greatly deteriorated "owing to intermarriage," and indicated that the outlook was "hopeless imbecility."[6] The Commissioner's successor, some twenty-three years later, came to contrary conclusions.

It might be expected that signs of degeneracy which were observed twenty-three years ago would be even more noticeable now; and certainly

I saw none. Possibly former observers have been prejudiced by the theory that intermarriage over a period of years inevitably results in degeneration. This, I believe, is by no means the case when the original stock is sound: and in this instance it seems reasonable to suppose not only that the original stock was hardy and robust, but that it was strengthened and adapted to its environment by the admixture of Tahitian blood.[7]

This view is supported by the authoritative findings of Dr. Shapiro, who points out that inbreeding, while it may increase the chance of the appearance of a latent defect, had resulted in no visible ill effects on the Pitcairners, with the possible exception of "degeneration of their dentitions." Some have sought to attribute this defect to Midshipman Young of the Bounty, described by Bligh as having "lost several of his fore teeth" at the age of 22, with the remainder "all rotten." (See p. 234.)

Dr. Shapiro found the Pitcairners robust and healthy, with good medical records, and few abnormalities. His "subjective impressions" of mental and psychological character are in line with his physical data. Two or three were "distinctly below par mentally—a small proportion in a group of two hundred. Several were dull but able to manage their affairs efficiently enough. The rest seemed to me to fit into the average range of intelligence." A dozen Pitcairners of notable superiority of personality received commendation.

More recent visitors, notably the Johnsons, corroborate Dr. Shapiro's conclusions, but the search for stigmata has not completely ceased. Infusions of new blood by intermarriage with outlanders have sharply lowered the index of inbreeding in recent decades.

It was Dr. Shapiro's observation as of 1934 that, "The newer blood has not added anything noticeably superior to the population. In fact, the finest individuals appear to be those from the purest Pitcairn strains. It is regrettable that the original population were not kept unadulterated."

The situation has now reached the stage where, "Today there are native-born Pitcairn Islanders who have only the faintest trace of "Bounty" blood in their veins."[8]

The "controls" which made the Pitcairn laboratory of inbreeding uniquely valuable have been shattered. But not before a long-held folk belief was demolished.[9]

❦ CROSS-CULTURATION ❦

When English sailors who cook their fish set up housekeeping with Polynesian women accustomed to eating fish raw, what results? Do all eat it in the same style, do they compromise by cooking fish slightly, or do they avoid trouble by simply eschewing fish? And, if they maintain their separate ways while alive, how do succeeding generations prepare their fish? The result, whatever it may be, is known to anthropologists and sociologists as "cross-culturation" or "culture adjustment." Pitcairn society provides a notable instance of this process.[10]

Whether fish is eaten raw or cooked may depend on many circumstances. For example, on whether husband and wife live in the land of one of them or elsewhere, on whether the fish they know are available there, on whether one spouse or the other is domineering, or on whether cooking fuel is readily available. In a new community, like the Pitcairn of 1790, foreign to both husbands and wives, many decisive "culture adjustments" were required almost immediately.

What type of shelter should be used? What crops should be favored? How should labor be divided between the sexes? Should they sit on chairs or mats? Should the land be divided and worked separately, or should ownership and work be communal? How should they be governed?

Most of the answers to these questions are dealt with under specific topics and they will be only briefly summarized here.

HOUSING

The housing which resulted on Pitcairn from a combination of the British conception of a cottage and the materials available and missing might be designated as an original adaptation. The use of sturdy plank walls was clearly English, the thatched roof Polynesian. The scarcity of nails, glass, mortar, and cement resulted in ingenious contrivances and substitutions, such as the sliding shutters foreign to both England and Polynesia.

THE HOUSEHOLD

Since the women were all Polynesian, it is not surprising to find that many of the household arts followed their ways. Thus, the underground oven, the calabash, tapa-making, dress style, hats, "linens," lighting, and weaving were patterned on Polynesian models. But the furniture was British, with a nautical accent. Instead of the mats common in Tahiti, the mutineers manufactured chairs or stools, tables, and beds (more frequently bunks) "as best they could," and used sea chests for storage. In considering such Polynesian adoptions as tapa-making and lighting with doodoee or candle nuts, it must be remembered that the raw materials were available on Pitcairn, more like Polynesia than like England, and that English alternatives were not at hand.

FOOD

The Polynesian pattern of preparing meals twice a day, once in the late morning and once in the early evening, prevailed. The method of food preparation and the dishes served, yams in a dozen different guises, vegetables and fruits cooked in coconut milk,* and pillihai, were likewise largely of Pacific origin. But raw fish, to return to our original unanswered question, "seemingly was neglected on Pitcairn," despite the high esteem in which it was held over wide areas of the Eastern world. Dr. Shapiro found this "a matter of wonder . . . where raw-fish eaters controlled the kitchen. Had it once become established in the island diet, nothing could have shaken its hold, and it would have survived to this day among the islanders as one of the major requisites to the enjoyment of life."

---

* Coconut "milk" is not the water inside the nut. As used in Polynesian cookery, "It is made by steeping the flaked meat of a ripe coconut in hot water, then kneading it. The creamy liquid that results imparts a delicate flavor to whatever is cooked in it, seems to tenderize meats." Marden.

THE POSITION OF THE WOMEN

It is difficult to classify the role of women on Pitcairn; what evolved may be considered an original adaptation, in part. As in both British and Polynesian cultures, all the domestic chores, including the arduous tapa-making, were assigned to the women. In addition, they were required to share the heavy work on the plantations with men and children.

As in both civilizations, their treatment by their spouses varied from one couple to the next. In many respects their civic position was superior to that of women in either parent culture; they inherited land equally, were equally included in the compulsory schooling, and they voted in the first Pitcairn election in 1838, long before the Anglo-Saxon countries enfranchised their women. As described by Surgeon Bennett in 1834, Pitcairn women "bear an influential sway both in domestic and public politics . . . are intelligent, active, and robust, partake in the labours of their husbands with cheerfulness. . . ."

Much was made by early visitors of the fact that Pitcairn women, like the Tahitians, did not eat with the men, but took their meal after the men finished. It is doubtful if this custom was universally followed in the absence of visitors, and unlikely that it derived from the taboo which enforced it on Tahiti, rather than from habit.

In this connection, it is interesting to note the comment of Pitcairner Rosalind Young:

> . . . a feeling of unaccountable shyness . . . prevented the women in those early times from sitting down to the same table with strangers. At the present day [late nineteenth century] most of the island women, inheriting the same dispositions from their mothers, when an occasional visitor happens to share their hospitality, would much prefer to "stand and wait" than act the part of hostess by sitting down with their guests.

AGRICULTURE

The emphasis given the yam and the pig and treeborne products, such as coconuts, in the Pitcairn agronomy are reminiscent of Tahiti. The tools, metal hoes, spades, and mattocks, while elementary as

223

measured against even plow culture, were an English contribution so well adapted to the Pitcairn terrain that they are still in use, and were a distinct improvement over the stone and wood implements available to the Polynesians before the metal-rich Westerners arrived. Wheelbarrows were the only Island conveyances until very recently. Pitcairn now boasts two tractors and two motorcycles.

CLOTHING

Clothing followed Polynesian models in the early days on Pitcairn by reason of climate and the resources available. After exhaustion of whatever supplies were brought to Pitcairn, recourse was had to the bark of the paper mulberry or breadfruit tree for the making of tapa—nothing else was available. The basic costume was the maro (loincloth) for men and the pareu (skirt) for women. Sometimes a mantle was thrown over the shoulders. Hats for protection against the sun were devised from coconut leaves and pandanus, occasionally adorned with cock's feathers, and, in the case of the women, reached a level to draw forth high praise from Captain Pipon. "Linens" or bed clothing were made of tapa.

When commerce developed with Western ships, Pitcairn clothing become conglomerate; it depended more on whatever castoffs whalers and Royal Navy boats might provide than on any tradition. In the absence of visitors, the Pitcairners might revert to the native Polynesian simplicities; when a ship arrived they were inclined to show off every vestige of Western sartorial splendor they had acquired, even though they might possess only part of a costume, such as a waistcoat. Later developments saw the shirt and pants become the standard costume for men, the housedress for women, a triumph of the practical over the picturesque. Bare feet remained an Island trademark.

FISHING AND BOATING

The mutineers fashioned fishhooks of European style, but used fish line made from tree bark. They picked up spear fishing from the Polynesians, but ignored other Polynesian fishing lore and practice. The first canoes devised were dugouts, but did not use the Polynesian outrigger principle. The whale boats which became the Pitcairn work-horses were definitely a Western contribution, invaluable in the heavy Island surf. A later borrowing from the West was the engine for the boats.

ARTS AND PLAY

Polynesian survivals included dances and music, although there are clear indications that Island concern for the Pitcairn image of propriety prevented visitors from arriving at the true extent thereof. Captain King described being entertained in 1819 with ''an Otaheitan dance, which consisted of various writhings and distortions of the body, by no means obscene, yet in no respect pleasant.'' Captain Beechey reported the use in 1825 of gourds, the ''Bounty'' copper fish kettle, and musical wood (porou) by Pitcairn musicians.

From the Western world came the single tune introduced by John Adams, which was used for all hymns until 1850. The hymn-singing tradition was later supplemented by Western instruments, such as the organ and the harmonium.

Play patterns borrowed surfriding from Polynesia, kite-flying from both Tahiti and England. A notably British contribution of more recent times is cricket.

Music on Pitcairn is no longer confined to hymns. The benefits of Western civilization have arrived in the form of ''hill billy'' and jazz music. The phonograph and radio have widened the musical horizon.

RELIGION

One of the most unpredictable results of cultural adjustment took place in the emergence as a ''state religion'' of John Adams' version of the Divine Revelation according to the Church of England, in face of the fact that he was its sole exemplar in a community consisting of himself and a half-score Polynesian women and some twenty-three half-caste children. Considering the heavy odds against such an outcome, it is not difficult to understand why it was regarded as in the nature of a miracle.

EDUCATION AND LANGUAGE

Since book learning had no place in the unlettered Polynesian society, it was almost inevitable that schools and schooling, conducted in English, must follow English models. But the institution of compulsory education on Pitcairn in the 1830s, long in advance of most of the Western world, is in the nature of a surprise.

So, too, is the survival of English as the ''official'' language on Pitcairn, but the development of Pitcairnese was a logical outcome of a bilingual society in which each component had fluency only in its native tongue and a halting and fragmentary acquaintance with the other's language. Pitcairnese might have taken over completely if the position of English had not been reinforced by the increasing contacts with English-speaking whalers, men-of-war, and passenger vessels, and by the incorporation of Pitcairn into the British orbit.

LAW AND GOVERNMENT

Law and government on Pitcairn evidence a British cast, but with many indigenous adaptations. Thus, primogeniture, quite logically, was replaced by distribution of land to all the children of the landowner, and women's suffrage was instituted far in advance of more industrialized communities. A strong distaste for authoritarian rule is a prominent feature of island history.

❦ AMELIORATION OF INEQUALITY ❦

GOODS

''Tahitian contributions outweighed the English . . . in developing the characteristic life of the first generation of Pitcairn Islanders,'' is the evaluation of Dr. Shapiro. The outstanding Tahitian contribution, though it has received the least attention, is what might be called, lacking any term of art, "amelioration of inequality," both with regard to goods and land.

In the England from which the mutineers derived, the best social expedients developed for dealing with the universal problem of inequality were the workhouse and the clammy hand of private charity, both wholly inadequate to the task. On Tahiti, a sense of family, broad enough to include every member of the community, constituted insurance against starvation. (See p. 171.) This characteristically ameliorative Polynesian viewpoint prevailed on Pitcairn.

A common community stock of food and other articles was maintained, to be drawn upon by those in need. While some of the reports indicate the keeping of accounts with a view to repayment, no suggestion has been found of any penalties for failure to repay. Indeed, if one is to trust the report of Bechervaise, withdrawals from the "general store" were made "to supply the wants of all without regard to the quantity each has put in."

According to this 1825 visitor, no "purchase" from touching ships was "private . . . all tend to the general comfort, and to the general stock." This is, of course, the predecessor of the famous Pitcairn "share-out," described by many twentieth century visitors, such as Marden. "When a ship comes in, a certain amount of fruit is contributed to a common fund by every householder. As community property, the fruit is traded en bloc to the ship's steward for staples such as wheat flour, potatoes, onions, or sugar. The articles so obtained are divided on the courthouse square into 48 equal heaps, one for each household." Again there is no indication of penalty for failure of an unlucky household to contribute to the stock of fruit.

LAND

Inequality of crops, dependent in part on the vagaries of fortune, might level out to some degree from one year to the next. Inequality of land ownership was built into the varying fertility of Pitcairn families and could only be aggravated by the passage of time.

Visitors were not long in noting dramatic differences in the amount of land owned; what they did not explain was how this situation failed to result in the development of classes, *i.e.*, landlord and tenant, or landowner and hired worker—or in explosion. Either or both of these developments would seem likely on a tiny island, with a limited arable area and increasing population, individual emigration being rarely feasible.

Curiously enough, no explanation of this phenomenon has appeared until very recently. The statements hereafter quoted, the only ones found, are illuminating on this significant point, if not as comprehensive as one might desire.

A Guide to Pitcairn (which acknowledges indebtedness to Mr. Maude) notes that since the system of land ownership ''has never been studied in detail it is impossible to decide whether theory differs from practice'' and, consequently, qualifies subsequent remarks as ''a synthesis of observers' reports.''

The ''synthesis'' describes complaints voiced from time to time as

. . . more likely to be inspired by resentment of inequality than by actual want. Nevertheless, the pattern of agriculture and settlement place a premium on flattish, fertile land close to Adamstown and in it, and a system known as "borrowing" has been developed to meet scarcity, under which an owner grants usufructuary rights to the borrower, for food gardens or for housing, for as long as he remains on Pitcairn. . . . the pattern of usage is one of widely separated plots. A count made several years ago disclosed that there were over 150 garden plots, varying in size from a fifth to a third of an acre, cultivated by 37 families. The pattern today is probably little changed but, as an official soil survey in 1957 disclosed that over five times that area of land was suitable for development as gardens, it is likely that choice plays some part in the patchwork.

Maude (4) explains that the inequalities in land ownership

. . . mattered less as long as, in accordance with Tahitian custom, anyone had the right to plant and thereafter use coconut and fruit trees, irrespective of who owned the land on which they stood, and while in any case land was freely loaned for gardens to anyone who asked. But as European ideas came to supplant Tahitian the position of those with insufficient land of their own for the support of their families became more and more disadvantageous, and many of them were among the first to leave for abroad.

This view is supported by Mr. Schubert, who has served as schoolmaster and education officer on Pitcairn.

From earliest times it has been customary for any Islander to be free to plant coco-nut, orange and mango trees on anyone's land, and retain their ownership; each family possesses a registered mark which is chipped into the trunk of the tree. . . . However, with the growing sophistication of the Islanders, the tendency to plant only on family property is growing. . . . Some of the later arrivals among the strangers are landless, although they can always make a verbal agreement with one of the larger landowners for the use of enough land for subsistence crops. This, of course, is not a very satisfactory method of obtaining land, but it is the best evolved to date. . . . the ownership of land has become rather a vexed question.

It appears that "borrowing" of, and tree planting on, the land of others was adequate until recent times to counter the disruptive potentialities of sharp inequalities of land ownership. It is interesting that this expedient was derived from the placative and accommodative Tahitian culture, in contradistinction to the English emphasis on "mine and thine," and that its effectiveness became weakened "as European ideas came to supplant Tahitian."*

Culture adjustment on Pitcairn, given the unique factors prevailing, was predestined to produce a highly distinctive, if unpredictable, society. It did.

☙ HEALTH ☙

The plight of remote and doctorless communities draws ready sympathy from urbanites conditioned to readily available medical help. "What do they do in serious illnesses?" Like others in the same situation, the Pitcairners did what they could. Home remedies and treatments, sometimes involving use of native herbs and plants, were used, and the services of the more knowledgeable commandeered. Where these did not suffice, it was a case of recover or die, unless a happy chance made available the ministrations of a visiting physician.

The health history of Pitcairn sounds two seemingly contradictory notes; claims of Pitcairn freedom from disease alternate with reports of virulent epidemic infections, sometimes with high mortality.

The early voyagers found the Pitcairners notably robust and healthy. The catch was that their lack of previous exposure to many

---

* For an interesting parallel of Pitcairn "borrowing," see Firth, Raymond, *Primitive Polynesian Economy*, London, 1939, pp. 58 and 263, and the same author's *We, the Tikopia*, London, 1936, particularly p. 400.

diseases made them highly vulnerable to infections acquired on contact with outlanders. Infections acquired during the short stay on Tahiti in 1831 were blamed for seventeen deaths in a group of eighty-six. After the return, the Pitcairn Island Register Book records recurring bouts of what Nobbs called ''influenza.''

The ubiquitous Nobbs, in one of his multiple capacities, was Pitcairn's nearest equivalent to a doctor after his arrival in 1828. His Register entry for March 27, 1845, provides an insight into the course of disease and the state of medicine on Pitcairn:

> . . . respecting the salubrity of the island; it is generally supposed to be a healthy spot . . . but the reverse is found by experience to be the fact. Asthmas, Rheumatism, Consumption, Scrofula and last but not least Influenza under various modifications is prevalent. Five times within the last four years have the fever been rife . . . it has not been so severe latterly . . . This I attribute to the teacher's not giving them emetics as soon as the disease attacked them; since then he has invariably given them vomits on the first appearance of the disease; which seems to prevent any considerable degree of cough.
>
> . . . in this last sickness . . . only one person complained of cold and he was but slightly affected. The first person attacked was a man of full habit of body, plethoric and subject to fits, he had attended Divine service in the morning. . . after evening service I found him under the influence of a raging fever; his eyes seemed ready to start from their sockets and the heat of his skin caused a disagreeable sensation to those who touched him;—he complained of violent pains in his head, back and thighs and said he felt as if "live things were creeping between his flesh and skin." Fearing it might bring on one of the fits to which he was subject the teacher bled him, and gave him a sudorific which had a good effect; the next day a dose of calomel and jalap was administered, and two days after that he was well; though very weak.
>
> I do not think the fever was infectious; and though in the space of six days not less than sixty out of one hundred and twenty-two were attacked yet I attribute it solely to the peculiar state of the atmosphere: whenever we have been visited by this epidemick the circumstances, as respects the weather have been invariably the same. A long drought succeeded by two or three weeks of wet; and the wind settling into the north west; in fact a north west wind is always the precussor [sic] of rheumatism, catarrh, and slight febrile affection. Bleeding is not to be recommended; vomits are the sovereign remedy, for certainly no community of persons secrete greater quantities of bile than the inhabitants of this island. March 31st. There is now but one person sick and she is recovering. . . .

Whatever could be said of pastor-teacher-recorder-doctor George Hunn Nobbs, and a very great deal was, it must be credited to him that he supplied in devotion to his patients a considerable part of what he may have lacked in medical training and paraphernalia. He won particular praise for two months of dogged attendance on over one hundred patients in an 1849 epidemic which closed the school and suspended all but one public service on each Sabbath. Mortality was confined to one infant.

Much deadlier was the epidemic which followed a stay on Pitcairn by the crew of the "Bowdon," shipwrecked on Oeno in April of 1893. The spreading infection (enteric fever) claimed the first of twelve victims in August and the last in October. Six were children. In 1959, an influenza epidemic affected all but a few Islanders, but there was only one death.

Despite the dramatic tolls of the 1831 and 1893 epidemics, the number one killer on Pitcairn over the years was probably accident. This is surprising only until the accidental deaths are particularized; it then becomes clear how naturally they develop from the terrain and situation of Pitcairn. The very first death in the settlement, according to Beechey's account, occurred when Williams' wife, Fasto, fell from a precipice while collecting birds' eggs. It was this fall which precipitated the carnage following Williams' demand for a replacement. Several other deaths of the pioneer women are attributed to the identical cause, and other fatal falls punctuate Pitcairn history.

Accidental deaths resulted also from an attempt in 1853 to fire a salute from an old "Bounty" gun, from shootings, from the falling of a tree, from being washed from a rock, and, most frequently, from handling of boats in the turbulent Pitcairn waters.

Typical of many such accidents was the one which occurred during a 1921 visit of Sir Cecil Rodwell, High Commissioner for the Western Pacific. Two of three longboats put out to a heavy sea successfully; the third was caught by a wave, dashed against the rocks and smashed. Fisher Young, church leader and schoolteacher, and his uncle Christian were killed.

Analyzing 114 deaths listed in the Pitcairn Book of Records from 1864 to 1934, Dr. Shapiro found 19 assigned to accident, and six more which could logically have been given this cause, to give accidents a total of almost 22 per cent of the deaths. Four of the six cases involved lockjaw, then almost invariably fatal on Pitcairn. Shapiro was understandably skeptical of the causes assigned for non-accidental deaths by the Book of Records, but it is interesting to note that, after accidents, "consumption" with 12, "typhus" with 12, and "old age" with 7, led the list. "Heart trouble" was assigned as cause in only 3 deaths.

Of the 114 deaths, 2 represented still births and 17, infants less than a year old. The resulting rate of 56 per thousand births is a "remarkably low" infant mortality for a doctorless community.

To doctors on touching ships, the Pitcairners were indebted for medical aid eagerly availed of, and outlanders are indebted for descriptions of the Island health picture. Thus Dr. George Lyman, who accompanied Shapiro,

> . . . was besieged by the elderly sufferers from chronic conditions common to old age and by the possessors of warts, encysted splinters, benign tumors, and such like, eager for minor surgical operations. On the whole, he found the islanders very healthy and free from any endemic diseases. The ailments for which he was consulted are of a kind that might occur in any random lot of Europeans of equivalent ages. His diagnoses included high blood pressure, cancer, osteomyelitis, fibroma, asthma, arthritis, varicose veins, arteriosclerosis, and tuberculosis.

A physician on board the Johnsons' "Yankee," Dr. Rufus Southworth, offered his services to Pitcairn and spent six months on the Island. Such medical windfalls, as well as a number of others of shorter duration, were welcomed by the Islanders, but did not completely meet needs, nor avert criticism of the British Government for failure to provide regular services by a physician. One writer attributed three deaths within a single year (one case necessitating an amputation, two others involving the appendix) to lack of medical care.[11]

The most recent picture is improved by the presence of a certificated nurse and a dispensary.

> The Seventh Day Adventist Church, which appoints the Missionary, ensures that the wife of each missionary is a trained nurse. In cases that cannot be treated by a nurse a ship's doctor is called. Sometimes he will give advice by radio after hearing the symptoms of the case. At other times a ship will call at the Island and the patient will either be taken out to the ship for examination—perhaps by X-ray—and treatment, or, if the patient is seriously ill, the doctor will come ashore. Each year a number of the Islanders, on the average about five, have to go to New Zealand for medical treatment, appendicitis being the most common cause.[12]

"With the willingly-given assistance of surgeons from passing ships, which call at the island on an average of one approximately every ten days . . . Pitcairn is better situated for medical assistance than many small, rural communities.''[13]

From 1956 to 1960 an average of 180 non-epidemic medical cases were treated in the government dispensary. Almost half were for minor ailments such as colds, bruises and cuts, and a fourth involved eye, ear and skin infections and injuries. A few surgical cases were taken to New Zealand; expenses were met by government loan or grant when necessary.[14]

None of the studies encountered have included an analysis of Pitcairn longevity. The fact that one can readily bring to mind a number of Pitcairn notables (Susannah, Nobbs, Buffett, Elizabeth Young (nee Mills), Thursday October Christian II, among others) who died in their late seventies, eighties, and nineties suggests that the prospects of long life on Pitcairn, barring accident, were not inferior to those in the Western world.

❦ TEETH ❦

The teeth of the Pitcairners have been the subject of a copious stream of comment from the early days of the Colony, when they were extravagantly praised by visitors, to the time at the end of the nineteenth century (and beyond) when it was noted that missing teeth were becoming characteristic of even the younger Islanders. Legend and the travelers' tales have it that the dental endowment of the Polynesians was of a notable excellence, that of the English notoriously poor. Add to the inconclusiveness of both notions the special conditions of Pitcairn, the crossbreeding of the two races, the dietary habits developed by the Pitcairners, the intensive inbreeding, and the lack of dentistry and dental hygiene, and it is easy to understand why it was difficult to affix the blame for dental deterioration.

The first British visitors to Pitcairn (1814) describe the women as having "invariably beautiful teeth." Indicating that sound teeth were not confined to one sex, Captain Waldegrave reported (1830) that the Pitcairn men tore off the husks of coconuts with their teeth in order to offer the milk to their visitors. Many further expressions of admiration could be quoted down to the middle of the century, when

Brodie noted that "both men and women have fine teeth, especially the latter."

These dazzling testimonials are in striking contrast to later developments. A century after the dental feat witnessed by Waldegrave, one of the first things to catch the eye of Dr. Shapiro on his visit to Pitcairn in 1934 was the large number of missing teeth and the consequently toothless jaws of the Islanders.

> Not one adult woman out of sixty examined had a complete set of teeth, and nineteen had all the teeth missing. Thirty-seven, or roughly sixty-one per cent, had lost ten or more teeth. I actually found five men out of sixty who still had full dentures. Eight had become edentulous and thirty-one, or about 52 per cent, had lost ten or more teeth. It is difficult to account for this dental condition. The diet appears to be adequate, although no investigation of the chemistry of the food was undertaken. The same situation prevails on Norfolk where more meat and fish are consumed. It is true that the English have notoriously bad teeth which may be an important factor in the shocking dental degeneracy on Pitcairn. Its English origin is supported by the case of Edward Young, one of the mutineers, who had already lost his incisor teeth at the age of twenty-four.* . . . Young's loss suggests either fisticuffs or a congenital defect. If the latter hypothesis is true, it is not difficult to see that the close inbreeding practiced on Pitcairn might spread and intensify the defect among all the population.

Whatever the various explanations, lay or professional, for dental deterioration on Pitcairn may lack of conclusiveness is more than compensated by variety. Native daughter Rosalind Young suggested insufficient cleanliness and diet. Native daughter Emily McCoy offered the insufficient use of grains and the plentiful supply of sugar cane. Captain Henry Dyke noted that the front teeth were not "lost but broken off" and attributed it to diet. J. S. Neill, in his administrative report, blamed a deficiency in fats and lack of oral hygiene, and noted that outlanders "resident for any period, who adopt the local diet are soon troubled with dental caries and a loss of teeth."

Mrs. Routledge offered Dr. Keith's statement that Pacific Islanders were extremely liable to the loss of teeth from disease, as evidenced by every skull from Easter Island. "Tooth trouble is even

---

* The complete portrait of Young in the *Description of the Pirates* drawn up by Bligh at Timor, and difficult to come by, not only mentions that Young "has lost several of his fore teeth," but adds *"and those that remain are all rotten."* (Italics supplied.) This significant detail was edited out of Murray's curtailed version of the *Description*, which probably accounts for its omission in the subsequent literature.

more prevalent in Easter Island than in the slums of our great towns.'' One explanation even blamed the consumption of too many oranges by the Pitcairners. Dental science apparently provides no unanimous verdict which disposes of the question.*

Some relief from edentulosity reached the Islanders in the 1930s with the coming of New Zealand dentist Cooze, a Seventh Day Adventist, who sought to regain his health on Pitcairn and furnished many Pitcairners with dentures.

Later, Islander Hilda Christian learned to make and fit dentures in New Zealand, with results admired by subsequent visitors. Currently dental services are available to Pitcairners from a fellow Islander, Elwyn Christian, trained in Fiji. *A Guide to Pitcairn* notes an average of sixty tooth extractions annually in the late fifties, and the filling of over six hundred teeth in the period from 1957 to 1960.

⚜ "OUR OWN MASTERS"—AND GOATS ⚜

As wood follows its appointed grain, the will to do things in one's own way attends mortal man. It is notoriously intransigent among islanders in general; in the case of the Pitcairn Islanders, it is authenticated not only by their human and island condition, but by descent from a breed of men so intent on their own way that they become outlaws to attain it. Even before they reached Pitcairn, they had sounded their motto at Tubuai: "The ship is moor'd and we are now our own masters."

The pursuit of their own grain is a continuous thread of the history of Pitcairn Islanders. It can be traced in scores of incidents, such as the resistance to dictator Hill's attempts to convert the Islanders to Wesleyanism, the rejection of attempts by outlanders to introduce cattle and sheep culture, and the return from two complete migrations that presumably wrote an end to the Pitcairn community. ("They had a longing to be back to the Island, where nobody could

---

* Tahitian dental deterioration curiously parallels Pitcairn experience. In *Tahiti* (1961), Barnaby Conrad notes that young Tahitian women typically lack full dentures.

interfere with them, however good and kind the intention, and however necessary, perhaps, the interference.'')

A former schoolteacher on Pitcairn, Mr. E. Schubert, speaking of
a Men's Club formed on the Island, remarked, ''. . . immediately the
organizer left the Island, it died, as do most organizations instituted
by temporarily resident strangers (e.g., an Education Officer or
Missionary).'' He further reports that Pitcairners sometimes return
from New Zealand ''with some progressive ideas and attempt to apply
them. The reaction of the majority of the 'stay-at-home' Islanders is
to accuse their would-be leaders of 'making big.' As the average
Islander hates to be so accused only the strongest will persevere with a
new idea.''

The love for indigenous as opposed to outlander ways has persisted despite strong countervailing influences: the keen desire for
outlander approval; the need for trade with, and assistance from,
outlanders; awe of the British Government; and genuine respect for
the achievements and products of more industrialized communities.

In the continuing battle between Pitcairn preferences and the
recommendations of outlanders, the Islanders were not invariably on
the side of unreason; frequently proposals made were not germane to
their situation. To cite one example: noting the depth of the rich
volcanic soil of Pitcairn, twenty inches in some places, visitors more
than once suggested that deeper working of the earth would increase
its productivity. The Islanders, restricted to hoe and spade by the
nature of their terrain, could only smile politely at the visions inspired
by experience in plow cultures—and sharpen their hand tools.

On the other hand, there were instances in which a neutral could
sympathize with the exasperation of colonial administrators at the
unwillingness of the Islanders to act in what seemed obviously their
best interests.

EPIC OF THE GOATS

Nothing better epitomizes Pitcairn adhesion to its own ways than
the epic of the goats.

Goats arrived at Pitcairn on the ''Bounty,'' along with chickens, pigs, and rats. At various times, largely at the instigation of
outlanders, unsuccessful efforts were made to introduce cattle (as well

as sheep, rabbits, and other animals) into the Island economy. The Islanders did not share the British lust for beef, nor did they favor cow's milk, preferring that of the coconut. This may have influenced their conclusion that Pitcairn was unsuitable for cattle, although it could be supported by logical reasons.*

The Pitcairn pigs are long gone—a sacrifice to Seventh Day Adventism. The sheep and cattle are gone—as a result of the fact or belief that they were unsuited to Pitcairn. The goats remain, prideful descendants of authentic "Bounty" lineage.†

From the beginning, the goats were not fenced in, as were the chickens, but allowed to roam the Island with outlaw freedom. They found a primordially predestined habitat in the upper reaches of the mountainous Pitcairn landscape, soon becoming as happily wild or as wildly happy as their undomesticated ancestors. That is when they were not being shot at by the Pitcairners, who were faced with the pleasant necessity of combining sport and husbandry in order to realize a harvest of the goats. Or when not being harried by the dogs later introduced.

Let it not be thought that the goats were a matter of minor concern on Pitcairn, even though they were largely ignored in the beginning save for sporadic hunts. They were later the subject of a considerable portion of Pitcairn legislation. The laws provided, among other things, that "Dogs chasing goats may be killed for the first offence, in the act anywhere," that the shooting of goats was confined to designated areas, that suitable men would be appointed "to act as goat masters," that no one should chase or catch kids or goats without the sanction of one of the goat masters, that no one should kill kids or

---

* A lively farce with pointed moral could be fashioned out of the many attempts of the Westerners, beginning with Cook, to introduce cattle into Polynesia. The British offered the cattle with the air of men bringing salvation; the Tahitians accepted them with the mingled feelings of men required to show gratitude for a munificent and well-intentioned gift of dubious value. What to do with these strange creatures, whom they would gladly have traded for a handful of nails, must be left to the future; as it turned out, the policy adopted was to ignore them as long as their depredations did not become intolerable. When the mutineers came from Tubuai to Tahiti for the first time, to acquire livestock and supplies, the Tahitians happily relinquished the cow and bull left by Cook. The bull died on the way back to Tubuai; the cow was consumed.
† The "Bounty" lineage of the current Pitcairn goats is evidenced by the fact that, after the total migration to Norfolk in 1856, sailors from the shipwrecked "Wild Wave" "found wild goats" on Pitcairn in 1858. See Knowles, Josiah N., *Crusoes of Pitcairn Island,* Los Angeles, 1957.

goats unless accompanied by two other men, that the ears of kids and goats killed must be shown to one of the Internal Committee or a goat master, that each family should keep no more than six (or four or two) breeding nannies, that families not residing on the Island, but expecting to return, "have the same privelage [sic] to keep four breeding nannies . . . the committee being informed of the care-taker's name," and that goats suffering from "Big Bubby" must be either isolated or killed unless heavy with kid, when the goat masters may allow it to remain until after kidding.

It is not clear whether the original "Bounty" goats had been regarded as communal property; the legislation cited makes it abundantly evident that private ownership of goats had become institutionalized. This is borne out by the fact that branding of goats became the rule; in 1934 Dr. Shapiro counted 63 family goat brands, usually various forms of ear-slitting.

If one gains from the foregoing the seemingly justified impression that goats were much cherished by Pitcairners, he will hardly be prepared to learn that they cared nothing for the milk of the goat, and that they not infrequently told visitors that they were not particularly fond of goat meat. Why then did they cling to goats so tenaciously, despite the ease with which they eschewed cattle and sheep, and even pigs?

This is not the first time the question has been asked, by Pitcairners as well as outlanders. The "foreign" point of view, shared by some Islanders, is stated by Mr. Schubert: "Goats have always had a greater nuisance than utility value on Pitcairn. Besides increasing the Island's natural tendency to soil-erosion, they have ravaged many gardens."

Developments as of 1957 in Pitcairn goatology are described in Luis Marden's report of a meeting of a Pitcairn men's club which discussed "anything." ". . . someone brought up the question of goats. The chairman looked resignedly heavenward and everyone laughed. Goats are a sore point on Pitcairn.

". . . There are now 400-odd goats on Pitcairn, confined to the southern half of the island by a five-foot-high fence.

"Anti-goat Pitcairners say:

" 'They nuisances, do lots of damage.'

"Pro-goaters say . . .:

" 'If war come, ships cut right off, and we'll go stranded with no meat.' Pitcairners remember vividly the war years, when they were almost completely isolated.

"A goatmaster, elected each year, is in charge of all island goats. With eight helpers he brands the new kids as they come along. No household may keep more than two breeding nannies. The goatmaster also organizes shoots when the people need fresh goat meat. . . .

"Both schoolteacher Wotherspoon and Pastor Hawkes try to convince the people that the goats must go for the good of the land. They remain, by and large, unconvinced."

The latest indications, from the semi-official *A Guide to Pitcairn,* suggest that the pro-goaters are fighting a losing rearguard action. At the end of 1962, the number had been reduced to 58, but they were still a

> . . . contentious problem. They are not eaten very often; they are not milked; and they occasionally damage food gardens. But the principal case against them is that by eating bushes, young trees and grass they have contributed to pockets of soil erosion and inhibit conservation and the regeneration of forest. Against this catalogue of criticism stands a body of islanders who regard the goats as a reserve stock of food for emergencies, and legislation enacted in 1960, to secure more effective control and reduction of goats, was designed to meet both points of view. Whether it will succeed entirely is still in doubt, but the goat defenders realize it serves notice on them and that, if it fails, the elimination of the goats must inevitably follow.

Elimination of goats on Pitcairn? Perhaps. Inevitable? Goats and Pitcairners have been butting the inevitable for the best part of two centuries.*

ꙮ THE PITCAIRN BREED ꙮ

APPEARANCE

The physical appearance of the Pitcairn men is dramatic and distinctive, as described by the Johnsons on the first meeting (and verified by photographs):

---

* A recent (1966) communication from Pitcairn indicates that some of the Island anti-goaters have had a change of heart.

Swarthy skins, beards, old clothes, lined faces, and the heavily-muscled bodies of seamen combined in a general impression that was rather alarming. We might have been back a century and a half and these men the mutineers themselves for all their appearance. . . . the people show many English characteristics, though their skins are mostly dark. They all have very few teeth, many front ones missing, and their feet are huge. The pitiful assortment of old clothes is the greatest drawback in general appearance.

Anthropologist Shapiro had

expected to see definite indications of the Tahitian contribution to their mixed Anglo-Polynesian origin. Instead, the men, *en masse,* were more like a group of Englishmen—dock workers—with ugly, knobby hands and feet, roughened and calloused by labor. They wore nondescript garments . . . Battered officers' caps were clapped on mops of shaggy hair. Blue sea-jackets rubbed shoulders with ancient tweed coats. And hardly a pair of trousers matched its companion jacket. Shirts, open at the throat, revealed strong muscular necks and hairy chests. A glance at their bare feet explained why shoes were unnecessary. . . . large prominent noses slightly beaked, heavy brows defined by bony bars above the eyes, giving the forehead a pronounced slope in profile. The complexion was ruddy and weather-beaten and the hair dark, although with a suggestion of fairer color here and there.

These descriptions of the Pitcairners of the 1930s echo in part those of the first visitors. A notable difference exists in the matter of teeth; these which were the subject of admiration in the first half of the nineteenth century. It is possible also that inbreeding had tended to intensify individuality of appearance.

PHYSICAL PROWESS

The physical prowess of Pitcairners is celebrated in so many reports over the years as to disarm skepticism. Beechey speaks of the "robust" and Pipon of the "athletic" young men, but it remained for mid-nineteenth century reporters to dramatize these descriptions with concrete examples.

Two of the strongest men on the island, George Young and Edward Quintal, have each carried at one time, without inconvenience, a kedge anchor, two sledge hammers, and an armourer's anvil, amounting to upwards of six hundredweight. Quintal, at another time, carried a boat, twenty-eight feet in length. . . . They [the Pitcairners] frequently swam round their little island [approximately five miles]. When the sea beat heavily on the island, they have plunged into the breakers, and swum to sea beyond them . . . pushing a barrel of water before them. . . .[15]

Captain Wood, H.M.S. "Pandora," after an 1849 visit, brought back stories of an eighteen-year-old woman carrying hundred pound weights of yams for a considerable distance over precipitous hills "where one unaccustomed to such exercise would scarcely be able to scramble," of a sixty-year-old Pitcairner who carried a six-foot officer up the steep and slippery ascent from Bounty Bay which the officer had been unable to negotiate, and of Captain Wood himself making the same ascent "in the arms of a damsel."[16]

These tributes to the strength of the Pitcairners are corroborated by more recent reports, which indicate that the Islanders have lost none of their prodigious prowess in the twentieth century. "The greatest measurable accomplishment that we know of occurred when the Islanders unloaded from a steamer forty-five tons of cargo, brought it ashore through heavy surf, and then landed it and carried it on their backs up to the village. We have seen the men start up the 400-foot climb with a 200-pound sack, and the women with 100 pounds."

INDUSTRIOUSNESS

Nowhere is the unreliability of travelers' reports more striking than in references to the indolence of "the natives." To name just one example, were the reader to swallow whole the early voyagers' emphasis on Tahitian idleness, one would have to explain their impressive fleet of giant war canoes, among other things, as the result of a miracle.

This consideration makes one reach for the salt shaker in assessing reflections on the industriousness of the Pitcairners which are sprinkled through the record. As early as 1853 B. Toup Nicolas, British Consul at Raiatea, in a generally laudatory report, stated that "the men seemed to allow the women to work harder than themselves. . . . there is a want of energy apparent in all they do. . . ." This

241

criticism reached its zenith toward the end of the nineteenth century, when preceding headshakings of visiting British captains were climaxed by the statement in a government report that the Pitcairners "do absolutely nothing all day."

If such extravagance were not self-defeating, much evidence indicates its falsity. The early economy of Pitcairn, with heavy emphasis on laborious yam culture, demanded frequently unremitting labor of a very strenuous kind. The development of commerce with touching ships involved the upkeep of a fleet of whale boats and the wrestling of cargo down and up the taxing "Hill of Difficulty," to say nothing of rowing through the heavy Pitcairn surf to and from the ships and dragging the long boats out and in. The muscles noted by visitors did not develop from doing "absolutely nothing." When the curio industry became the Islanders' main support, whittling and weaving became an accompaniment to conversation.

The Islanders' long-time friends, the Johnsons, have it that "nowhere in the world is a higher standard of a day's work. . . . when a Pitcairner puts his hand to the oar or to the saw or to the hoe or to the axe, what results!"

But it would perhaps be as misleading to picture the Pitcairners as constantly working as it would be to describe them as constantly idle. They shared the Tahitian "high standard of leisure." What probably confused some of the visitors was the intermittent nature of the demands of the Pitcairn way of life. The crops on which the Islanders depended, particularly yams, were seasonal, so that sowing, harvesting, and storing might call for prodigious exertion for a time, to be followed by a complete absence of urgency. Similarly, the approach of ships would produce strenuous and hurried labor for as long as was needed to gather the produce to be taken out, the rowing of the whale boats to and from the ship, the loading and unloading, the housing of the heavy and clumsy boats, and the struggle up the steep incline with the cargo. After such an event, absent pressing business, the Pitcairners might be inclined to take it easy for a while. Westerners whose notion of work was geared to a time clock or an assembly line might consider such relaxation as indicative of "Polynesian" laziness, whereas to the Islanders it was as essential as the work they had finished and might be called upon to resume at any moment. The Pitcairners harbored no unnatural appetite for labor, but were capable of maximum effort when it was required.

QUALITY

Beyond appearance, physique, industriousness, hospitality, and island parochialism, what is the quality of the Pitcairner—the intelligence, the personality? Here we tread treacherous ground, booby-trapped with the subjective.

Thus, Hall, after a two-day stay in 1933, in a magazine article lamented the deterioration of the Pitcairners in the tones of the incurable dreamer whose vision has been violated by reality. "Adamstown of today is anything but the Adamstown of the early nineteenth century, with its neat, well-kept houses and gardens and plantations. It is a huddle of forlorn habitations occupied by people who seem to have no hopes for the future, except in the religious sense."[17] In this passage Hall assigns the alleged degeneration of the Pitcairners to inbreeding, lack of contact with the outside world, and the fact that the Island is too small for "isolation without deterioration." He indicts the British Colonial Office for neglect and the failure to provide teachers "from outside to arouse their minds, to drive from their faces the vacant expression common to nearly all of them."

The very next year, 1934, brought anthropologist Shapiro, likewise keenly aware of Pitcairn's romantic past, to the Island for a ten-day visit in which he scrutinized the Pitcairners with a practiced, if much more sympathetic, eye. Dr. Shapiro noted what apparently distressed Hall, a "suggestion of shanty white about these islanders—the not quite neatly built houses, the cast-off clothing, the necessarily makeshift furniture, the air of utilizing the junk shop, . . ." but arrived at a much kindlier view of the Pitcairn personality:

> The mental and psychological qualities of the islanders tend rather to elude exact measurement. I had no time to administer psychological tests, even if there were any adequate for the special environment in which the Pitcairners live. I have, therefore, only subjective impressions, and these are perhaps biased in favor of the islanders. Actually I knew of only two or three who were distinctly below par mentally—a small proportion in a group of two hundred. Several were dull but able to manage their affairs efficiently enough. The rest seemed to me to fit into the average range of intelligence.
>
> As I think back to the individuals I knew on Pitcairn, I am impressed by the relatively large number of men such as Parkins Christian, Fred Christian, Edgar Christian, Norris Young, and Arthur Herbert

Young and of women such as Mary Ann McCoy, Ada Christian, Margaret Lucy Christian, and Harriet Warren, who possessed qualities of leadership or traits of personality that raised them above the levels of their neighbors.*

This view is supported by the testimony of the Johnsons, particularly impressive because their Pitcairn experience covered twenty-one years and involved lengthy stays and intimate contacts with the Islanders. Their earthy New England outlook is complemented by outgoing natures designed to evoke genuine responses, and their years of roving the seas and meeting the humble and celebrated of many nations has not diminished the value of their judgment:

"The magistrate, Parkin Christian,† would have been a leader anywhere. He was the most convincing proof of the good stock of the island. . . . We met others too of real quality. . . . Many of our old friends have died in the twenty-one years we have known Pitcairn. Many of the young people have migrated to New Zealand. But outstanding people still remain on Pitcairn."

One of the most convincing evidences of the quality of Pitcairners is their ability to win the friendship of men of substance, demonstrated in word and deed. The long roll includes Beechey, Barrow, Moerenhout, Admiral Moresby and his son, Rev. Murray and Rev. Drew, Dr. Shapiro and the Johnsons, to say nothing of the hundreds of anonymous correspondents and well wishers.

---

* One note echoed and re-echoed by British Navy captains and government officials down the years was the importance of wise and firm leadership to the welfare of Pitcairn. (One sometimes receives the impression from their lamentations that the lack of such leadership was a condition peculiar to Pitcairn.) It would be fatuous to argue the desirability of good leadership, but it must not be forgotten that an overly strong hand was almost certain to evoke the cry of, "We are our own masters" from the egalitarian Islanders. Even Adams had not always enjoyed his own way, and Nobbs was subjected to sniping at home and abroad from the beginning of his Pitcairn career. The dictatorial reign of Hill foundered on the opposition of an aroused Pitcairn parent. While the leadership after the return from Norfolk of Simon Young was criticised as lacking in forcefulness, that of the subsequent leader, James Russell McCoy, created opposition for contrary reasons. The way of the would-be-leader of Pitcairn was strewn with the prickly fruit of the Island sense of individual sovereignty. Leadership suited to Pitcairn was that of example and achievement, rather than leadership which relied on the issuance of orders and directives. Considering the small population and the absence of any class born or trained to rule, it is surprising that the Islanders were able to generate as much leadership as they developed, from Adams to Parkin Christian, and beyond.

† The Johnsons' regard for Parkin Christian is indicated by their naming of their second son, Robert Parkin Johnson, for this Pitcairn leader.

244

It seems fair to conclude from this and other testimony that the Pitcairn community compares favorably in intelligence and adaptation to the human condition with much more advantaged communities in the mainstream of modern life. If lacking in elegance and cosmopolitanism, there are compensations. To quote the Johnsons yet one more time: ''The spirit of the community eclipses its defects . . . through the whole group spreads a delightful and rare feeling of good will. This small concentrated colony has learned to live together peacefully.''

⚜ NOTES: PART SIX ⚜

1. Nicoll, J. M., *Three Voyages of a Naturalist,* London, 1908.
2. Routledge, Mrs. Scoresby, *The Mystery of Easter Island,* London, 1919.
3. Keith, Dr. Arthur, "The Physical Characteristics of Two Pitcairn Islanders," *Man,* August 1917, vol. 17, p. 121 ff.
4. Dr. Shapiro's findings, summarized in Chapter 10, "Anglo-Polynesian," of *Heritage of the Bounty,* are the primary authority; only a few of them are mentioned herein.

   Scattered references to the appearance and physical characteristics of Pitcairners are frequent in the literature. Photographs of the Islanders of widely varying quality, roughly corresponding to their age, will be found in Young, Fullerton, Shapiro, Marden, and the books and articles of the Johnsons.
5. "The Great Revolution in Pitcairn" (in *The Stolen White Elephant,* 1882).
6. Parliamentary Paper, C.S.9148, February 1899.
7. Rodwell, Sir C. (Great Britain—Colonial Reports, Miscellaneous, No. 93), London, 1921.
8. Schubert, E., "Pitcairn Island Today," in *The Pitcairnese Language.*
9. Shapiro, Chapter 11, "Breeding and Inbreeding," is the most valuable authority on inbreeding. His findings corroborate his previous study of Pitcairn Island descendants on Norfolk, *Descendants of the Mutineers of the* "Bounty," Bishop Museum, Honolulu, 1929.

   The literature is full of observations corroborative of Dr. Shapiro's findings; contrary suggestions derive largely from the effort to find a scapegoat for whatever imperfections visitors found in the Pitcairners.
10. The most considered and thorough treatment of cross-culturation on Pitcairn will be found in Shapiro, Chapter 7, "Early Victorian Eden." The accounts of the voyagers and the "standards" contain descriptions of cultural adjustments and adaptations, with natural emphasis on the picturesque. Social attitudes were and are more difficult to capture, although frequently of the highest significance.

11. Greene, Marc T., "Lonely Isle," *Asia,* December 1945, vol. 45, p. 588.
12. Schubert.
13. *A Guide to Pitcairn.*
14. References to the health of Pitcairners are scattered throughout the literature. The entries by Nobbs in the Pitcairn Island Register Book contain descriptions of epidemics, treatments, and health notes, as well as reports of accidents, by the one who functioned as the Island's nearest equivalent to a physician from the 1830s to emigration to Norfolk in 1856. The most comprehensive treatment (to 1934) will be found in Shapiro, pp. 173–174, 220 ff.

    Murray quotes many letters of Nobbs which flesh out the health picture during his stewardship. Young gives a sketchy Islander's view of the later years of the nineteenth century. Some information is contained in the official reports cited herein and in *A Guide to Pitcairn.* The Johnson books and articles include material of value. And see Ferdon, which reports medical findings showing a generally favorable picture of Pitcairn health in 1956, although noting obesity of the women and a high incidence of dental caries.
15. Quoted by Murray, p. 155.
16. Quoted by Murray, p. 156.
17. *Atlantic Monthly* for May 1934, vol. 153, p. 572 ff.

The Pitcairn literature is suffused with "impressions" of the Islanders which range from gushing admiration to harsh criticism. Pertinent material will be found in the voyagers' accounts, the "standards," and the official reports.

❧ A SELECTIVE BIBLIOGRAPHY ❧

I. The "Standards"

The "standards" are the books, comprehensive to the date of publication, which have had the widest circulation, although some are not readily accessible at this time.

Barrow, Sir John. *The Eventful History of the Mutiny and Piratical Seizure of H.M.S. BOUNTY.* London, 1831. Reprinted in *The World's Classics,* with an introduction by Admiral Sir Cyprian Bridge, in editions from 1914 to 1960.

Belcher, Lady. *The Mutineers of the Bounty and Their Descendants in Pitcairn and Norfolk Islands.* London, 1870.

Brodie, Walter. *Pitcairn Island and the Islanders in 1850*. London, 1851.

Murray, Rev. T. B. *Pitcairn: The Island, the People, and the Pastor*. London, 1853, and various subsequent editions.

Shapiro, H. L. *The Heritage of the Bounty*. New York, 1936. Reprinted in the Natural History Library in paperback in 1962.

Young, Rosalind Amelia. *Mutiny of the Bounty and Story of Pitcairn Island, 1790–1894*. Oakland, California, 1894.

II.   VOYAGERS' AND SETTLERS' ACCOUNTS BEFORE 1856

These form the principal "source material" for the history of the first half century of the Pitcairn Colony, and particularly for its first decade.

Bechervaise, J. *Thirty-Six Years of a Seafaring Life*. Portsea, 1839.

Beechey, Captain F. W. *Narrative of a Voyage to the Pacific and Bering's Strait*. 2 vols. London, 1931.

Bennett, F. D. *Narrative of a Whaling Voyage*. 2 vols. London, 1840.

Buffett, John. "A narrative of 20 years' residence on Pitcairn's Island." *The Friend* (Honolulu), vol. 4 (1846), pp. 2–3, 20–21, 27–28, 34–35, 50–51, 66–68.

Delano, Captain Amasa. *The Voyages and Travels of Amasa Delano*. Boston, 1817. (Though suspect, this is the most complete account of Mayhew Folger's discovery of the Pitcairn Colony.)

Fryer, Master John. *Narrative of the Mutiny*, undated manuscript, United Service Institute.

Jenny(1) (One of the women who settled Pitcairn.) Interview with, reported in Sydney *Gazette* for July 17, 1819.

Jenny(2) Interview with, reported by Otto von Kotzebue in *A New Voyage Round the World*. 2 vols. London, 1830.

Jenny(3) Interview with, reported in the Bengal *Hurkaru* for October 2, 1826 and reproduced in the *United Service Journal*, Part 2 (1829), pp. 589–593.

King, Captain Henry. Extract from Journal. *Edinburgh Philosophical Journal*, vol. 3, pp. 381–388. (1820)

Bibliography

Moerenhout, J. A. *Voyages aux îles du Grand Océan.* Paris, 1837.

Newell, G. (First Officer of the "Sultan"). Extract from the "Private Journal," published in the *New-England Galaxy,* vol. 4, January 12, 1821.

Pipon, Captain P. Holographic account in *Banks Papers,* Brabourne Collection, vol. 1, pp. 17–51, M. L. Ref. A77, in the Mitchell Library of Sydney. This account has been quoted in part frequently, most completely in Mackaness, pp. 216–219.

Pitcairn Island Register Book, with introduction by Sir Charles Lucas. London, 1929.

Shillibeer, Lieut. J. *A Narrative of the Briton's Voyage to Pitcairn Island.* London, 1818.

Waldegrave, Captain W. *Journal of Royal Geographic Society* (1833). Vol. 3, pp. 156–168.

III.   OFFICIAL REPORTS AND CORRESPONDENCE AND RECORDS

"Correspondence relating to the Condition of the Pitcairn Islanders" presented to both Houses, February 1899. C. 9148. London, 1899.

Simons, R. T. "Pitcairn Island." Cd. 2937. London, 1905.

Rodwell, Sir Cecil. "Report on a Visit to Pitcairn Island." Colonial Reports, Miscellaneous, No. 93. London, 1921.

Pilling, H. G. "Report on a Visit to Pitcairn Island." Colonial No. 53. London, 1930.

Neill, J. S. "Pitcairn Island: General Administrative Report." Colonial No. 155. London, 1938.

A Guide to Pitcairn, published for the Government of the Islands of Pitcairn, Henderson, Ducie and Oeno, by the South Pacific Office, Suva, 1963.

    While not strictly an official report, this valuable brochure is not out of place in this list, and brings the picture nearly up to date.

Pitcairn Island Civil Recorder, 1792 c.a. 1963.

Records of the Local Government, 1819–1948.

IV.   MISCELLANEOUS

Fullerton, W. Y. *The Romance of Pitcairn Island*. London, 1923.

Hall, J. N. *The Tale of a Shipwreck*. New York, 1934.

Johnson, Captain and Mrs. Irving.
Westward Bound in the Schooner Yankee. New York, 1936.
Sailing to See. New York, 1939.
Yankee's Wander World. New York, 1949.
Yankee's People and Places. New York, 1955.

Mackaness, George. *The Life of Vice-Admiral William Bligh*. Sydney, 1931 (revised edition, 1951). Though but incidentally concerned with Pitcairn, it contains a wealth of pertinent information and documentary quotations. On Bligh and the mutiny, it is the most exhaustive, if far from the last, word.

Maude, H. E.(1) "In Search of a Home: From the Mutiny to Pitcairn Island (1789–1790)," *Journal of the Polynesian Society,* vol. 67, pp. 106–16.

Maude, H. E.(2) "Tahitian Interlude," *Journal of the Polynesian Society,* vol. 68, pp. 115–38.

Maude, H. E.(3) "A Social and Administrative History of Pitcairn Island." Typescript, 1941.

Maude, H. E.(4) "The History of Pitcairn Island." (A chapter in *The Pitcairnese Language,* New York, 1964.)

McKee, Alexander. *H.M.S. Bounty,* New York, 1962.

Montgomerie, H. S. *William Bligh of the "Bounty," in Fact and in Fable,* London, 1937.

Morrison, James. *Journal of James Morrison,* London, 1935.

O'Brien, Frederick. *Atolls of the Sun,* London, 1922.

Shapiro, H. L. *Descendants of the Mutineers of the Bounty*. Bishop Museum, Honolulu, 1929.

V.   OUTSTANDING MAGAZINE ARTICLES

Selections are winnowed from scores of articles on the basis of unusually valuable text or illustrations or both.

Bibliography

Ferdon, Jr., Edwin N. "Pitcairn Island, 1956." *Geographical Review,* vol. 48, pp. 69–85, January 1958.

Hancock, W. K. "Politics in Pitcairn." *Nineteenth Century,* vol. 109, pp. 575–587, May 1931 (later reprinted in book of same title, London, 1947).

Johnson, Captain and Mrs. Irving. "Westward Bound in the Yankee." *National Geographic Magazine,* vol. 81, pp. 23–44, January 1942.
"The Yankee's Wander World." *National Geographic Magazine,* vol. 95, pp. 26–33, January 1949.

Marden, Luis. "I Found the Bones of the Bounty." *National Geographic Magazine,* vol. 112, pp. 725–789, December 1957.

McCoy, Emily. "The Pitcairn Island Miracle in Ethnology," *Independent,* vol. 57, pp. 712–719, September 22, 1904.

Shafter, Richard A. "Pitcairn Island Through Native Eyes," *Travel,* vol. 90, p. 11, January 1948.

Young, Rosalind Amelia. "The Mutineers of the Bounty, 1859–1880," *Scribner's Monthly,* vol. 22, pp. 54–63, May 1881.

✹ INDEX ✹

257

Williams, John, 9; flogging of, 11; history and character of, 46; wife of dies, 63; appropriates Toofaiti as replacement, 64, 65; killing of, 66

Yams, importance and culture of, 95, 96
Young, Midshipman Edward, support by of Christian, 25; history and char-acter of, 44 ff.; hides out during "massacre," 67; shoots Niau, 67, 68; complicity in "massacre," 45, 69n; death of, 69, 70; journal of, 71, 72
Young, Rosalind Amelia, character and school services of, 151, 191
Young, Simon, service as school teacher and religious leader, 149, 191

DATE DUE

2 -12			
JAN 3 0 1974			
SEP 1 2 1974			
GAYLORD			PRINTED IN U.S.A.